The Dance Vocabulary of Classical India

Raga – Nrtya Series No. 8

The Dance Vocabulary of Classical India

By

MANDAKRANTA BOSE,

M.A. (Cal.) et U.B.C. B. Litt. D. Phil. (Oxon.)

With a Foreword by

LATE PROFESSOR THOMAS BURROW

Boden Professor of Sanskrit, Oxford University

Sri Satguru Publications

A Division of:

INDIAN BOOKS CENTRE

DELHI • INDIA

Published by :
SRI SATGURU PUBLICATIONS
Indological & Oriental Publishers,
A Division of :
INDIAN BOOKS CENTRE
40/5, Shakti Nagar,
Delhi-110007.
INDIA

ISBN 81-7030-439-3

Second revised edition–1995

Typeset by:
ABC *for* **DTP**
Delhi-34 Ph : 7183087

PRINTED IN INDIA

To the memory of

my father

Dr. Makhan Lal Roychoudhuri

Preface to the First Edition

The dance in India is an ancient art and most fortunately it has not only survived the centuries but has prospered in the present. The classical dances of India are widely practised and regarded as art-forms descended unchanged from the earliest ages of Hindu culture. The esteem that this changelessness indicates needs to be explained.

In ancient India the dance was presumed to be of such aesthetic richness that it was thought to be a direct gift of the gods to men. If we cut through the wrappings of allegory that make so much of Indian historiography bewildering, we realise that the dance with its allied arts, music and drama was important enough for the ṛṣis or sages, that is, the intellectual class, to have taken it up as an area of speculation. This explains why so much was written on it. In a society in which education was mainly a matter of verbal instruction, the extensively textual transmission of the theory and techniques of dancing and its allied arts shows how anxious were the authors to save the art-forms from destruction or corruption. One may note then that the student of Indian dancing must use their writings as primary sources. I would indeed go further and claim that to reconstruct the dances of ancient India one may have no better guides than these authors. Some sculptural, iconographical and literary materials still exist, but they are not nearly as exhaustive as the treatises. I have therefore drawn upon them rather than upon other sources to explain the terms that belong to the technique of classical Indian dancing.

Any sort of acquaintance with classical Indian dancing shows that these terms do need explanation. In dealing with them one cannot just leaf through a text and pick out a movement described under that term. For one thing, texts vary in describing movements. For another, a less obvious kind of confusion arises when we discover that several different categories of action possess one name between them. Precisely what, for instance, is the recita? Is it a movement of one hand or two hands, or one foot or both, of the trunk or of the body as a whole? The answer is that it is all these. When the potentiality of such terms in creating confusion is recognised, my point is made.

In translating the definitions my results are often awkward yet I have tried through them to describe the movements as clearly as possible. However, even the best of such efforts cannot be good enough. What, for instance, may this mean: "Puṣpagaṇḍikā: Songs are sung, accompanied by music, and the recitation of verses of diverse metres take place. Men and women act contrary to their nature" (p. 16). Apart from the odd language, which may be in itself a barrier to communication, the definition does not really describe anything well enough to be visualised. With nothing but this definition to go upon, no one could perform the Puṣpagaṇḍikā, and this is but one of many such instances. In dealing with these there is nothing there for me but to face it out with an apology.

A part of this difficulty is due to the obsessive attention given by the authors of the Sanskrit texts to minute details of physical action. They think of nothing of prescribing independent action for the eyelashes. The effect when not altogether grotesque, is of acrobatics rather than of art. But to see the art in it, it is necessary first to bring such strange directions to scale and understand that they do not occupy sufficient time to be noticeable. Secondly, we must allow that movements such as these are fractional portions of an unified choreographic sequence. And lastly, it is not difficult to admit that when these movements are performed by a dancer with a truly supple body they blend into a smooth, fluid harmony.

With these difficulties in view I have refrained from commenting on the feasibility of performing these actions or upon their aesthetic validity. I have thought it best to classify the movements accoring to the parts of the body involved, putting the limbs in one class, the torso in another, the eyes, the hips, the nostrils in yet others. The classification is thus fairly extensive as it has to be in order to achieve facility of reference.

Much of this work arose out of my researches at Oxford on classical Indian dancing. I take this opportunity to express grateful thanks to my supervisor Professor Thomas Burrow who spent countless hours so that I might begin to understand the intricacies of working on Sanskrit texts. I am deeply grateful to him for his kindness in writing a Foreword for this work. My thanks are also due to the Library staff of the Indian Institute, Oxford, for their courtesy and help, to the India Office Library, London, to the Bibliotheque Nationale, Paris, to the Asiatic Society, Calcutta, and to the staff of the National Library, Calcutta. It is a pleasant duty to acknowledge my debt to Sri Surajit C. Das who has seen the book through the press with such good care.

M.B.

Calcutta
June, 1970

Foreword

Mrs. Mandakranta Bose has over the past ten years devoted her attention to a careful and systematic study of the corpus of Indian writings in Sanskrit dealing with dancing. Of these some nineteen texts have been studied in detail the earliest of which, the *Nāṭyaśāstra* of Bharata, may be as early as the third century A.D. Already at this period a most elaborate tradition had been developed, the details of which are set forth and classified in that work. The work of Bharata proved so influential that most of the later works are based on it though interesting variations occur. There is also a separate tradition, South Indian in origin, which is described in one or two works, and this is separately examined in the present treatise.

The elaborate treatment of the subject by Bharata and his successors involved the creation of an extensive technical vocabulary, and the present work is mainly devoted to the classification and elucidation of these technical terms. Their number is enormous, and they are for the most part defined in the Sanskrit treatises, though by no means always in the same terms, and not always too clearly. There is also the question of textual corruption in the transmission of the works, and it is well known that the *Nāṭyaśāstra* in particular has suffered in this respect. Under these circumstances Mrs Bose has provided just what is needed, namely a classified reference book of all the technical terms with full reference to all the texts in which they occur, and English renderings of the definitions given by them. The work has been prepared with great care and it provides a very full and reliable account of the subject. It will prove to be indispensable to all who are interested in Indian dancing and its history.

The Oriental Institute
Oxford **T. Burrow**
11 July 1970

Contents

List of Abbreviations

A Dar : Abhinaya Darpaṇa.

Ad. Lib. ed. : Adyar Library Edition.

Ad. Lib. Bulletin : Adyar Library Bulletin.

ASS : Ānandāśrama Sanskrit Series.

Abhg : Abhinavagupta.

AP : Agni-Purāṇa.

KN : Kallinātha.

KSS : Kāśī Sanskrit Series.

G.O.S. : Gaekwad's Oriental Series.

TSS : Trivandrum Sanskrit Series.

DR : Daśarūpaka.

NN : Nartana Nirṇaya.

ND : Nāṭya Darpaṇa.

NLR : Nāṭaka Lakṣaṇa Ratnakośa.

NŚ : Nāṭya Śāstra.

Nśsam : Nātya Śāstra Saṁgraha

NRK : Nṛtyaratnakośa.

Nṛdh : Nṛtyādhyāya

Bhp : Bhāvaprakāśa

Mānas : Mānasollāsa.

VDP : Viṣṇu - Dharmottara - Purāṇa.

SDar : Saṅgīta Darpaṇa.

SDām : Saṅgīta Dāmodara.

SUS : Saṅgātopaniṣatsāroddhāra.

SMak : Saṅgīta Makaranda.

SR : Saṅgīa Ratnākara.

SSam : Saṅgīta Samayasāra.

SD : Sāhitya Darpaṇa.

HR : Hasta Ratnāvalī.

Additional Notes

P. 3: The likelier dates of *Abhinayā Darpaṇa* and *Sangīta Makaranda* seem to be around early medieval times (12th/13th centuries). See Mandakranta Bose, *Movement and Mimesis* (Dordrecht, Boston, London: Kluwer Academic Publishers, 1991), pp. 26-30, 34-37.

P. 8, line 5: The traditions described in these two texts cover a number of regions. They are mostly from the south but some came also from the north.

P. 112, line 20: The terms syanditā and apasyanditā can be read as spanditā and apasyanditā as well. It is hard to differentiate between sya and spa in nāgarī. Either could be correct. The terms occur in the text a number of times.

Pp. 204-6: Mukhacāli described in *Nartananirṇaya* and *Sangītádarpaṇa* seems to be the same as Rangmanch ki Tukra in the Kathak style. See Bose, 1991, pp. 205-6; see also Maya Rao, "The Hastas in Kathak," in *Classical and Folk Dances of India,* Part III, Bombay, 1963, pp. 44-47.

Pp. 203, 220: Vaṭu appears in today's Odissi repertoire.

Pp.214-15: The Svarābhinaya described in the *Nartananirṇaya* also appears in today's Odissi repertoire.

Pp. 217-18; Dharu is still practised in Andhra and is being developed by dancers of Kuchipuḍī.

Pp. 220: Movements such as kuḍupa and lāvaṇī can be found in Kathak style and the description of the Jakkaḍī dance can be compared to the Ghungat gat in Kathak. See Bose, 1991, Kluwer, pp. 194-215.

References to *Nartananirṇaya* appear as folio nos. in the India Office Library, London, manuscript. For the reader's convenience, these references are keyed below to my edition of the text (*Nartananirṇaya*, ed. M. Bose, Calcutta: General Printers, 1991), given by chapter and verse. Some references did not appear in the original edition.The error was mine.

Movements of the body

	folio nos..	*verse nos.*
śiras	14b015a	4.244-58
dṛṣṭi	16a-17a	4.258-85
bhru	17a-b	4.286-91
mukharāga	17b	3.292-97
bāhu	18a	4.298-304
hasta	19b-22b	4.305-374
hastakaraṇa	23a	4.375-81
cālaka	23a	4.382-83
pracāra	23b	4.383-84
hastakarma	23b	4.384-87
hastakṣetra	23b	4.387-88
kaṭi	24a	4.389-93
caraṇa	24b	4.394-403
sthāna	25a-26a	4.404-32
cārī	28a-32b	4.432-527
karaṇa	32b-33b	4.528-50
recaka	33b	4.551-55

Dances in the Deśī tradition

Dances of Bandha category

Urupa	43b-45b	4.719-60
Dhuvāḍa	45b	4.761-77
Viḍulāgava	45b-46b	4.777-94
Bhramarī	47b	4.794-98

Śabdanṛtya	47b-48a	4.799-804
Svaramaṇthanṛtya	48b-49a	4.805-19
Gītanṛtya	49a	4.815-25
Gharghara	50a	4.826-37
Cindunṛtya	50b	4.838-50
Dharu	50b-51a	4.851-67
Dhruvapada	51a-b	4.867-74

Dances of anibandha category

Nāmāvali	51b-52a	4.878-79
Yati	52a	4.880
Neri	52a	4.881
Sālanganeri	52a	4.882
Sukīrṇaneri	52a	4.882
Bhāvaneri	52a	4.882-3
Naḍaneri	52a	4.883
Kaivartana	52a	4.884-85
Muru	52a	4.885-86
Raṭṭamuru	52a	4.886-87
Tālarupaka	52a	4.887-88
Guṇḍāla	52b	4888-89
Malaka	52b	4.889-90
Natajānuka	52b	4.890
Maṇḍī	52b	4.890-91
Muḍupa	52b	4.891-92
Muraṇḍāri	52b	4.892-93
Kuḍupa	52b	4.893-94
Tiripakaraṇa	52b	4.895-96
Lāvaṇī	52b-53a	4.896-97
Vaṭu	53a	4.897-98

Other Deśī dances

Jakkaḍī	53a	4.899-902
Rāsa	53a-b	4.903-11

Preface to the Second Edition

It has been over two decades since I wrote this book and it represents my first work in the sixties at Oxford in the arts of dance and drama in the Sanskritic tradition. My guide to the study was Professor Thomas Burrow whose unstinted help has inspired me through my life. Since those early days I have continued my studies and published in many areas of the field but this, my earliest work, has remained as useful to me as at first. I am gratified that it has also remained in constant demand as a reference book for researchers in the art of the classical dance of India. As far as I know, this is still the only book that gives a full descriptive glossary of technical terms of classsical Indian dancing based on Sanskrit texts.

It has been out of print for a number of years and I thought of bringing out an extensively revised edition. However, I realized that with the greater knowledge and insight I have gained in the field, I would have to write an entirely new book. So, I decided to bring out the original book with a few revisions that seemed absolutely necessary and I hope this will be helpful to those who wish to study the dance traditions recorded in the Sanskrit texts. The publisher of the second edition, Mr. Sunil Gupta, decided to give the book a new title which seemed a good idea to me. So here I present my old friend with a new name.

This book was written when I had access to only twenty-one Sanskrit texts on the subject. Since then more texts have become available to me. One of the many texts that were then unedited and unpublished, is *Nartananirṇaya,* a mine of radically new information, which I have since then edited and published. Obviously, from this and other sources I have gathered much more information which has enriched my knowledge and helped me to correct a number of errors of oversight or sheer carelessness in the first edition. To remedy these I have added a page of errata. The description of lāsya needed some correction, which too is incorporated in the present edition. The bibliography has been thoroughly updated. I have also added a short overview of my findings over a period of three decades. A brief description of the recorded history and evolution of dance will, I believe, further our knowledge of the art. However, I do not intend to repeat myself by presenting here what appears in my recent work, *Movement and Mimesis* (Dordrecht: Kluwer Academic Publishers, 1991). Yet, I feel it necessary to bring out some salient points of my conclusions and I will try to do that in the next few pages.

When we begin searching for the recorded history and evolution of the concepts of the art as well as the descriptions of its techniques we come across nearly thirty texts that deal with dance. These texts span a period of nearly twenty centuries. After studying them in depth we realize that three texts are of vital importance in our understanding of the evolution of the art-form. These texts are the *Nāṭyaśāstra* of Bharata, *Sangītaratnākara* by Śārangadeva and *Nartananirṇaya* by Puṇḍarīka Viṭṭhala, marking three periods of evolution, respectively the beginning of the Christian era, the early and the late medieval period. The other texts, although they often record more detailed descriptions, are conceptually speaking virtual reiterations of these three texts.

The first of these texts, the *Nāṭyaśāstra* of Bharata which is generally taken to have been written around the second century A.D.,[1] was in its time and still remains the framework for every writer on dance. This text records a tradition which was obviously recognized by scholars and art critics of Bharata's time. This tradition of dance was recorded as an art for lending beauty to a play and was used in the preliminaries of the presentation of a play. Bharata describes the techniques of the art in the minutest detail and conveys the idea of dance by using five terms; nṛtta, tāṇḍava, piṇḍībandha, sukumāraprayoga and abhinaya. By nṛtta he understood the body movements that produce beauty and he used tāṇḍava as a term synonymous with nṛtta. Piṇḍībandha refers to group dances performed by groups of female dancers who formed into ritualistic patterns to invoke the blessings of different deities. Sukumāraprayoga means a graceful style of presenting the same movements sthat are used in nṛtta. The term abhinaya denotes the method of expressing ideas through gestures.[2] Although Bharata mentions the existence of regional styles, he does not include them in his book but refers to Kohala's work,[3] which was supposed to have recorded the regional styles. Unfortunately, Kohala's work has not come down to us, so we have to wait till the advent of much later texts for information regarding the regional tradition. From the first ten centuries of the Christian era very few texts have survived and the only two extant texts dealing with dancing are *Viśṇudharmottara Purāṇa* and *Abhinavabhāratī,* the commentary on the *Nāṭyaśāstra,* both of which follow Bharata in their descriptions of dancing.

It is not until Śārangadeva wrote his work *Sangītaratnākara* in the thirteenth century,[4] that we find a text describing the regional tradition in a systematic and detailed way. In the evolution of the art of dance Śārngadeva's contribution is just as important as Bharata's. Not only does he recognize and describe the tradition recorded by Bharata but also gives it the name mārga. It is also he who for the first time records the regional tradition, calling it Deśī and describing it in the same detail as mārga. From his time dance begins to be recognized as an art in its own right, not as an art subsidiary to drama. He uses a different term nṛtya,[5] to signify the communication objectives of dance movements. He identifies tāṇḍava and lāsya as separate categories with sub-categories and classifies body movements into three separate divisions by parts of the body, namely, aṅga, upāṅga and pratyaṅga. His final contribution is his emphasis on the aesthetics of presentation whereby individually conceived imaginative effects may be achieved through bodily motion. He realized that there is more to body movements than merely the beauty of form. The texts that were written between the thireenth and fifteenth centuries mostly follow Śārangadeva.

The *Nartananirṇaya* of Puṇḍarīka Viṭṭhala, written in the late sixteenth century,[6] stands at a transitional point in the history of Indian dancing. As a treatise that deals exclusively with deśī dance styles it is a major source of our knowledge of the state into which dancing had evolved by the sixteenth century. The deśī style had not been recognized by Bharata as integral to what he considered to be the central tradition of the art, the authority of which he sought to establish by invoking a divine origin for it.[7] However, through the centuries after Bharata the styles he had described lost their pre-eminence and were gradually replaced in importance by regional and popular styles. Eventually, there came a time when the new ways of dancing became the established tradition. It is that time, a watershed in the history of dancing in India, which is marked by *Nartananirṇaya.* The contribution of this text is two fold: first it provides a full and detailed record of the later tradition of dancing, from which present-day classical styles seem to be directly descended. Secondly, it conceives the art in two conceptual categories, termed by him bandha and anibandha, whereby he marks an entirely original distinction with deep aesthetic implications regarding the relationship between the dancer and his or her art. Throughout the history and evolution of dance, its literature has been given to categorizing the art in many ways. Most texts follow either Bharata or Śārangadeva in providing a rigorously prescriptive account of dance forms. Puṇḍarīka's use of the terms bandha and anibandha is a major step in categorizing dancing in terms of the dancer's creative originality and freedom. According to him, bandhanṛttas are set pieces with every movement in their structured sequences clearly specified for the dancer. By contrast, anibandhanṛttas are flexible in both form and content within broadly specified frameworks of aesthetic purpose. Puṇḍarīka's emphasis here seems to be not so much on the movements themselves as on the dancer's freedom to compose dances using them. By studying the descriptions of individual dance compositions found in this text it is possible to see how our contemporary styles such as Kathak, Odissi, Bhratanātyam and Kucipuḍī grew out of styles and techniques of Puṇḍarīka's time.[8] The details of this process are fascinating but this is not the book to deal with them.

My work through the years in this field is reflected in my later study which took shape in the eighties, again at Oxford. But, as I mentioned earlier, the present book still remains useful. I am grateful to Sunil Gupta for bringing out this edition which I hope will serve as the basic tool of reference to the researchers in the field.

Vancouver, April 15, 1994
Bengali New Year 1401 **Mandakranta Bose**

REFERENCES

1. Bose, M., 1991, *Movement and Mimesis,* p. 7.
2. *Ibid.,* pp. 108-130.
3. *NŚ.* 37.18.
4. Nijenhuis, 1977, p. 12; *SR.* vol. iv, tr. Raja and Burner, 1976, Preface, p. ii.
5. Nṛtya was first used by Dhanañjaya in his Daśarupaka. See Bose, 1991, p. 155.
6. *Nartananirṇaya,* ed. M. Bose, 1991, Introduction, p. xxxv.
7. *NŚ.* 4.260.
8. See Bose, M., 1991, *Movement and Mimesis,* pp. 194-215; *Nartananirṇaya,* ed. M. Bose, 1991, Introduction, pp. li-lix.

CHAPTER ONE

Introduction

The purpose of this glossary is to assist the student of Indian dancing to understand its technicalities. No mere glossary can present the process, the essence of which is mobility, but it is hoped that the various parts of that process are explained in the following pages. In other words, this is in no way a descriptive introduction to the art of dancing but an explanation of its technique. In order to make this explanation as full as possible the meaning of class-names and basic concepts is given at the beginning. The method adopted is not one of a continuous alphabetical arrangement. The terms have been arranged under classheadings, each class being arranged alphabetically. To facilitate reference a complete alphabetical index has been given at the end.

It must be clearly understood that the technical terms discussed here have not been collected from the living tradition of classical dancing in India, though it is of course true that some of these terms are in living use. The immediate source of the terminology is however, the body—a fairly large one—of Sanskrit treatises dealing with dancing. Nineteen texts of this nature have been studied in a comparative manner and the information given in the following pages is the result of that collation. It can be safely stated that the earliest, the *Nāṭyaśāstra* of Bharatamuni, has an archetypal status, for the later texts are directly derived from it. The accounts and explanations given in them have little difference with the *NŚ* that can be called significant. The difference consists mainly in details of classification or in emphasis. It is therefore possible in the case of individual technical terms to arrive at definitions or explanations that are valid with reference to all texts.

Separate mention must be made of the following two texts: *Nartananirṇaya* and *Saṅgīta-Darpaṇa.* These texts include a large body of terms that are entirely different from those found in the texts of the Bharata tradition. These are not even etymologically similar to the terms of that tradition, which we may call the classical tradition. It is possible that the tradition represented by these terms arose in different localities or in different times. Since these terms form a distinctly different group they have not been incorporated in the main body of the present work, but presented in an appendix.

In the following lines the textual sources are briefly described.

The oldest available work is the *Nāṭyaśāstra,* which is believed to have been written by Bharata not later than the third century A.D.[1] It is a treatise on dramaturgy and includes elaborate directions for dancing.
chapter of this book is devoted entirely to dance poses. The fifth, the chapter that discusses the preliminaries of a play, has references to dancing. Chapters eight to twelve deal with the movements of the various parts of the body. The nineteenth chapter discussses the Lāsyāngas which are a form of histrionic representation, but of such graceful nature that they may be regarded as a kind of dancing.

The next treatise that we come across is an Upapurāṇa, the Viṣṇudharmottara-Purāṇa. The text has been placed by its editor between the second half of the fifth and the first half of the seventh, century A.D. (circa 450-650 A.D.)[2] But it is possible that it is of a different date. The third khaṇḍa or section of this book discusses various arts including dancing. The section on dancing can be called Nṛttasūtra in accordance with the colophon of the thirty-fourth chapter. The Nṛttasūtra begins at chapter twenty and ends at chapter thirty four. The first twenty ślokas define Nāṭya and Nṛtta. Ślokas twenty-one to thirty-five deal with dance poses and composite forms of dance. Chapter twenty-three discusses the Sthānas meant for men and women. Chapters twenty-four to twenty-six discuss Aṅga, Upāṅga and Hastakarmas. Chapter twenty-nine discusses Gatis or different gaits for men and women. Chapters thirty-two and thirty-three deal with Rahasyamudrā and Nṛttaśastramudrā. The tradition that it discusses is the same as in the *NŚ*.

Abhinaya Darpaṇa (written between the fifth and the thirteenth century A.D.)[3] of Nandīkeśvara treats in detail the Āṅgika Abhinaya which includes postures and movements of the hands and the feet. It defines Nāṭya Nṛtya and Nṛtta and describes Abhinaya which includes Āṅgika Abhinaya. Though in dealing with the gestures of the hand, *ADar.* follows the *NŚ*, yet some of the movements described, most notably those of the feet, belong to a different tradition.

The *Agnipurāṇa* was written in about the seventh century A.D.[4] It deals, among other things, with dancing in chapter 341. Though it has certain technical terms which can not be found in any other text, yet it generally agrees with the *NŚ*. It mentions the terms without discussing them in detail. About the movements of the feet it merely says that there are many and thus ends the chapter.

Saṅgīta Makaranda of Nārada, dated sometime between the seventh and eleventh centuries A.D.,[5] has two sections, one on Saṅgīta and the other on Nṛtya. The last chapter of Nṛtya section deals with dancing in a few ślokas, describing some movements of the hands and the feet. This text describes a tradition of dancing altogether different from those described by other treatises. The text is very corrupt and most of it is too obscure to be explained.

In *Daśarūpaka* (tenth century A.D.),[6] Dhanañjaya presents, in the form of a manual, the rules for dramatic composition. The first chapter of this book mentions two forms of dance, Nṛtta and Nṛtya as arts auxiliary to drama and gives brief descriptions. In the third chapter the author defines Lāsya, a gentle dance, and gives the names of its forms, called Lāsyāṅgas following Bharata.

Nāṭakalakṣaṇaratnakośa of Sāgarnandin (tenth century A.D.)[7] is a treatise on dramaturgy which discusses in passing, certain topics connected with histrionics. It describes ten Lāsyāṅgas as members of Bhāṇa, which is thought to be a major dramatic form. Some of the minor types are reported to be in the Kaiśikī Vṛtti, a graceful style that includes dancing, while others are described as having ten Lāsyāṅgas which are movements very similar to dancing. Some others are described as forms of dance-drama.

Naṭya-Darpaṇa, written by Rāmacandra and Gūṇacandra (1100-1175 A.D.),[8] deals with dramaturgy. In the third chapter of this book the authors speak of Āṅgika which they later discuss fully in their own commentary on their work. In this discussion they deal with Āṅgika Abhinaya in general and mention some of the technical terms of the *NŚ* without going into details. At the end of the commentary the authors give the names of thirteen other Rūpakas of which five seem to be forms of dance-drama and two others contain dancing.

The fourth section of *Mānasollāsa* or *Abhilaṣitacintamaṇi* (1131 A.D.),[9] a treatise by the Cālukya king Someśvaradeva, deals with the Vinodas or royal pastimes. The sixteenth chapter of this section deals with Nṛtya. Besides discussing the movements of the limbs the Nṛtyavinoda discusses the Deśī style of dancing. This text is thus one of our few authorities on the Deśī style.

Bhāvaprakaśa of śāradatanaya (1175-1250 A.D.)[10] is a compendium of all critical works from that of Bharata down to that of Kṣemendra in the eleventh century. It deals with dramaturgy and the allied arts. A section of the fourth chapter is devoted to Drṣṭi. The seventh chapter discusses the forms of drama, which of course includes music and dancing. The ninth chapter discusses twenty other types of dramas which the author calls Nṛtyabhedas. The tenth chapter mentions some technical terms of dancing.

Saṅgitaratnākara of Śārṇgadeva (thirteenth century A.D.)[11] is a work on music and dancing, closely following the *NŚ* and Abhinavagupta's commentary on it, with some fresh material added. The seventh chapter of this text discusses dancing, outlining two traditions. In reporting one it follows the *NŚ* but the other is taken from a totally different tradition.

Sāhityadarpaṇa of Viśvanātha Kavirāja (14th century A.D.)[12] is a history of literary theories which contains a chapter on drama-turgy. This chapter, the sixth, is a lengthy discussion on dramaturgy of which histrionics is thought to be a part. It discusses Lāsyāṅgas following Bharata in describing Bhāṇa which is a major type of drama.

Saṅgīta Samayasāra of Pārśvadeva (14th century A.D.)[13] is a treatise on music and dancing. The sixth chapter of this book deals with dancing and acting. The author defines Nṛtta and Abhinaya and then he discusses Āṅgika Abhinaya. He first enumerates different Aṅgas, Upāṅgas and Pratyaṅgas and other movements. Then he discusses some of them. He also discusses Nṛtya in detail; by Nṛtya he means dances in the Deśī style. At the end of this chapter, the author discusses another tradition which can be found in *SDar.* and in the last part of *NN.*

Saṅgitopaniṣat Sāroddhara of Sudhākalaśa, as he himself says, was composed in Samvat 1406, i.e. A.D. 1350 as an abridgement of his earlier work Saṅgītopaniṣad, composed in Samvat 1380, i.e. A.D. 1324.[14] This text discusses dancing in its fifth and sixth chapters. The fifth deals with Aṅgas Upāṅgas and Pratyaṅgas while the sixth discusses dance poses mainly. After the discussion of dance poses, the author says that in his age those who danced did not know the texts on dancing, and those who knew the texts were not themselves dancers. He thinks that without practical experience, the theorists can not have complete knowledge of dancing. The dancers have their own notes on dancing, mostly in their own argot and they learn dancing through their argot only. The author quotes some of these notes which he calls Nartakabhāṣa.[15] The modern editor of this text says that this Nartakabhāṣā is known as Parasi in Gujarat and Rajasthan. According to the editor, the author's references are to this.[16] We may also note that Nartakabhāṣā i.e. professional argot of this nature is known as Bol in Bengal. The tradition that is discussed here, follows the *NŚ*.

Saṅgīta Dāmodara of Śubhankara is believed to have been written in the fifteenth century A.D.[17] This book is mostly a collection from ancient works on music and dramaturgy and contains very little that is original. In the fourth chapter it deals with dancing and drama. In discussing the art of dancing, the author discusses the Mārga style after Bharata and uses the term Aṅgahāra for it. He also discusses the Deśī style which according to him is Nṛtya.

Nartana Nirṇaya is a text on dancing by Puṇḍarika Viṭṭhala written to please the Emperor Akbar.[18] From this it appears that this book was written sometimes in the sixteenth century A.D. Nothing is said about its actual date in the text. It is as yet unpublished but the following manuscripts are extant:

(1) A ms. at the Asiatic Society Library in Calcutta; this ms. consists of 86 folios, well-preserved and legible though there are some scribal errors and omissions. The colophon has the spelling Nartakanirṇaya and this has

caused the title to be misspelt in the Society's catalogue.

(2) A ms. in the India Office Library, London. This ms. consists of 107 leaves. It is full of scribal errors but it is kept in a very good condition. The script is in Devanāgarī. The text has a few ślokas which can be found in the *NŚ*.[19]

In the first thirty-three folios *NN* gives the same views on dancing as the *NŚ* with a few variations while the last twenty-one folios report a different tradition, though in describing the basic movements, it follows the *NŚ*. The tradition can also be found in *SDar*, in the last half of *SSam* and in the description of the Deśī style in *SR*.

(3) A fragment, which has been edited by Dr. Priyabala Shah for the Rajasthan Oriental Research Institute. As the fragment bears no title and as the editor has not discovered its relationship with the *NN*, she calls it *Nṛttasamgraha*. The fragment in fact consists of 13 folios which correspond with the last 13 folios of the *NN*.

Saṅgīta Darpaṇa, by Dāmodara, is a work of the seventeenth century A.D. (1704 Samvat).[20] I have examined a ms. of this work at the Bibliotheque Nationale in Paris and an incomplete ms. at the Bodleian Library, Oxford. The Paris ms. contains 225 leaves and the script is in Devanāgarī. The Nṛtyādhyāya is a part of the *Bodleian* ms., which like the Paris ms., is in Devanāgarī script and is in very good condition. Nṛtya is discussed in the last chapter of this work which quotes ślokas from *SSam*, *SR*. and *ADar*.[21]

The tradition that this book represents seems to be the same as that which appears in the last part of the *NN*. This tradition is also described by *SSam* in a short section at the end of the sixth chapter. The same tradition is revealed in the description of the Deśī style in *SR*.

The author of *NN* is from Karṇāṭaka, as it appears from his own writings.[22] The author of *SDar* refers to the dances of South India while describing certain forms of dancing towards the end of this book.[23] From this it can probably be assumed that these two books describe traditions which was prevalent in India at that time.

SDar shows a confusing lack of order. In the middle of discussing one matter the author becomes involved in others that arise and, leaving his original subject, turns to them and returns to his subject only after considerable digressions.

Nāṭya Śāstra Saṁgraha is a compilation of the texts on the theory and practice of Nāṭya in Marathi made by Utke Govindācārya on the orders of the Maratha kings of Tanjore.[24] The name is given by the editors who think that the work was done sometime in the late eighteenth century.[25] Only the first two volumes of this text have been available to me. The first deals with Aṅgas, Upaṅgas and Pratyaṅgas while the second deals with the Cārīs and Sthānas. The first volume is entirely based on *SR*. In most of the places it copies *SR* outright. The section dealing with the hand-gestures, after giving the list and description given by *SR*, also mentions some gestures following *ADar* and others that can not be found in any other text. The second volume is based, according to the editors, on *Saṅgīta Muktāvalī* (Devendrācārya), *Sṛṅgāraśekhara* (Bhallāṭa), *Saṅgīta Darpaṇa* (Dāmodara) and *Saṇgīta Makaranda* (Vedasūri).[26]

Hasta Ratnāvalī is a ms. written in the nineteenth century.[27] It describes hand-gestures. The authors, Rāghava Rāya, says that his work is based on *Śrīhastamuktāvalī*. Lists of different hand-gestures are given, all of which agree with the lists given by Śubhāṅkara in his *SDām*. Śubhaṅkara refers to a book of his authorship which he calls *Śrīhastamuktāvali*, and it is highly likely that this is the text followed by Rāghava Rāya. *HR* seems to be a virtual copy of *Śrīhastamuktāvalī*. The few differences will be recorded in the chapter on hand gestures. The ms is in the Bodelian Library, Oxford and it is in very good condition. The script is in Bengali but the handwriting is difficult to decipher. I have depended to a considerable extent upon Aufrecht's account in his catalogue.

Besides the books mentioned above, many others have chapters on dancing. These are, however, mostly in ms. and even the only one that is published, *Saṅgītarāja,* has not been available to me. There are a few other texts which mention dancing while discussing various other subjects such as the Viṣṇu and the Skanda Purāṇas. The fifth section of the Viṣṇu Purāṇa contains a detailed biography of Kṛṣṇa, and the thireenth chapter of this section describes the Rāsa festival of Kṛṣṇa, which is a form of dancing accompanied by songs, a festival that exists even to-day.

In the Skanda Purāṇa, the third (3.3; 3.20), the fifth (5.2; 5.3; 5.11; 5.13), the sixth (6.188; 6.254) and the seventh khaṇḍas (7.11; 7.270) mention dancing. The fifth khaṇḍa (5.3) contains some technical terms. The sixth khaṇda (6.254) describes how Śiva danced to please Pārvati while other gods accompanied him on instruments.

These books do not discuss the forms of dancing and as such are left out from the present study. There are occasional references to dancing in many other texts but as they have nothing concrete on the art and merely mention it, they are also left out.

CHAPTER TWO

Forms of Dancing: Nṛtta, Nṛtya, Mārga, Deśi, Tāṇḍava, Lāsya

Nṛtta and Nṛtya are the two terms used by the theorists to mean two different types of dancing. Nṛtta does not seek to convey meaning and is intended to be no more than an exercise pleasing to the eye consisting of graceful and beautiful but highly stylised movements of the body.[1] Nṛtya has the form of Nṛtta with dramatic overtones added to it. That the difference between these two types of dancing is the difference between the classical and the popular style, is the opinion of some of the later theorists.[2]

That people knew of both the terms is evident from the use of the terms in the Vedic and other literature, but Bharata does not seem to have used the term Nṛtya. The two ślokas in which it can be found,[3] seem to be interpolations. It can probably be said that Bharata was concerned with the form of dance and as such he has discussed Nṛtta, and not Nṛtya. Moreover, if we agree with the theorists who define Nṛtya as a popular style, we may explain the absence of the term Nṛtya in Bharata, who states himself that though he knew of many popular styles, he does not discuss them.[4]

Another text, the *VDP,* has also discussed Nṛtta, and not Nṛtya. But from the time of *ADar* the term Nṛtya was being generally used by the theorists to denote an independent art and in all the later treatises, both the terms are found. *Abhg,* however, has used Nṛtta in his commentary on the *NŚ*, in order to be consistent, as K.M. Varma points out,[5] with the *NŚ*, which does not use the term Nṛtya.

It is curious to note that the term Nāṭya has often been used in the earlier texts to mean Nṛtya. Amarasiṃha, in his *Amarakośa,* gives the term Nṛtya as a synonym for Nāṭya.[6] *BhP* in one context, says that Nṛtta and Nṛtya are also called Nāṭya as they are performed by Naṭa in the preliminaries of a play.[7] Kālidāsa, in his *Mālavikāgnimitraṃ*, has used Nāṭya for Chalita, which is a type of Nṛtya,[8] although he has also used Nāṭya to mean a dramatic representation in the same text.[9] Perhaps, the synonymity of the terms Nṛtya and Nāṭya is illustrated by the term Bharatanāṭyaṃ, which is a branch of dancing.

Nartana is another term which in some texts means dancing. Amarakoṣa has given Nartana as a synonym for both Nṛtya and Nāṭya.[10] In the medieval period several terms appear in a rather confusing way. *Mānas* divides Nartana into six categories which are Nāṭya, Tāṇḍava, Lāsya, Lāghava, Viṣama and Vikaṭa[11] while *SR* has cited the last three varieties as varieties of Nṛtta.[12] This text equates Nartana with Nāṭya *BhP* differentiates Nṛtta and Nartana and says that Nartana is simple movements of the body while Nṛtta is constituted of the more complicated Karaṇas and Angahāras.[14] *NN* divides Nartana into Nāṭya, Nṛtya, and Nṛtta of which Nṛtta is again divided into Viṣama, Vikaṭa and Laghu.[15] In the *SDar*, Nartana is divided into Nṛtya, Nṛtta, Nāṭya, Tāṇḍava, Lāsya, of which Nṛtya is thought to have five forms, namely, Viṣama, Vikaṭa, Laghu, Peraṇi and Gauṇḍalī.[16] *DR* and *SR* consider that Nṛtta is Tālalayāśraya and Nṛtya is Bhāvāśraya while Nāṭya is Rasāśraya.[17] *BhP,* however says in one context that Nṛtta and Nṛtya have each two divisions, Mārga and Deśī, the Mārga style of both forms being Bhāvāśraya and the Deśī style being devoid of Bhāva.[18] Thus Śāradātanaya differs from others in maintaining that in one form at least, the Mārga, Nṛtta, which usually has no

Bhāva, can be Bhāvāśraya, while Nṛtya, which usually has Bhāva can in one form, the Deśī, be devoid of Bhāva. In another context, the same author says that Rasa-pradhāna Mārga Nṛtta is danced by a Naṭa while Bhāvāśraya Mārga Nṛtya is danced by a Nartaka,[19] That Nṛtta can be Rasāśraya while Nṛtya remains Bhāvāśraya is further mentioned by the same author in another context.[20] K.M. Varma reports that Kumbha Rāṇā and Vipradāsa "say that Rasa is to be manifested by Nṛtya while Bhāvas are accompanying it and similarly Bhāva is made to be manifested by Nṛtya while Rasa is accompanying it. Both these things are possible, and in either case it retains the name Nṛtya. Thus in order to distinguish them, they name former variety as Nāṭya-Nṛtya and the later as Mārga-Nṛtya. At the same time they retain and reserve the word Deśī for Nṛtta, in the same fashion as Dhananjaya and Dhanika do."[21]

We may now consider Mārga and Deśī, the two broad divisions of Nṛtta and Nṛtya mentioned above. Mārga is the classical style of dance described in the *NS*, which does not recognise Deśī dance. Later, however, Deśī developed so well that it was recognised as an independent style of serious dance. A discussion of it appears in *SR*, although its main concern is the Mārga tradition. In discussing Mārga dance *SR* follows the *NŚ* or to be more precise, it follows *AbhG's* interpretation of the *NŚ NN* also discusses both the traditions, Mārga and Deśī.

The importance of the Mārga style can be the more fully appreciated when we see that though Deśī was an independent style, yet its development was based on the methods of Mārga. But the acceptance of Deśī as a serious style can be seen in the fact that in some texts Nṛtya has been specifically used to mean the Deśī style.[22] *Mānas*, in its "Nṛtyavinoda," discusses the Deśī style while *DR.* says that Nṛtya is Mārga and Nṛtta is Deśī.[23] *SR* and *SDar*, are also of opinion that Nṛtya is Mārga.[24]

The division of Nṛtta and Nṛtya into Tāṇḍava and Lāsya was perhaps developed after Bharata though these terms occur in the *NŚ*. But Tāṇḍava as defined by the later writers, was perhaps not known to Bharata, who seems to have meant Nṛtta by this term.[25] Nor can Lāsya be found to denote what the later writers think it to be. Of course, references to "sukumāraprayoga," which is the essence of the type of dance known now as Lāsya, can be found in the *NŚ*[26] but the "sukumāraprayoga" and Lāsya are never associated. Tāṇḍava and Lāsya are discussed very thoroughly by some of the later writers who sometimes also divide dance into Masṛṇa, Uddhata, Viṣama, Vikata, Laghu, and so on.

By Tāṇḍava Bharata means only Nṛtta, which is constituted of such difficult poses as the Karaṇas and Angahāras[27] and the term has no other meaning. The word Lāsya is used only when the *NŚ* describes Lāsyāngas, which are essentials to Bhāṇa, one of the ten types of drama.[28] Ten Lāsyāngas are mentioned and from their descriptions they do not seem to constitute a style of dancing by themselves, but appear rather to be certain graceful movements contained in the technique of Bhāṇa. Besides this, Bharata mentions "sukumāraprayoga" which is the essence of Lāsya, being a feature of the dance of Pārvatī. But the nature of the "sukumāraprayoga" is not explained. Bharata defines Cārī and Mahācārī, in the discussion of the Purvaraṅga, as movements expressing Sṛngāra and Vīra Rasas respectively.[29] The distinction is similar to that between Tāṇḍava and Lāsya. This shows an awareness that one type of dance requires graceful movements, and this perhaps led to the recognition of Lāsya as a separate style.

The *VDP* gives Tāṇḍava and Lāsya as two parts of Nṛtta which are further divided into Bāhya and Ābhyantara. Bāhya does not follow any precise rule while Ābhyantara does so.[30] The distinction seems to be the same as that between Deśī and Mārga.

ADar mentions Tāṇḍava and Lāsya as two styles of dancing, one virile, and the other graceful.[31] *DR* says that Nṛtta and Nṛtya have each two divisions. namely, Tāṇḍava and Lāsya. Nṛtta and Nṛtya are in any case, auxiliary to drama.[32]

Mānas describes Tāṇḍava and Lāsya as two of the six forms of dancing done by men and women respectively.[33] *BhP* differentiates Tāṇḍava and Lāsya as Nṛtta and Nṛtya.[34] Perhaps Nṛtta, because it is strenuous, is kept for men and thus becomes Tāṇḍava; Nṛtya being more graceful, is reserved for women and becomes Lāsya. Since Nṛtya contains Abhinaya, it is less rigid than Nṛtta, and Lāsya is a suitable name for movements that have the quality of Lāsyāngas. Pārvatī may thus be associated with Lāsya because there was "sukumāraprayoga" in her dance. Several varieties of Tāṇḍava and Lāsya are mentioned, *SR.* says that Nṛtta and Nṛtya have both Tāṇḍava and Lāsya and mentions ten forms of Deśī Lāsyāngas.[35] *SUS* differentiates Nṛtta and Nṛtya as dances being performed by men and women respectively. The distinction is similar to that made by others between Tāṇḍava and Lāsya.[36]

SDām discusses Tāṇḍava and Lāsya as divisions of Nṛtya which is a Deśī style, according to it, and Tāṇḍava and Lāsya are dances for men and women respectively. Each of these styles is divided into two.[37] *NN* describes Tāṇḍava and Lāsya as forms of both Nṛtta and Nṛtya.[38] *SDar.* describe them as forms of Nartana which are being performed by men and women respectively.[39]

Tāṇḍava

The *NŚ* calls Taṇḍu the originator of Tāṇḍava which is, it says, composed of forceful Karaṇas and Aṅgahāras.[40] *BhP* states that it is accompanied by songs and Ārabhaṭṭi Vṛtti is one feature of it. It also says that Vardhamānaka, Āsārita and other songs and the appropriate instruments, should accompany Tāṇḍava. It has three subdivisions. It can also be

Deśī dance of two varieties. It should also be noted that none of these two Deśī Tāṇḍavas is forceful. The following are the forms of Tāṇḍava described in *BhP*.

(i) **Uccaṇḍa :** This is very forceful and quick. Karaṇas, Aṅgahāras, Akāśacārīs and Bhramarīs are performed and Raudra, Bibhatsa and Bhayānaka Rasa are evoked. (*BhP* pp. 298-9. 11-5.7, 21:2).

(ii) **Caṇḍa :** This is not very vigorous and is danced to a slow tempo. Bhūmicārīs, Karaṇas and Aṅgahāras are performed and Vīra and Raudra Rasas are evoked (*BhP* pp. 298-9. 11.16-7, 3, 9-10).

(iii) **Pracaṇḍa :** This is forceful, full of Karaṇas that involve jumping and Bhramarīs. Raudra and Bībhatsa are its Rasas (BhP p. 298-9. 11. 19-20, 0, 8-9).

(iv) **Prāpaṇa :** This is a form of Deśī Tāṇḍava (*BhP* pp. 301).

(v) **Preraṇa :** This is also a form of Deśī Tāṇḍava (*BhP* pp. 301).

Mānas describes Tāṇḍava as a virile form of dancing[41] *SR* agrees with the *NS* and *BhP* in describing the form of Tāṇḍava and adds songs of Dhruvā type to the description. This does not say anything about its sub-divisions or classification into Deśī.[42]

SDām. believes that Nṛtya is always Deśi and Tāṇḍava is a kind of Nṛtya which is danced by men. It has two divisions, Peraṇi and Bahurūpa.

(i) **Peraṇi :** Peraṇi is characterised by a multitude of movements but no acting (*SDām* pp. 69). *SR* describes it in greater detail but the character is the same. (*SR* 7.1316-25). *SDar* has the same description as the *SDām,* (*SDar* 53a). None of these two books define it as a Deśī Tāṇḍava.

(ii) **Bahurūpa :** This was promoted by Varuṇa. It is of such diverse forms that it has been compared with a scattered pearl necklace (*SDām* pp. 69).

Lāsya

Lāsya is not defined by the *NŚ*. It gives a list of ten Lāsyāngas auxiliary of Bhāṇa, and discusses them. The *VDP* says that Lāsya, a form of Nṛtta, can be performed either on the stage or outside it.[43] *ADar* mentions Lāsya as a dance of Pārvatī in its story of the mythological origin of dramaturgy.[44] Lāsya is not defined in *DR* and mentioned merely as a division of Nṛtta and Nṛtya.[45] *Mānas* describes Lāsya as a graceful style consisting of Aṅgahāras.[46]

BhP has exhaustive discussions on Lāsya defining it as a form composed of delicate Karaṇas and Aṅgahāras. Songs accompany it and Kaiśiki Vṛtti is added to it.[47] There can be four types of Lāsya, namely, (i) Śṛnkhalā, (ii) Latā, (iii) Piṇḍī and (iv) Bhedyaka. (*BhP* pp. 297).

(i) **Śṛnkhalā :** It consists of ten types of Lāsyangas. The Lāsyāngas referred to, are the same as those found in the *NŚ* (*BhP* 297).

(ii) **Latā :** It is of three types, known as Rāsakas: Daṇḍa, Maṇḍala and Nāṭyarāsakas (*BhP* pp. 297).

(iii) **Piṇḍī :** It seems to have no divisions but apparently can also be a Tāṇḍava dance, and when so, has many divisions (*BhP* pp. 297).

(iv) **Bhedyaka :** This again has ten Lāsyāngas, which are those mentioned in the *NŚ*. (***BhP***. p. 297).

In another context, *BhP* refers to the Bhāṇa type of drama and says that it employs ten Lāsyāngas whih are again those mentioned in the notes on Śṛnkhalā and Bhedyaka, i.e., the Lāsyāngas mentioned in the *NŚ*.[48] *BhP* seems to mean that these Lāsyāngas constitute Lāsya. It says once more that apart from these Lāsyāngas there are, according to some writers, four Nṛtyabhedas: (i) Gulma, (ii) Śṛnkhalitā, (iii) Latābandha and (iv) Bhedyaka, *BhP* says that Gulma is the same as Piṇḍi and describes both.

(i) **Gulma :** It is danced together by a group of dancers in a slow tempo. (*BhP* p. 246).

(ii) **Śṛṅkhalitā :** It is danced in form of a chain and in a comparatively faster tempo (*BhP* p. 246).

(iii) **Latābandha :** It is danced to a tempo neither too slow nor too fast, the partners holding each other (*BhP* p. 246).

(iv) **Bhedyaka :** Each dancer, in a group of dancers, plays her own part to a fast tempo (*BhP* p. 246).

These Nṛtyabhedas mentioned seem to be the same as the four classes of Lāsya mentioned at the beginning, the names of which, Sṛṅkhalā, Latābandha, Piṇḍī and Bhedyaka, occur also in the *NŚ*. But the *NŚ* views them as classes of Pīṇḍībandha, and says that Śṛṅkhalā is Gulma, i.e., a group. It uses the terms Latā and Latābandha synonymously. The *NŚ* does not describe these in detail but defines them. It states that the various Piṇḍīs are designed to please gods, and each bears the name of a god or a goddess.[49] The *VDP.* repeats this view.[50] *ND* describes these four classes of Lāsya while describing the Rāsaka type of dance-drama.[51]

It seems that *BhP* begins with its own interpretations of the views given in the *NŚ* on those movements that are graceful and delicate. It also seems to take the Lāsyāngas mentioned in the *NŚ* to mean parts of Lāsya, because they are delicate movements. But later it seems that *BhP* believes that Lāsya is made up of not only these but four other types of movements, which it calls Nṛtyabhedas.

SR defines Lāsya as a dance consisting of delicate movements that arouse erotic sentiment.[52] *SDām* says that Lāsya is a division of Nṛtya, which it considers to be a Deśī form of dance, and it is danced by women. It gives two subdivisions of Lāsya which are Churita and Yauvata.

(i) **Churiṭa :** The hero and the heroine dance with embraces, kisses and dramatic acting in the middle of an act (*SDām* p. 69).

(ii) **Yauvata** : The dancers dance with delicate movements and overpowering charms (*SDām* p. 69).

Lāsyāngas

The *NŚ* enumerates and defines Lāsyāngas while describing the Bhāna type of drama. In that connection a śloka is found in the G.O.S. edition of the *NŚ*[53] which says that Lāsya has a form similar to that of a Bhāṇa and it is to be danced by only one person. The text says that there are ten Lāsyāngas as follows: The G.O.S. edition actually describes twelve.

Geyapada, sthitapāṭhya, āsīna, puṣpagaṇḍikā, pracchedaka, trimuḍhaka, saindhava, dvimuḍhaka, uttamottamaka and uktapratyukta—these ten features characterise lāsya.

Where the male singers, being seated in the seats sing dryly [i.e., uttering meaningless syllables] being supported by stringed instruments and drums, it is known as *geyapada.*

Where a separated woman, her body burning with the fire of love, remains withdrawn and reads prākṛta [verses], it is *sthitapāṭhya.*

When [a woman] sits, without any musical instrument around her, without stretching out her body and is overcome with anxiety and sorrow, it is *Āsīna.*

Where songs are sung in different metres, where geya [the composition to he sung] is dependent on gāna [the regional style, as opposed to traditional gāndharva style[1] abounding in manly movemnts, it is *puṣpagaṇḍikā.*

That is known as *pracchedaka* in which women, although wronged by lovers, are attached to their lovers, being struck by the moonlight [in love].

Trimuḍhaka is a nāṭya [performed by women] composed of gentle and tender words, adorned with even metres and abounding in manly emotions.

Where a person has failed to keep a tryst, recites prākṛt to the accompaniment of karaṇas, it is *Saindhavaka.*

Where a song is presented with mukha and pratimukha [=exposition and progression] [song] in a series of caturaśrapada adhering to bhāva and rasa and arriving at a different meaning, it is known as *dvimudhaka.*

Uttamottamaka is known to be dependent on many rasas [expressed through] a variety of ślokas and is adorned with [feminine movements], such as helā and hāva.

Uktāpratyukta is derived from anger or pleasure and [often] contains words of censure. If [should also] contain a variety of expressive songs. (*NŚ*. 19. 121-35)

The last two lāsyāṅgas, which appear in the R. Kavi's edition seem to be interpolations which do not appear in any other text that follow Bharata.

(xi) **Citrapada :** A woman, burning with the fire of love, consoles herself by looking at her lover's picture (*NŚ* 19.136).

(xii) **Bhāvika :** A woman, burning with the fire of love, sees her lover in a dream and expresses different Bhāvas (*NŚ* 19.138).

DR gives a list of ten Lāsyāngas which agree with the list of the *NŚ*. It does not discuss them in detail and instead of Dvimūḍhaka, Dvigūḍhaka is mentioned as a Lāsyānga.[54]

NLR gives the same list of ten, but Vaimūḍhaka, Uttorottaka and Dvimuktaka are substituted for Trimūḍhaka, Uttomottaka and Dvimūḍhaka respectively. The author describes them in detail as follows.

(i) **Geyapada :** The same as in the *NŚ* (*NLR* 11.2853-5).

(ii) **Sthitapāṭhya :** The performance of Bhūmicārīs and recital of Carcarī is suggested (*NLR* 11.2856-7).

(iii) **Āsīnapāṭhya :** A woman recites a piece of poem from her seat with gestures of hand, foot and eyebrow (*NLR* 11.2862-3).

(iv) **Vaimūḍhaka :** It is performed by a man in a woman's dress with delicate movements (*NLR* 11.2864-5).

(v) **Puṣpagaṇḍikā :** It is a dance, performed to get to know the mind of men, accompanied with song, instrumental music and rhythmic beat (*NLR* 11.2867-8).

(vi) **Pracchedaka :** A woman, as though moonstruck, clings in anguish and love to her lover in spite of his faithlessness (*NLR* 11.2871-2). According to Rāhūla, quoted by *NLR* this portrays the situation in which a woman accidentally sees another woman being courted by her lover and her consequent indignation tortures her (*NLR* 11.2872-4).

(vii) **Saindhava :** In this form of Lāsya, the woman wears conchshell bracelets and uses dialects, songs and instrumental music of the Sindhu country (*NLR* 11.2879-80).

(viii) **Uktapratyukta :** This is simple dialogue (*NLR* 11.2881).

(ix) **Uttorottaka :** The description agrees with that of Uttomottaka, given by the *NŚ* (*NLR* 11.2887-8). But this text also believes that this may show a lover, afraid that her beloved may not come to her, going to her house (*NLR* 11.2895-6).

(x) **Dvimuktaka :** This Lāsyānga has Mukha-Pratimukha, and graceful Cārīs are performed in order to express Bhāvas (*NLR* 11.2897-8).

ND gives the same list of Lāsyāngas as the *NŚ* without discussing them.[55] *SD* also gives a list of ten Lāsyāngas that gives Trigūḍha and Dvigūḍha for Trimuḍha and Dvimūḍha. It discusses them as follows.

(i) **Geyapada :** The same as in the *NŚ* (*SD* 6.214-5).

(ii) **Sthitapāṭhya :** The same as in the *NŚ* (*SD* 6. 215).

(iii) **Āsīna :** To the description of the *NŚ* it is added that there should be no instrumental music in it, *SD* 6.216).

(iv) **Puṣpagaṇḍikā** : Songs are sung, accompanied by music, and the recitation of verses of diverse metres take place. Men and women act contrary to their nature (*SD* 6.217).

(v) **Pracchedaka** : This agrees with the view of Rāhūla, quoted in *NLR* and adds that the singer should accompany herself on the Vīṇā (*SD* 6.218).

(vi) **Trigūḍhaka** : This agrees with the description of Vai-mūḍhaka of *NLR* (*SD* 6.129).

(vii) **Saindhava** : This agrees with the *NŚ* (*SD* 6.129-20).

(viii) **Uttomottaka** : The same as the NŚ, but adds that the song should be sung in anger or pleasure. (*SD* 6.220).

(ix) **Dvigūḍha** : This agrees with both the *NŚ*, and *NLR* (*SD* 6.221).

(x) **Uktapratyukta** : The same as in the *NŚ* (*SD* 6.221-3).

Lāsyāngas, described in SR, are Deśī and the text gives a list of ten of them. They are described as follows.

(i) **Cālī** : (Cāli is the simultaneous movement of the feet, hips, thighs and arms.) It should be soft, graceful and attractive following the Tālās. (It should be neither too fast nor too slow, and done in triple measures (*SR* 7.1207-8)).

(ii) **Cālibaḍa** : Cāli is done quickly with straight movements (*SR* 7.1209)).

(iii) **Laḍhi** : It is soft and graceful and contains simultaneous oblique movements of the hips and the arms (*SR* 7.1209-10)).

(iv) **Sūka** : (It is a rhythmic movement full of Hāva and can be performed slowly or quickly. The ears of the dancer should shine with beautiful earrings

(*SR* 7.12 No. 11)).

(v) **Urongaṇa :** (It is the graceful oblique movement, slow or fast, of the shoulders and the breasts (*SR* 7.1211-12)).

(vi) **Dhasaka :** This is to lower the breasts gracefully in a rhythmic way (*SR* 7.1212)).

(vii) **Aṅgahāra :** It is the gradual bending of the body to the likeness of a bow (*SR* 7.1213)).

(viii) **Oyāraka :** (It is a slightly oblique and downward movement of the head (*SR* 7.1214).

(ix) **Vihasi :** It is a smile full of Śṛngāra Rasa. It has an extremely subtle and novel charm (*SR* 7.1214-5)).

(x) **Mana :** It is performed in the Sthāya Tāla, *SR.* 7.1215. *SDām.* discusses the ten Lāsyāṅgas used in Bhāṇa in the following manner.

(i) **Geyapada :** The heroine sings and is accompanied by instrumental music (*SDām* p. 86).

(ii) **Sthitapāṭhya :** This agrees with the *NŚ* in prescribing Cārīs and Caccatpuṭa. This also suggests recitation and Pāṇikalā hand-gesture (*SDām* p. 86).

(iii) **Āsīnapāṭhya :** The heroine sits and acts with graceful movements of the hands, feet and eyebrows (*SDām* p. 86).

(iv) **Vaimūḍhaka :** Men, dressed in women's dress clothes act Lāsya (*SDām* p. 86).

(v) **Puṣpagaṇḍikā :** Lāsya is performed with various graceful movements. *Or* : The heroine tries to understand the hero and in order to do so, she sings in various ways (*SDām* p. 86).

(vi) **Pracchedaka :** A woman sings to the accompaniment of the Vīṇā in grieving over the separation from her hubsand who loves another woman. *Or* A woman, seeing her husband attached to another woman, becomess jealous (*SDām* p. 86).

(vii) **Uttarottaram :** The simple conversation of a woman with her lover who she pretends is beside her (*SDām* p. 86).

(viii) **Uktapratyukta :** The heroine abuses the hero (*SDām* p. 87).

(ix) **Vimūḍhaka :** The heroine sings and dances gracefully (*SDām* p. 87).

(x) **Saindhava :** The dancer dances and sings songs which are appropriate to the Sindhu country (*SDām* p. 87).

SDām again describes Lāsyāṅgas as forms of Nṛtya, with their origin in Karṇāṭa. They are full of hand gestures and movements of the other parts of the body.[56] Then it describes this form of nine other Lāsyāṅgas, most of which agree with *SR's* list of the dancing which it calls Māṇḍalī.[57] This text also gives a list of Deśī Lāsyāṅgas, most of which agree with *SR's* list of the Deśī Lāsyāṅgas. They are Cāli, Cālibaḍa, Uroṅgana, Dhaṣaka, Naṭi (*SR* has Ladhi), Tukaṁ (*SR.* gives Sukaṁ), Nati, Rekhā and Dyotita.[58] Nati and Dyotita can not be found in *SR* while Rekhā[59] is not described as a form of Lāsyāṇga in *SR.* The descriptions generally agree with *SR.* and Nati seems to be the same as Aṅgahāra in *SR.*[60] while Dyotita seems to be the same as Vihasi.[61] While discussing these Lāsyāṅgas, the author discusses Mana, given by *SR*, which is not found in the list.[62] This description, however, does not say anything about Sthāya Tāla but agrees with the rest of the description, given by *SR.*

Dancing has also been classified as Sukumāra, Viddha, Uddhata, Madhura, Viṣama, Vikaṭa and Laghu. The terms Sukumāra and Viddha occur in the *NŚ*[63] as two sorts of performances, but it must be noted that there the author has Nāṭya not dancing, in mind. The *VDP* classifies Nṛtta as Sukumāra and Viddha[64] and says that Viddha is a Uddhata or virile dance performed by men while Sukumāra is a graceful style practised by women. The distinction is similar to Tāṇḍava and Lāsya. *Māṇas.* shows that Lāghava, Viṣama and Vikaṭa are divisions of Nartana. Lāghava is a form which is danced for merriment and Karaṇas such as Svastika and Añcita are performed. Viṣama is done by the recital of various verses and is devoid of bending movements. Moving about, the throwing and trembling of the body accompany it. Vikaṭa is the performance of contorted movements of the face, the hand, the belly, the feet and the eyes. The result is a strained Nṛtta.[65]

SR describes Viṣama, Vikaṭa and Laghu as varieties of Nṛtta and defines them. Viṣama is dancing (with straight limbs, according to the commentator), round and round with ropes. Vikaṭa is ludicrous in form. Laghu is constituted by Añcita and other minor Karaṇas.[66]

SDām mentions the Utplutikaraṇas under Viṣama.[67]

BhP uses Madhura and Uddhata to mean Lāsya and Tāṇḍava.[68]

NN describes and defines Viṣama, Vikaṭa and Laghu as varieties of Nṛtta following *SR* and says that Laghu must have jumping movements.[69]

SDr cites Viṣama, Vikaṭa and Laghu as forms of Nṛtya.[70]

Some texts discuss certain minor types of drama that contain dancing or movements similar to dancing. The *AP.* has a list of twenty-seven major and minor kinds of drama and the names of some Nṛtyabhedas appear among the minor.[71] The Avaloka of *DR* mentions seven such types, calling them Nṛtyabhedas.[72] Also *NLR* in its description of minor types of drama, refer to plays that have dancing and though it does not call them Nṛtyabhedas, yet the descriptions agree with those of *DR.*[73] *ND* discusses thirteen minor types of drama of which seven contain dancing.[74] *BhP.* gives the longest list of twenty Nṛtyabhedas.[75] *SD.* has a list of eighteen minor dramas some of which contain dancing.[76] *SDām* includes in its list of "Nṛtye Ratnanakṣatramālā," twenty-seven Rūpakas and Uparūpakas. Of seventeen Uparūpakas, seven contain dancing.[77] This subject has been very fully dealt with by D.R. Mankad in *Types of Sanskrit Drama.* The following is the list of these dramas given in the above mentioned texts.

(i) Ullopyaka (*BhP* 266); Ullāpyaka (*NLR* 11.3213-6, *SDām*, p. 95). Ullāpya (*SD* 6.282-3); (ii) Kalpavallī (*BhP* p. 268); (iii) Kāvya (*BhP* p. 262; *DR* p. 4; *NLR* 11.3151-3; *ND* p. 215; *SD* 6.284-5; *SDām* p. 96); (iv) *Goṣṭhī* (*BhP* 3. p. 256); (v) *Dombi* (*BhP* p. 257; *DR* p. 4); (vi) Toṭaka (*BhP* p. 255); (vii) Durmallikā (*BhP* 267); (viii) Nartanaka (*ND* p. 214); (ix) Nāṭikā (*BhP* p. 255); (x) Nāṭyarāsaka (*BhP* p. 263; *NLR* 11.3210-2; *ND* p. 215; 6.277-9; *SDām* p. 96); (xi) Pārijātaka (*BhP* p. 268); (xii) Prasthāna (*BhP* p. 262; *DR* p. 4; *NLR* 11.3148-50; *ND* p. 214; *SD* 6.280-1; *SDām* p. 95); (xiii) prekṣaṇa (*BhP* p. 263); (xiv) Bhāṇa (*BhP* p. 255; *DR* p. 4); (xv) Bhāṇikā, Bhāṇī, (*BhP* p. 62; *DR* p. 4; *NLR* 11. 3184-6; *ND* p. 215); (xvi) Mallikā (*BhP* p. 267); (xvii) Rāsaka (*BhP* p. 265; *DR* p. 4; *ND* p. 214; *SD* 6.288-90); (xviii) Lāsikā (*SDām* p. 96); (xix) Vilāsikā (*SD* 6.301-2); (xx) Śilpaka (*BhP* p. 257); (xxi) Śrigadita (*BhP* 258; *DR* p. 4; *SDām* p. 95); (xxii) Sallāpa (*BhP* p. 256). (xxiii) Hallisaka (*BhP* p. 266; *NLR* 11.3154-6; *ND* p. 214; *SD* 6.306-7; *SDām* p. 94).

This chapter is designed to indicate the variety of opinions that exist in the treatises on dancing.

The practical pursuit of the art, not unexpectedly, involves many directions and an attempt has been made to describe them in the following pages.

CHAPTER THREE

Movements of the Aṅgas, Upāṅgas and Pratyaṅgas

No unanimity can be claimed in the definitions of Aṅgas, Pratyaṅgas and Upāṅgas. Those parts of the body that are called Aṅgas in one text may well become Pratyaṅgas or Upāṅgas in another, or to increase the confusion, Pratyaṅgas may become Upāṅgas and Upāṅgas Pratyaṅgas. Fortunately, some degree of uniformity is reached in the case of some parts of the body, for most of our textual sources follow the *NŚ* in their accounts. Yet it should be again emphasised that even in works of such derivative nature, fresh views are constantly incorporated.

It is clear at any rate, that the terms "Aṅgā," Pratyaṅga" and "Upāṅgas" are class names, each denoting one class of parts of the body. It is equally obvious that Aṅga refers to the major limbs while Pratyaṅga and Upāṅga refer to smaller parts of the body. The confusion is due to the inability of the theorists to decide whether a part of the body is large enough to be an Aṅga or so small as to be a Pratyaṅga or an Upāṅga. In the following account the variety of opinion has been recorded in each instance.

The *NŚ* gives the following list of Aṅgas: Kaṭi, Pāda, Pārśva, Vakṣas, Śiras and Hasta. In some of the treatises we come across other parts of the body which were treated perhaps locally or in different periods of time, as Aṅgas. In the *VDP*, Grīvā, Mukha, Udara, Ūru and Jaṅghā are mentioned as Aṅgas while Hasta is in a unnamed class by itself. The *ADar* remarks that Grīvā is sometimes considered as an Aṅga, while *Mānas*, in which Skandha and Udara are Aṅgas calls Hasta and Pāda, Pratyaṅgas. The *SR* reports that Skandha is classified by some as an Aṅga, an opinion which it does not itself follow. The *SDām* adds to the class Jaṭhara (i.e. Udara) but calls Caraṇa (i.e. Pāda) a Pratyaṅga.[1]

We may say that the following have been regarded at one time or another as Aṅgas : Kaṭi, Pāda, Pārśva, Vakṣas, Śiras, Hasta, Grīva, Udara, Skandha, Ūru, Jaṅghā, Mukha.

All treatises, except the *AP* have used the term Upāṅga to indicate what we may call the minor parts which according to the *NŚ*, are Netra, Bhrū, Nāsā, Adhara, Kapola and Cibuka. Netra has four sub-divisions, such as Dṛṣṭi, Darśana, Tārā and Puṭa.[2] Most of the treatises have corresponding lists, though some mention a greater number of Upāṇgas.

The *VDP* gives no list and follows the *NŚ* entirely in discussing the Upāṅgas, the only difference being that it describes Darśanakarma as Dṛṣṭikarma and Cibuka as Danta, although the movements described as Dantakarma are the same as Cibukakarma.[3]

ADar mentions twelve Upāṇgas of which eight occur in the account of the *NŚ*, but four, Hanu, Daśana, Jihvā and Vadana do not. In speaking of Dṛṣṭi, it describes Darśanakarma, not the functions of Dṛṣṭi, as the other text do. There is no discussion of Dṛṣṭi in it. It takes Skandha to be a Pratyaṅga, but admits that other texts consider Skandha to be an Upāṅga. It also reports that other treatises include Pārṣṇi, Gulpha, Karāṅgulī and Padāṅgulī within their lists of Upāṅgas. No detailed description of the Upāṅgas, except Darśanakarma, appears in this text.[4]

The *AP* does not use the term Upāṅga, though it deals with the parts of the body known as Upāṅgas. *ND* refers, without going into details, to the same Upāṅgas as mentioned in the *NŚ* except Tārā and Darśana.[6] To the list of the *NŚ*, *Mānas* adds Hanu, Danta and Jihvā and drops Cibuka. Of Netra, only one subdivision, Dṛṣṭi, is described. Other Upāṅgas are discussed in detail.[7] *SR* gives almost the same list as given by *ADar.* with the difference that Anila is substituted for Hanu. In addition it refers to Skandha as an Aṅga, not Upāṅga. All are discussed in detail.[8]

The list of six Upāṅgas in *SSam* correspond to the list found in the *NŚ* but only Darśana is discussed in detail.[9] *SUS* follows the *NŚ* in general, but the movements of the eyes are all put under *Dṛṣṭi* and not Netra.[10] *SDām* is the only text that gives the following list of twenty-three Upāṅgas : Keśa, Stana, Dhammilla, Lalāṭa, Bhrū, Cakṣukoṇa, Netra, Tārā, Dṛṣṭī, Darśana, Śaṅkha, Karṇa, Hanu, Nāṣā, Kapola, Oṣṭha, Radana, Jihvā, Niḥśvāsa, Cibuka, Mukha, Mukharāga and Grīvā.[11] This includes almost all the parts of the body except those that appear as Aṅgas and Pratyaṅgas. It mentions all the Upāṅgas found in the *NŚ* except Puṭa. Some of the Upāṅgas named here, such as Keśa, Stana, Dhammilla, Lalāṭa, Cakṣukoṇa, Śaṅkha and Karṇa, are found in no other text. Hanu is mentioned also in *ADar.* and *Mānas.*; Radana in the *VDP*, *ADar*, *Mānas* and *SR*; Mukha in *ADar.* and *SR* and Mukharāga is referred to as an Upāṅga by *SR,* which is the only other text beside *SDām* that discusses Niḥśvāsa as an Upāṅga. Jihvā is mentioned as an Upāṅga also in *ADar.* *Mānas.* and *SR,* the last of which discusses it in detail. Grīvā is not listed as an Upāṅga except in *SDām.*

NN discusses Dṛṣṭi and says that Tārā and Puṭa follow the movements of Dṛṣṭi. Bhrū and Mukharāga are described in detail.[12] *SDar* gives the same list of Upāṅgas as the *NŚ* without giving details.[13] The only text that remains is *NŚSam.* but as it has merely copied *SR* in the matter of Upāṅgas, it need not be discussed here.[14]

With regard to the Upāṅgas, it is difficult to see how such parts of the body as Keśa, Stana, Cakṣukoṇa and others can have movements of their own, but for the sake of accurate reporting such doubts have been kept out of the present account.

A third class of the movements of the limbs of the body is known as the movements of the Pratyaṅgas. This is a late development, the class being accepted as an indepdendent one only in the later treatises. It denotes parts of the body smaller even than the minor limbs. The *NŚ* does not regard Pratyaṅga as an independent class but as a sub-class of Aṅga.[15] There are also other early texts, e.g. *VDP*, *ND*, which do not use the term Pratyaṅga though they discuss the movements known later as those of Pratyaṅgas. The importance attached by the later writers to Pratyaṅgas as an independent class can be seen in the fact that the *AP* has only two divisions, Aṅga and Pratyaṅga.

The texts that have discussed Pratyaṅgas are *ADar*, *AP*, *Mānas*, *SR*, *SSam*, *SUS*, *SDām* and *NŚSam*. *ADar* gives the list of six Pratyaṅgas which are Skandha, Bāhu, Pṛṣṭha, Udara, Ūru and Jaṅghā. It refers to four other Pratyaṅgas, i.e. Manibandha, Jānu, Kūrpara and Grīvā as items included in the list by other theorists. Skandha, the text says is sometimes considered as an Upāṅga by some other theorists.[16] It does not discuss the movements of these Pratyaṅgas in detail except Grīvā.

The *AP* gives a list of Aṅgas and includes in the list of the Pratyaṅgas those parts of the body that are called Upāṅgas in the earlier treatises.[17] None of these divisions are discussed in detail although some technical terms have been mentioned.

Mānas gives a list of six Pratyaṅgas which includes Bāhu, Manibandha, Karaśākhā, Jānu and Padāṅgulī. Udara and Skandha, which are considered as Pratyaṅgas by most of the texts, are put in the list of Aṅgas in this text. It is stated that Skandha is sometimes considered as an Upāṅga. In discussing the Karaśākhā, it deals with gestures of the hand which is described as an Aṅga in all other texts. *Mānas* also discusses Aṅghri as a Pratyaṅga but does not mention it in the list of Pratyaṅgas. The types of the movements of Aṅghri, discussed here, correspond to *SR's* list of Pratyaṅgas. Grīvā, Pṛṣṭha and Uru are not discussed in this text.[18]

SR discusses six Pratyaṅgas : Grīvā, Bāhū, Pṛṣṭha, Udara, Ūru and Jaṅghā. It mentions three others, Manibandha, Jānu and Bhūṣaṇa which, it says, are included in the list of Pratyaṅgas by some theorists.[19] One Pratyaṅga mentioned, Bhūṣaṇa, is not found as a limb of the body in any other text. Mukha, Kūrpara, Caraṇāṅgulī and Karāṅgulī are included in the list of Upāṅgas. Skandha is discussed in the list of Aṅgas, following, it is remarked, the practice of the others. *KN* quotes Kohala to describe Cālaka and Vartanā which are two types of movements of the arms. These have not been included in the present account beyond mentioning their names.

The list given by *SSam* corresponds to *SR* which has Grīvā, Bāhu, Pṛṣṭha, Udara, Ūru and Jaṅghā. It enumerates them without going into detail.[20] *SUS* gives almost the same list that we find in *SR* and *SSam*. It includes Aṁsa, and does not mention Bāhu in the list, which consists of Grīvā, Aṁsa, Pṛṣṭha, Udara, Ūru and Jaṅghā, all in detail.[21]

SDām, unlike any other text, gives a list of ten Pratyaṅgas, namely, Skandha, Bāhu, Kūrpara, Manibandha, Karāṅgulī, Ūru, Jānu, Jaṅghā, Caraṇa and Caraṇāṅgulī.[22] Caraṇa is considered to be an Aṅga by all other texts except *Mānas* which agrees with *SDām*. Udara is mentioned as an Aṅga. Grīvā and Mukha are mentioned as Upāṇgas. The list of Pratyaṅgas and Upāṅgas in this text, includes all possible minor limbs except Pṛṣṭha. It does not discuss Pratyaṅgas in detail. *NŚSam* merely copies *SR*.[23] *NN* discusses Bāhu and Mukharāga[24] while *SDar* gives the same list as the *NŚ*, but no detail.[25]

From this discussion it appears that Udara, Ūsru, Kūrpara, Karāṅgulī, Grīvā, Caraṇāṅgulī, Jaṅghā, Jānu, Pṛṣṭha, Bāhu, Manibandha, Mukha and Skandha may be taken as

Pratyaṅgas. Not all of these are, however, specified as Pratyaṅgas in every text and the *NŚ* discuss some without calling them either Aṅgas Upaṅga or Pratyaṅga. The following are the movements of Aṅgas, Upāṅgas, and Pratyaṅgas.

Movements of the Śiras

These are movements of the head; usually movements of the neck are included among these. The Śiras is considered to be an Aṅga.

(1) **Añcita :** The neck is slightly bent sidewise (*NŚ* 8.31; *VDP* 3.24.8; *SDam* p. 61; *SUS* 5.25; *SSam* 6.25; *Mānas* 16.4.989; *SR* 7.64; *NN* 15a; *NŚSaṁ* 60). *AP* : Acita (*AP*. 341.8).

(2) **Adhogata :** The head is bent down. *ADar, SR, SUS, NN, NŚSaṁ* have Adhomukha for Adhogata (*NŚ* 8.36; *AP* 341.8; *VDP* 3.24.12; *SDām* p. 61; *SUS* 5.25; *SSam* 6.27; *Mānas* 16.4.996; *SR* 7.73; *NN* 14b; *NŚSam*. 70; *ADar* 54).

(3) **Ardhagātra :** Too obscure to explain (*SMak* 2.4.35).

(4) **Avadhūta :** The head is bent down once (*NŚ* 8.30; *AP* 341.8; *VDP* 3.24.7; *SDām* p. 61; *SUS*. 5.24; *SSam*. 6.24; *Mānas* 16.4.986; *SR* 7.56; *NN* 14b; *NŚSaṁ*. 51).

(5) **Ākampita:** The head is moved slowly up and down. (*NŚ* 8.20; *AP*. 341.7; *ND* p. 189; *SDām* p. 61; *SUS* 5.27; *Mānas* 16.4.980; *SR* 7.59; *NN* 14b; *NŚSaṁ*. 55). *VDP*: To raise the head straight in a natural way. (*VDP* 3.24.I). In another śloka, the *NŚ* suggests that the head which is moved up and down, should be kept straight, *SSam* agrees with this description (*NŚ* 8.21; *SSam*. 6.20).

(6) **Ādhuta :** The head is obliquely raised upwards once. The G.O.S. edition of the *NŚ* has accepted the reading Ādhuta. M.M. Ghosh prefers Udvāhita.

VDP and *ADar* have Udvāhita while *AP, SUS, SSam* and *Mānas* have Ādhuta. *SR, NN* and *NŚSam* have both. In *SR, NN, NŚSam* Ādhuta and Udvāhita are two different positions of the head while the *NŚ* combines them into one and permits the use of either. According *SR* and *NŚSaṁ*, the head is lifted upwards once in Udvāhita and the same movement done obliquely is Ādhuta. *NN* agrees with the *NŚ* in describing Ādhuta, but in the case of Udvāhita, it agrees with *SR* and *NŚSam*. In the list of terms, *NN* gives Vādhuta but while explaining the action, calls it Ādhuta. (*NŚ* 8.27; *AP* 341.8; *VDP* 324.6; *SDām*. p. 61; *SUS* 5.26l; *SSam* 6.23; *Mānas* 16.4.987; *SR* 7.55,61; *NN* 15a.; *NŚSaṁ* 49, 57; *ADar* 52).

(7) **Ārātrikā** : The head is moved in a circular way touching the shoulders (*SR* 7.76; *NŚSaṁ* 74; *NN* 15a).

(8) **Utkṣipta** : The face is raised (*NŚ* 8.35; *AP* 341.8; *VDP* 3.24.11; *SDām* p. 61; *SUS* 5.25; *SSam* 6.26; *Mānas.* 16.4.996; *ADar* 63; *SR.* 7.72; *NŚSaṁ* 69; *NN* 15a).

(9) **Kampita** : To move the head quickly up and down several times. (*NŚ* 8.20; *AP* 341.7; *VDP* 3.24.2; *ND* 189; *SDām* p. 61; *SUS* 5.27; *SSam* 6.21; *ADar.* 60; *SR.* 7.58; *NN* 15a; *NŚSaṁ* 53). *Mānas* : Vidhura (*Mānas* 16.4.981; 978).

(10) **Ciguru** : The head should rest on the left hand and the dancer should move glancing sideways. Gamaka should be applied from time to time (*SMak.* 2.4.31).

(11) **Ciṭiboṭabaṇi** : In the description the action is given the name Viṭabhāṭāvaṇikrama. The text is obscure (*SMak* 2.4.37; 29).

(12) **Tiryaṇnatonnata** : The head is titled obliquely, then raised (*SR.* 7.74; *NŚSaṁ* 72; *NN* 15a).

(13) **Dhuta :** Slow movement of the head. *NN* says that this should be done obliquely (*NŚ* 8.24; *AP* 341.7; *VDP* 3.24.3; *SDām* p. 61; *SUS* 5.26; *SSam* 6.22; *ADar* 57; *SR* 7.52; *NN* 14b; *NŚSam* 46). *Mānas* : *Druta*: (*Mānas* 16.4.984).

(14) **Nihañcita :** The shoulder is raised and the neck is bent down. Though the G.O.S. edition of the *NŚ* gives this description in its footnote, it accepts another reading which means, "to raise the shoulder and to arch the eyebrow slightly." All other texts accept the previous description. (*NŚ* 8.32; *SSam* 6.25; *SR* 7.65; *NŚSām* 61). *NN* does not say anything about the neck (*NN* 15s). *AP; VDP; SDām; SUS* : Nikuñcita (*AP* 341.8; *VDP* 3.24.9; *SDām* p. 61; *SUS* 5.25; *Mānas* : Nyañcita. (*Mānas.* 16.4.990).

(15) **Parāvṛtta :** The face is turned backwards (*NŚ* 8.34; *AP* 341.8; *VDP* 3.24.10; *SDām* p. 61; *SUS* 5.24; *Mānas.* 16.4.993; *SR* 7.71; *NN* 15a; *NŚSaṁ* 67; *ADār* 61).

(16) **Parivāhita :** The head is alternately moved sideways. *VDP.* describes it as a circular movement of the head. (*NŚ* 8.27; *AP* 314.8; *VDP* 3.24.5; *SDām* p. 61; *SUS* 5.26; *Mānas* 16.4.992; *ADār* 64; *SR* 7.62; *NN* 15a; *NŚSaṁ* 58).

(17) **Pārśvābhimukha :** The face is turned sideways. (*SR.* 7.78; *NN* 15a; *NŚSaṁ* 75).

(18) **Prākṛta :** The G.O.S. edition of the *NŚ* and *SDām* have this term. This indicates a straight and natural posture of the head (*NŚ* 8.38; *SDām* p. 61).

(19) **Phaṇibālā :** Some words are missing from the text which is corrupt as well (*SMak* 2.4.36).

(20) **Boṭāvaṇi :** The dancer should walk keeping her head straight, lifting her hands and frowning. In the list of terms *SMak* gives the term as Boṭāvaṇi but while describing the action, calls it Boṭaveṇi (*SMak* 2.4.28, 30).

(21) **Recita :** To move the head obliquely (*SUS.* 5.24).

(22) **Lolita :** Explained as Parivartita also. The head is moved in all directions. (*NŚ* 8.37; *AP* 341.9); *VDP* 3.24.13; *SDām* p. 61; *SUS* 5.26; *Mānas* 16.4.999; *ADar* 55 *SR* 7.73; *NŚSaṁ* 71; *NN.* 15a). *AP* : Lalita *ADār* : Alolita.

(23) **Vidhuta :** A quick movement of the head. According to the *VDP*, the head should be shaken sideways. *Mānas* : The head is moved obliquely in all directions (*NŚ* 8.24; *AP* 341.7; *VDP* 3.24.4; *SDām* p. 61; *Mānas* 16.4.983; *NN* 14b. *NŚSaṁ* 48; *SR* 7.54).

(24) **Viṣamaka :** Mentioned as Viṣagātra in the description. The next is too osbcure to explain (*SMak* 2.4.34; 28).

(25) **Vīragātra :** Some words are missing from the description. In the list of the terms, *Smak* gives Vīragātra but while describing the action, calls it Varagātra (*SMāk* 2.4.28, 33.).

(26) **Sama :** The head is kept straight and notionless in a natural way (*ADar* 51; *SR* 7.77; *NN* 14b; *NŚSaṁ* 75).

(27) **Saṁagātra :** The head should rest on the right hand. The dancer should glance sideways and she must pause from time to time (*SMak* 2.4.32).

(28) **Skandhānata :** The head is bent towards the shoulder. (*SR* 7.75; *NN* 15a; *NŚSaṁ* 73).

Movements of the Netra

These are movements of the eyes. Netra is considered to be an Upāṅga which has four types of movements : Dṛṣṭi, Darśana, Tārā and Puṭa.

Movements of the Rasadṛṣṭis

(1) **Adbhūtā :** The eyelids are curled, the eyes are charmingly opened and raised in wonder (*NŚ* 8.51;

VDP 3.25.7; *Mānas* 16.4.1049; *SUS* 5.30; *SR* 7.392-3; *NŚSaṁ* 553; *BhP* p. 125; *NN* 16a).

(2) **Karuṇā :** The eyes are focused towards the nose with drooping lids. The pupils are full of tears and dull with sorrow (*NŚ* 8.50; *Mānas* 16.4.1048; *SR* 7.386-7; *NŚSaṁ* 547; *BhP* p. 125-6; *NN* 16a) *SUS* : Sakaruṇā (SUS 5.30). *VDP* : The pupils are not seen. (*VDP* 3.25.7).

(3) **Kāntā :** To glance sideways in joy and pleasure, arching the eyebrows. (*NŚ* 8.47; *VDP* 3.25.5; Mānas. 16.4.1045; *BhP* p. 125; *NN* 15b). *SR* adds that the eyes should be open and clear. (*SR* 7.383; *NŚSaṁ*. 544). *SDar* agrees with the *NŚ* and *SR* (*SDar*. 39a)

(4) **Bībhatsā :** The eyelids are contracted at the corners, the pupils are agitated, the eyebrows are still and close to each other (*NŚ* 8.54; *VDP* 3.25.9; *Mānas* 16.4.1052; *SR* 7.391-2; *NŚSam*. 552.; *BhP*. p. 126). *NN* : The eyelids are contracted while the pupils are agitated. (*NN*. 16a).

(5) **Bhayānakā :** The eyelids are raised and fixed. The pupils are moved (*NŚ* 8.48; *VDP* 3.25.6; *Mānas* 16.4.1046; *SR* 7.390; *NŚSaṁ* 551; *BhP* p. 126; *NN* 16a).

(6) **Raudrī :** The eyes are open, bloodshot and still, with the pupils and lids suggesting cruelty and harshness. The eyebrows are knitted suggesting a frown (*NŚ* 8.52; *Mānas* 16.4.1050; *SR* 7.387-8; *NŚSam* 548). *SUS, VDP NN, BhP* : Raudrā (*SUS* 5.30; *VDP* 3.25.8; *NN* 16a; *BhP* p. 125).

(7) **Vīrā :** The eyes are fully open, excited steady and majestic (*NŚ* 8.53; *VDP* 3.25.9; *SUS* 5.30; *Mānas* 16.4.1051; *SR* 7.388-9; *NŚSaṁ* 549; *BhP* 125; *NN* 16a).

(8) **Śāntā :** The eyes are steady and they look downwards.

(*NŚ* 8.55; *SUS* 5.30). *VDP* : The eyes are steady in meditation. (*VDP* 3.25.10). This occurs only in the *VDP SUS* and the G.O.S. edition of the *NŚ*.

(9) **Hāsyā :** The eyes are narrowed gradually and the moving pupils are partly sen (*NŚ* 8.49; *VDP* 3.25.6; *SUS* 5.30; *Mānas* 16.4.1047; *SR* 7.385; *NŚsaṁ* 546; *BhP* p. 125; *NN*. 16a).

Movements of the Bhāvadṛṣṭis

(1) **Adharā :** Not explained (*SUS* 5.28).

(2) **Abhitaptā :** The pupils look dull due to the movements of the eyelids. The glance is full of distress and pain (*NŚ* 8.72; *VDP* 3.25.16; *Mānas*. 16.4.1071; *BhP* p. 129; *NN* 16b; *SDar*. 39a). *SR* : The eyelids are agitated in pain (*SR* 7.416; *NŚSaṁ* 575).

(3) **Abhinanditā :** Not explained (*SUS* 5.29).

(4) **Ardhamukulā :** The eyes are half open and the pupils move slightly (*NŚ* 8.76; *BhP* p. 129; *Mānas*. 16.4.1075; *SR* 7.410-1; *NŚSaṁ* 569; *NN* 16b).

(5) **Ākekarā :** The eyelids are slightly contracted at the corners. They are joined together and they are half closed while the pupils are repeatedly raised (*NŚ*. 8.93; *VDP* 3.25.15; *Mānas* 16.4.1078; *SR* 7.420; *NŚSaṁ*. 578; *BhP* p. 129). *NN* : A distant look with the eyes contrcted at the corners. (*NN*. 16b-17a). *SUS* : Kekarā. (*SUS* 5.29).

(6) **Udvignā :** Not explained (*SUS* 5.30).

(7) **Kuñcitā :** The eyelashes and the eyelids are slightly contracted and the pupils are completely contracted (*NŚ* 8.71; *VDP* 3.25.20; *Mānas* 16.4.1070; *SR* 7.414; *NŚSaṁ*. 573; *BhP* p. 128). *NN*: The eyelashes, eyelids and pupils are slightly contracted. (*NN* 16b).

(8) **Kruddhā :** An angry glance with the eyelashes still and the eyes raised. The pupils are motionless and fixed upwards. The eyebrows are knitted (*NŚ* 8.57; *VDP* 3.25.12; *SUS* 5.28; *Mānas* 16.4.1056; *BhP* 127). *SR* suggests that the pupils should move a little (*SR* 7.398; *NŚSaṁ* 558.). *SDar.* agrees with *SR* (*SDar* 38a). *NN* does not say anything about the pupils or the eyelashes but agrees with the *NŚ* in describing the rest of the action (*NN.* 16a).

(9) **Krurā :** Not explained (*SUS* 5.29).

(10) **Glānā :** The eyebrows, the eyelashes and the eyelids droop. The eyes move slowly and feebly with sunken pupils (*NŚ* 8.67; *VDP* 3.25.23; *SUS* 5.29; *Mānas* 16.4.1066; *NŚSaṁ* 570; *BhP* p. 128; *NN* 16b). *VDP* : The eyes, full of tears, are closed. The eyelashes seem to have been clipped off.

(11) **Calā :** Not explained (*SUS* 5.29).

(12) **Jihmā :** The eyelids are lowered and slightly contracted. The pupils are concealed. Oblique and shy glances are cast slowly (*NŚ* 8.73; *VDP* 3.25.11; *SR* 7.413; *NŚSaṁ* 571; *BhP* p. 129; *NN* 16b.). *Mānas*: The eyes are harsh (*Mānas.* 16.4.1072).

(13) **Jugupsitā :** The eyelids are contracted and the pupils are hidden and the eyes turn away from what lies in front (*NŚ* 8.60; *SUS.* 5.30). *Mānas* : A distressed look (*Mānas.* 16.4.1059). *SR* describes this as an indistinct look (*SR* 7.400; *NŚSaṁ* 560). *BhP* describes it as an anxious look (*BhP* p. 127). *NN* agrees with the *NŚ* in describing the first part of the action (*NN* 16a).

(14) **Trastā :** The eyelids are raised in fear and the pupils tremble. The eyes are wide open in panic (*NŚ.* 8.94; *Mānas* 16.4.1080; *SUS* 5.29; *SR* 7.425; *NŚSaṁ* 583; *BhP* 129; *NN* 17a; *VDP* 3.25.18).

(15) **Dīnā :** The lower eyelid is slightly lowered, then pupils are still and full of tears and they move slowly (*NŚ* 8.56; *SUS* 5.28; *BhP* p. 127; *NN* 16a). *Mānas* and *SR* attribute this action to the upper eyelid which should be half closed. (*Mānas* 16.4.1055; *SR* 7.397; *NŚSaṁ* 557).

(16) **Dṛptā :** The pupils are motionless and the eyes are wide open. This steady glance shows firmness (*NŚ* 8.58; *VDP* 3.25.13; *SUS* 5.28; *BhP* p. 127; *SR* 7.399; *NŚSaṁ* 559; *Mānas* 16.4.1057; *NN* 16a).

(17) **Nimīlitā :** A glance through half closed eyes (*VDP.* 3.25.3).

(18) **Parimlānā :** Not explained (*SUS* 5.30).

(19) **Bhayānvitā :** The pupils move away from the centre in fear and almost start out of their sockets. The eyes are wide open (*NŚ* 8.59; *SUS* 5.28; *BhP* p. 127; *Mānas* 16.4.1058; *SR* 7.400; *NŚSaṁ* 559). *VDP* : Bhītā : The eyes are contracted and the pupils are moving (*VDP* 3.25.12). *NN* : The eyes are wide open and they trembe in fear (*NN.* 16 a).

(20) **Madirā :** There are three types of Madirā : Taruṇā, Madhyamā and Adhamā.

Taruṇā : The eyes are distended at the corners and the rolling pupils denote desire.

Madhyamā : The evelids are slightly contracted and the pupils are mobile, suggesting restlessness.

Adhamā : The pupils are slightly visible in winking eyes which are turned down. According to the *NŚ* the eyes may either wink very often or be steady.

(*NŚ* 8.82-4; *Mānas* 16.4.1081-4; *SR* 7.26-30; *NŚSaṅ* 584-7). *BhP* does not describe Madirā. (*BhP* 125). *VDP* does not divide it into three types, and prescribes for the eys full-bloomed and whirling pupils. (*VDP* 3.25.22). *NN* : Uttamā, Madhyamā and Adhamā. The descriptions agree with those in the *NŚ* (*NN* 17a). *SDar* : Madhurā : Only Taruna Mada is described in which it agrees with the *NŚ* (*ṢDar* 39a).

(21) **Maliṇā :** The eyelashes flutter. The eyelids flutter and the corners of the eyes are pale (*NŚ* 8.64; *VDP* 3.25.15; *SUS* 5.28.29; *BhP* p. 128; *NN* 16a). *Mānas*: The pupils turn away from the object in front. (*SR* 7.404-5; *NŚSaṁ* 563).

(22) **Mukulā :** The eyelashes flutter and their tips meet. The pupils meet in happiness. (*NŚ* 8.70; *VDP* 3.25.21; *SUS* 5.28; *Mānas* 16.4.1069; *BhP* p. 128; *NN.* 16b). *SR* : The pupils are tranquil (*SR* 7.409; *NŚSaṁ* 568).

(23) **Lajjānvitā :** The eyelashes are slightly contracted and the upper eyelids arẹ lowered in shyness. The pupils are cast down (*NŚ* 8.66). *VDP Mānas, SR NN, SDār* : Lajjitā (*VDP* 3.25.14; *Mānas* 16.4.1065; *SR* 7.407; *NŚSaṁ* 566; *NN* 16b; *SDar.* 30a). *BhP* : Lajjāvatī (*BhP* p. 128) *SUS* : *Salajjā* (*SUS* 5.28).

(24) **Lalitā :** The eyes are narrowed at the corners. The glance is charming, cheerful and loving. The eyebrows are knitted (*NŚ* 8.74; *SUS* 5.29; *Mānas* 16.7.1073; *SR* 7.419; *NŚSaṁ* 577; *BhP* p. 129; *NN* 16b). *VDP* : The eyes are opened at the corners. (*VDP* 3.25.22).

(25) **Vikośā :** The eyelids are wide open and the eyes do not wink. The pupils are restless (*NŚ* 8.80; *Mānas* 16.4.1079; *SR* 7.421-2; *NŚSaṁ* 579). *VDP* : Viśokā (*VDP* 3.25.19) *NN* does not say anything about the winking of the eys (*NN* 17a).

(26) **Vitarkitā :** The eyelids are raised, the pupils are fully open and they move downwards (*NŚ* 8.75; *SR* 7.415; *NŚSaṁ* 574; *BhP* p. 129; *NN* 16b). *Mānas.* :

Vitarkā : The eyes are half open. (*Mānas* 16.4.1074). *VDP* : Vitarkā : The pupils are motionless. (*VDP* 3.25.21).

(27) **Viplutā :** The eyelids tremble and then become motionless. The they droop ((*NŚ* 8.78; *VDP* 3.25.17; *Mānas* 16.4.1077; *SR* 7.424; *BhP* p. 129; *SUS* 5.29; *NŚSaṁ* 582; *NN* 17a). The directions in which the pupils are raised and agitated are discussed only in the *NŚ*.

(28) **Vibhrāntā :** The pupils are mobile and the glance is restless. The eyes are wide open (*NŚ* 8.77; *VDP*. 3.25.19; *SR* 7.423; *Mānas* 16.4.1076; *NŚSaṁ* 581; *NN* 17a). *SUS Bhrāntā* : *SUS* 5.29). *BhP* suggests keeping the eyes open and agrees with the *NŚ* in describing the rest of the action. (*BhP* p. 129).

(29) **Viṣaṇṇā :** The eyes are wide in dejection and they wink. (*NŚ* 8.69; *SUS* 5.28; *VDP* 3.25.17). *NN* : The eyelids are narrowed at the corners. The winking pupils can not be seen (*NN* 16b) *SR* and *Mānas* add that the eyes drop at the corners (*SR* 7.418; *Mānas* 16.4.1068; *NŚSaṁ* 576). *BhP* : The eyes do not wink (*BhP* p. 129).

(30) **Vismitā :** The eyelids are wide open and the eyes are still and raised in happiness producing a wide-eyes glance (*NŚ* 8.61; *VDP* 3.25.13; *Mānas* 16.4.1060; *BhP* p. 129; *SR* 7.401; *NŚSaṁ* 561; *NN* 16b).

(31) **Śaṅkitā :** The glance is sometimes steady and sometimes still. The eyes are sightly raised, obliquely open and the pupils are unsettled (*NŚ* 8.68; *VDP* 3.25.18; *SUS* 5.29; *BhP* p. 128; *Mānas* 16.4.1067). *SR*. : The glance is sometimes steady and sometimes still. The eyes look sideways seemingly directed forward, yet looking stealthily and withdrawing immediately from the object. (*SR* 7.408; *NŚSaṁ* 567). *SDar* follows *SR* (*SDar* 39a).

(32) **Śūnya :** The pupils and eyelids are kept normally. The glance is vacant and immobile and it does not see the object in front (*NŚ* 8.63; *SUS* 5.28; *Mānas* 16.4.1062; *BhP* p. 128; *SR* 7.403; *NŚSaṁ* 562; *NN* 16b). *VDP* : The eyelids and the pupils are still. The glance shows agitation (*VDP* 3.25.20).

(33) **Śrāntā :** The eyelids droop due to fatigue, the corners of the eyes are contracted and the pupils are lowered. (*NŚ* 8.65; *Mānas* 16.4.1064; *BhP* p. 128; *NN*. 16b.). *VDP* : The eyelids are slightly raised. (*VDP*. 3.25.16). *SR* : The eyelids are raised and the unsteady pupils move slothfully. The eyes are fixed on a nearby object. (*SR* 7.406; *NŚSaṁ*. 535). *SDar*. follows both the *NŚ* and *SR* (*SDar* 39a).

(34) **Sakāmā :** Not explained (*SUS* 5.30).

(35) **Sabhayā :** Not explained (*SUS* 5.30).

(36) **Sahajā :** Not explained (*SUS* 5.28).

(37) **Saumyā :** A level glance with steady pupils (*VDP* 3.25.14).

(38) **Sthirā :** Not explained (*SUS*. 5.30).

(39) **Snigdhā :** The eyes are pleasing and slightly open. The pupils are still and the eyebrows denote joy. (*NŚ* 8.57; *VDPA* 3.25.10; *SUS* 5.28; *Mānas*. 16.4.1053; *SR* 7.394-5; *BhP* p. 126; *NŚSaṁ* 554; *SDar* 39a). *NN* : The eyes are pleasing and the eyebrows denote joy (*NN* 16a).

(40) **Smerā :** Not explained (*SUS* 5.29).

(41) **Hṛṣṭā :** The pupils move inwards in the moving eyes which are slightly lowered and winking. They are full of joy (*NŚ* 8.55; *Mānas* 16.4.1054; *SUS* 5.28; *BhP* p. 126) *VDP* : The eyes are open and they move. They look through the corners. (*VDP* 3.25.11). *SR* adds "phulagalla" which means a full cheek (*SR* 7.396; *NŚSaṁ* 556). *NN* does not direct the dancer to lower the eyes (*NN* 16a).

The sixty-four Dṛṣṭi-Vikāras given by *BhP*

(1) **Añcita :** The pupils alternately move and stop. (*BhP* p. 120).

(2) **Abhilāṣi :** An expectant glance (*BhP* p. 120).

(3) **Alasa :** The eyes move away from the desired object (*BhP* p. 120).

(4) **Ānandi :** The eyelids join in pleasure (*BhP p.* 120).

(5) **Utkaṇṭhita :** The reddened eyes are full of tears at the corners (*BhP* p. 121).

(6) **Utkampa :** The eyebrows, eyelashes and pupils are moved (*BhP* p. 121).

(7) **Udañcita :** the eyes are open at the corners (*BhP* p. 121).

(8) **Ullāsi :** A glance expressing desire (*BhP* p. 121).

(9) **Kaṭhora :** A harsh look (*BhP* p. 122).

(10) **Kaluṣa :** The eyes show the strain of sleep or tiredness (*BhP* p. 122).

(11) **Kātara :** A helpless look (*BhP* p. 122).

(12) **Kuñcita :** The eyes are contracted to express love. (*BhP* p. 120).

(13) **Komala :** A graceful and calm look (*BhP* p. 122).

(14) **Cakita :** A restless glance (*BhP p.* 122).

(15) **Cala :** The glance quickly look at everything (*BhP* p. 122).

(16) **Taraṅgita :** The eyes are gracefully moved like waves (*BhP* p. 122).

(17) **Tarala :** The pupils are moved (*BhP* p. 122).

(18) **Tāni :** To look at a thing without knowing anything about it. (*BhP* p. 122).

(19) **Tribhaṅgi :** To look at things through "the middle, the root and forepart of the eyes," i.e., to look

straight ahead, and from the corners of the eyes (*BhP* p. 121).

(20) **Tryaśra** : Tribhaṅgi is done with an oblique glance (*BhP* p. 121).

(21) **Nibhṛta** : The eyes are cast down (*BhP* p. 121).

(22) **Nispanda** : A still glance (*BhP* p. 120).

(23) **Nīhañcita** : The nostrils are expanded and the eyes are raised (*BhP* p. 121).

(24) **Nyañcita** : Not explained (*BhP* p. 118).

(25) **Praṇayi** : A pleasing glance (*BhP* p. 122).

(26) **Prasanna** : A pleasing glance with smiling eyes (*BhP* p. 120).

(27) **Preṅkhola** : The eyes look at an object and then are drawn away from it. (*BhP* p. 122).

(28) **Premagarbhi** : A pleasing glance (*BhP* p. 122).

(29) **Madamanthara** : The pupils are moving and the reddened eyes are repeately closed (*BhP* p. 120).

(30) **Madhura** : A soothing glance (*BhP* p. 120).

(31) **Masṛṇa:** A glance expresing love (*BhP* p. 120).

(32) **Mahi** : A glance expressing greatness. (*BhP*. p. 121).

(33) **Mugdha** : A bright look (*BhP* p. 120).

(34) **Rukṣa** : A dull and colourles look. (*BhP* p. 122).

(35) **Lalita** : The eyes are slowly opened expressing affection (*BhP* p. 122).

(36) **Lola** : The eyes are moved (*BhP* p. 122).

(37) **Vakra** : The eyes are moved up and down at the corners (*BhP* p. 120).

(38) **Valita** : To draw away the eyes and then to look back obliquely and repeatedly (*BhP* p. 120).

(39) **Vikāśī** : A wide glance to look at things carefully. (*BhP* p. 120).

(40) **Vikūṇita :** The eyes are contracted and only a part can be seen (*BhP* p. 119).

(41) **Vikṛṣta :** The eyes are cast down sideways at the corners (*BhP* p. 121).

(42) **Vikṣepi :** Vyākṣepi is done at the sides (*BhP* p. 121).

(43) **Vidagdha :** A shrewd glance (*BhP* p. 121).

(44) **Vinata :** A straight, wide and cast down glance (*BhP* p. 121).

(45) **Vilulita :** A distressed look (*BhP* p. 122).

(46) **Visaṁsthula :** To look through the eyebeows, eyelashes and pupils (*BhP* p. 121).

(47) **Vistāri :** The eyes are open (*BhP* p. 120).

(48) **Visphārita :** A wide look with pupils wide open (*BhP* p. 121).

(49) **Vihasita :** The eyes are open and they do not wink (*BhP* p. 120).

(50) **Vihvala :** The pupils are agitated (*BhP* p. 121).

(51) **Vyākṣepi :** To look backwards through the corners of the eyes (*BhP* p. 121).

(52) **Vyāsaṅgī :** The eyes look at a distant object (*BhP* p. 121).

(53) **Samanmatha :** An excited glance (*BhP* p. 121).

(54) **Saspṛha :** A glance expressing desire (*BhP* p. 122).

(55) **Sākuta :** A glance full of meaning ((*BhP* p. 120).

(56) **Sotka :** A distant glance expressing love (*BhP* p. 121).

(57) **Soprāsa :** An anxious look (*BhP* p. 122).

(58) **Sotsuka :** To look back again and again (*BhP* p. 121).

(59) **Stimita :** A fixed glance (*BhP* p. 120).

(60) **Sthira :** A glance fixed at a distant object (*BhP* p. 120).

(61) **Snigdha :** A graceful look (*BhP* p. 120).

(62) **Sphita** : The eyebrows, eyelashes and pupils are shining (*BhP* p. 121).

(63) **Smera** : The eyebrows, eyelids and pupils are quivering (*BhP* p. 120).

(64) **Hlādi** : A glance that effaces all sorrows (*BhP* p. 122).

All these express the Śṛṅgāra Rasa but some may also express the Adbhūta and Hāsya Rasas (*BhP* p. 122).

Dṛṣṭis, expressing the Raudra Rasas

(1) **Utphulla** : The eyes are open with the eyelashes separated (*BhP* p. 123).

(2) **Uddhura** : To look at a certain thing with a desire to know everything about it (*BhP* p. 123).

(3) **Uvartita** : The eye brows are raised (*BhP* p. 122).

(4) **Udvṛtta** : The eyelids are raised and the eyes are open. The pupils move inwards (*BhP* p. 123).

(5) **Ullola** : The eyes are raised (*BhP* p. 123).

(6) **Kuṭila** : The eyes are frowning (*BhP* p. 123).

(7) **Caṭula** : To look at a disagreeable object (*BhP* p. 123).

(8) **Niṣṭhura** : The pupils are hidden under the eyelids (*BhP* p. 123).

(9) **Vivartita** : The pupils are rolled upwards (*BhP* p. 123).

(10) **Viśliṣṭa** : To look at nothing due to anger (*BhP* p. 123).

(11) **Śuṣka** : A dim glance (*BhP* p. 123).

(12) **Stabdha** : The eyes are still (*BhP* p. 123).

Dṛṣṭis expressing the Śoka Rasa

(1) **Ārta** : A vacant look (*BhP* p. 123)

(2) **Jaḍa** : A feeble and still look (*BhP* p. 123).

(3) **Tapta** : The eyebrowss and eyelids are closed. The eyes are dull (*BhP* p. 123).

(4) **Tānta** : A fatigued look (*BhP* p. 123).

(5) **Savyāgra** : An eager look (*BhP* p. 123).

(6) **Savyātha** : A painful glance (*BhP* p. 123).

(7) **Sasambhrama** : The eyes are agitated (*BhP* p. 123).

Dṛṣṭis expressing the Vīra Rasa

(1) **Akṛtrima** : A natural look (*BhP* p. 124).

(2) **Anupaskṛti** : The eyes show affection through the corners (*BhP* p. 124).

(3) **Anulvaṇa** : An agitated look (*BhP* p. 124).

(4) **Avikriya** : A still glance (*BhP* p. 124).

(5) **Avyāja** : A clear look (*BhP.* p. 124).

(6) **Asambhrānta** : A glance that notices the subtlest things (*BhP* p. 124).

(7) **Dhīra** : A majestic glance (*BhP* p. 123).

(8) **Bandhura** : The eyes are slightly opened (*BhP* p. 123).

(9) **Manthara** : The eyes are opened (*BhP* p. 123).

(10) **Sagarva** : The eyes are raised with pupils still (*BhP* p. 124).

(11) **Saharṣa** : The eyes look as if they want to speak (*BhP* p. 124).

Dṛṣṭis expressing the Bībhatsa and Bhayānaka Rasas

(1) **Anutseka** : The eyelids and the corners of the eyes are cast down (*BhP* p. 124).

(2) **Arocaka** : The eyes are contracted at the corners (*BhP* p. 124).

(3) **Āviddha** : The eyes look upwards and downwards (*BhP* p. 124).

(4) **Vikṛṣṭa :** To look vacantly at the sky (*BhP* p. 124).

(5) **Viddha :** The corners of the eyes and the pupils are cast down (*BhP* p. 124).

(6) **Vinigīrṇa :** The eyes are open and they are full of tears (*BhP* p. 124).

(7) **Viniṣkrānta :** The eyes want to leave their sockets. (*BhP* p. 124).

(8) **Vilohita :** The text is too obscure to explain (*BhP* p. 124).

The Darśanakarmas

(1) **Anivartita :** A fixed gaze (*SUS* 5.34).

(2) **Anuvṛtta :** To observe carefuly (*NŚ* 8.108; VDP 3.25.50; *SSam* 6.120; *SR* 7.457; *NŚSam* 617). *ADar:* To look quickly up and down. (*ADar* 77).

(3) **Avalokita :** To look downwards. (*NŚ* 8.109; *SSam* 6.122; *ADar* 78; *SR* 7.458; *NŚSam* 618) VDP : To look backwards. (*VDP* 3.25.51) *SUS* : To look straight *SUS* 5.33).

(4) **Ālokita :** A sudden look (*NŚ* 8.108; *VDP* 3.25.50; *SSam* 6.121; *SR* 7.460; *NŚSam* 620). *ADar* : To look quickly with widely opened eyes. (*ADar* 69).

(5) **Ullokita :** To look upwards. (*NŚ* 8.109; VDP 3.25.51; *SUS* 5.34; *SSam* 6.122; *SR* 7.459; *NŚSam* 620; *ADar* 75).

(6) **Nivartita :** To look round (*SUS* 5.33).

(7) **Pralokita :** To look sideways (*NŚ* 8.109; *ADar* 72), SR *NŚSam*, Pravilokita (*SR* 7.460; *NŚSam* 621).

(8) **Pratilokita :** Not explained (*SSam* 6.119).

(9) **Mīlita :** The eyes are half closed (*ADar* 74).

(10) **Lokita :** To look at all directions (*VDP* 3.25.51).

(11) **Vilokita :** To look backwards (*NŚ* 8.109; *SSam* 6.121; *SR* 7.459; *NŚSam* 619). *VDP* : To look sideways.

(*VDP* 3.25.51). It is the same as Pralokita. *SUS* : An eager look (*SUS* 5.33).

(12) **Vṛtta :** To look again (*SUS* 5.34).

(13) **Sama :** The eyes are charming and serene (*NŚ* 8.107; *VDP* 3.25.49; *SUS* 5.34; SSam 6.120; *SR* 7.456; *NŚSam* 615). *ADar*: To look charmingly like a nymph. (*ADar* 67).

(14) **Sācī :** To look obliquely and to cover the eyes with the lashes (*NŚ* 8.107; VDP 3.25.49); *SUS* 5.33; *SSam* 6.118; *SR* 7.457; *NŚSam* 616). *ADar* : To look obliquely moving the eyes. (*ADar* 70).

In *SR* these are described as "Viṣayābhimukhāni Tārākarmāṇi," i.e. those movements in which the eyes are focused on objects, not those in which the eyes are not focused.

Movements of the Tārā

(1) **Udvartana :** To turn away the pupils (*VDP* 3.25.45).

(2) **Calana :** To oscillate the pupils (*NŚ* 8.99; SUS. 5.37; *SR* 7.450; *NŚSam* 609). *VDP* says that this must be done in an oblique way (*VDP* 3.25.43).

(3) **Niṣkrāma :** The pupils seem to start out, (*NŚ* 8.100; *VDP* 3.25.44; *SUS* 5.37; *SR* 7.451; *NŚSaṃ* 611).

(4) **Pātana :** To look downwards (*NŚ* 8.99; *VDP* 3.25.44): *SUS*, *SR*; *NŚSam* : Pāta (*SUS* 5.38; *SR* 7.449; NŚSaṃ 609).

(5) **Praveśana :** To draw in the pupils (*NŚ* 8.99; *SUS* 5.36; *SR* 7.450; *NŚSaṃ* 610). *VDP* : Saṃpraveśana. (*VDP* 3.25.43).

(6) **Prākṛta :** The pupils are kept normally (*NS* 8.100; *VDP* 3.25.45; *SUS* 5.38; *SR* 7.451; *NŚSaṃ* 611).

(7) **Bhramaṇa :** To move round the pupils (*NŚ* 8.98; *VDP* 3.25.42; *SR* 7.449; *NŚSaṃ* 608). *SUS* Bhrama (*SUS* 5.37).

(8) **Valana** : To move the pupils obliquely (*NŚ* 8.99; *SUS* 5.37; *SR* 7.449; *NŚSaṃ* 609). *VDP* : To move the pupils (*VDP* 3.25.43).

(9) **Vivartana** : To turn the pupils aside (*NŚ* 8.100; VDP 3.25.44; SR 7.450; NŚSaṃ 610). *SUS* : To raise the pupils. (*SUS* 5.38).

(10) **Samudvṛtta** : To raise the pupils (*NŚ* 8.100.; *SR* 7.451; NŚSaṃ 611) SUS : The eyes seem to start out (*SUS* 5.36).

Movements of the Puṭa

(1) **Unmeṣa** : To separate the eyelids (*NŚ* 8.112; VDP 3.25.34; SR 7.442; *NŚSaṃ 601)*.

(2) **Kuñcita** : To narrow the eyelids (*NŚ* 8.113; SUS 5.40; SR 7.442; *NŚSaṃ* 600). *VDP* : Ākuṇcita. (*VDP* 3.25.35).

(3) **Nimeṣa** : To close the eyelids (*NŚ* 8.112; *VDP* 3.25.34; *SUS* 5.41; *SR* 7.442; *NŚSaṃ* 601).

(4) **Pihita** : To keep the eyelids still. (*NŚ* 8.114; *VDP* 3.25.37; *SR* 7.442; NŚSam 603).

(5) **Praṣrta** : To stretch the eyelids (*NŚ* 8.112; SUS. 5.41; *SR* 7.441; *NŚSaṃ* 599). *VDP* : Prasārita (*VDP* 3.25.32).

(6) **Bhrānta** : The eyelids are moved (*SUS* 5.42).

(7) **Vitālita** : To strike the eyelids accidentally. (*NŚ* 8.114). It is also described as Tāḍita. (*VDP* 3.25.37). Vitāla (*SUS* 5.42). Vicālita (SR 7.442. ASS ed.; *SR* 7.445. Ad. Lib. ed). and Vitāḍita (*SR* 7.440. Ad. Lib. ed). *NŚSaṃ* uses both Vitalita and Vicalita (*NŚSam* 604).

(8) **Vivarita** : To raise the eyelids (*NŚ* 8.113; *SUS* 5.41; *VDP* 3.25.35; *SR* 7.443; *NŚSaṃ* 601).

(9) **Viśleṣa** : The same as Unmeṣa (*SUS* 5.40).

(10) **Sama :** To keep the eyelids normally (*NŚ* 8.113; *VDP* 3.25.36; *SUS* 5.41; *SR* 7.446; *NŚSaṃ* 605).

(11) **Sphurita :** To tremble the eyelids (*NŚ* 8.113; *VDP* 3.25.36; *SUS* 5.42; *SR* 7.443; *NŚSam* 602).

Movements of the Bhrū

These are the movements of the eyebrows which are considered to be Upāṇgas.

(1) **Utkśepa :** To raise the eyebrows together or one after the other (*NŚ* 8.120; *VDP* 3.25.54; *SUS* 5.44; Mānas. 16.4.1029; *NN* 17b; *SR* 7.435; *NŚSaṃ* 593).

(2) **Kuñcita :** To bend the eyebrows slightly together or one after the other (*NŚ* 8.122; *SUS* 5.45). *VDP* Mānas; *SR*; Nikuñcita. (*VDP* 3.25.56; *NN* 17b; Mānas 16.4.1031; *SR* 7.437; *NŚSaṃ* 595).

(3) **Catura :** To move the eyebrows in a pleasing manner. (*NŚ* 8.120; *VDP* 3.25.55; *SR* 7.439; *NN* 17b; *NŚSaṃ* 597) *SUS* : To raise the eyebrows slightly. (*SUS* 5.44) Mānas : To raise the corners of the eyes. (Mānas 16.4.1031).

(4) **Pātana :** To lower the eyebrows together or one after the other (*NŚ* 8.120; *VDP* 3.24.54; *SUS* 5.45; Mānas 16.4.1030); *SR* 7.434; *NŚSaṃ* 592). Mānas SR; *NN*: Patita (*NN* 17b).

(5) **Bhrūkuṭti :** To raise the inner end of the eyebrows. (*NŚ* 8.121; *VDP* 3.25.55; *SUS* 5.44; *NN* 17b; Mānas 16.4.1030; *SR* 7.438; *NŚSaṃ* 596).

(6) **Recita :** To raise one eyebrow (*NŚ* 8.122; *VDP* 3.25.56; *SUS* 5.44; *NN* 17a-b; *SR* 7.437; *NŚSaṃ* 594). *Mānas:* Sphurita. (*Mānas* 16.4.1032).

(7) **Sahaja :** To keep the eyebrows normally (*NŚ* 8.123; *SUS* 5.45; Mānas 16.4.1032; *NN*; 17a; 7.433; *NŚSam* 591). *VDP*: Svābhāvika (*VDP* 3.25.57).

Movements of the Nāsā

These are the movements of the nose, an Upāṅga.

(1) **Natā :** The nostrils are repeatedly contracted (*NŚ* 8.131). *VDP*; *SUS*; Mānas : The nostrils are contracted. (*VDP* 3.25.63; SUS 5.48; *Mānas* 16.4.1086) *SR* : The Nostrils are contracted and expanded (SR 7.467); *NŚSaṃ* 629).

(2) **Mandā :** According to the *NŚ*, "Mandā tu Nibhṛtā" which may mean either that the nostrils are drawn in or that the nostrils are at rest (*NŚ* 8.131). *VDP* : The nostrils are drawn in (*VDP* 3.25.63). *SUS* : Nibhṛtā : The nostrils are at rest (*SUS* 5.47). Mānas: The nostrils are a little drawn in (*Mānas*. 16.4.1087). According to *SR*, however, Mandā is the state of nostrils while breathing in and out. (SR 7.468; *NŚSam* 630).

(3) **Vikūṇitā :** The nostrils are contracted (*NŚ* 8.130; *SUS* 5.47; *Mānas* 16.4.1090; *SR* 7.470; NŚSaṃ. 632). *VDP*: Kūṇitā. (*VDP* 3.25.64).

(4) **Vikṛstā :** The nostrils are dialated (*NŚ* 8.131; SUS. 5.47; *Mānas* 16.4.1088; *SR* 7.469; *NŚSaṃ* 631). *VDP*: The nostrils are contracted. (*VDP* 3.25.64).

(5) **Socchvāsā :** The air is drawn in. (NS 8.131; *VDP* 3.25.64; *SUS* 5.48; *Mānas* 16.4.1089; *SR* 7.470; *NŚSaṃ* 633).

(6) **Svābhāvikī :** The nose is kept normally. (*VDP* 3.25.64; *Mānas* 16.4.1091; *SR* 7.466; *NŚSaṃ* 6528). *SUS* : Sahajā : (*SUS* 5.47). *NŚ* : Samā. (*NŚ* 8.132).

The Anilas

These are described in *SR* alone, though *SDām* mentions the term. It means breathing and is regarded as an Upāṅga. The following types are found in SR :

(1) **Ullasita** : The breath is drawn in slowly and gently through the nose. (*SR* 7.478; *NŚSaṃ* 640).

(2) **Cala** : Warm, long drawn and audible breathing through the mouth. (*SR* 7.475; *NŚSaṃ* 637).

(3) **Nirasta** : Breathing out once audibly. (*SR* 7.477; *NŚSaṃ* 639).

(4) **Pravṛddha** : To breathe audibly through the mouth. (*SR* 7.476; *NŚSaṃ* 638).

(5) **Prasṛta** : Long drawn and audible breathing through the mouth during sleep. (*SR* 7.482; *NŚSaṃ* 644).

(6) **Vimukta** : The breath is held for a long time and then let out. (*SR* 7.479; *NŚSaṃ* 641).

(7) **Vismita** : The breath is held with an effort as the mind is wandering elsewhere (*SR* 7.480; *NŚSaṃ* 642).

(8) **Skhalita** : To let out a deep breath in sorrow (*SR* 7.481; *NŚSaṃ* 643).

(9) **Svastha** : Natural breathing (*SR* 7.474; *NŚSaṃ* 636).

These nine anilas are, according to *SR*, mentioned by Kohala. *SR* refers to Māruta and give another list of ten Anilas but with few details. They are : Sama, Bhrānta, Vilīna, Āndolita, Kampita, Stambhita, Ucchvāsa, *Niḥśvāsa*, Sūtkṛta and Sītkṛta. (*SR* 7.83-7).

Movements of the Kapola

These are the movements of the cheek, an Upāṅga. *AP* which does not categorise any class as Upāṅga, places this among Pratyaṅgas.

(1) **Kampita** : Trembling cheeks (*NŚ* 8.138 ; *VDP* 25.59; *SUS* 5.50; *Mānas* 16.4.1094; *SR* 7.463; *NŚSaṃ* 623).

(2) **Kuñcita** : The cheeks are contracted (*NŚ* 8.138; *VDP* 3.25.59; *SUS* 5.50; *Mānas* 16.4.1095). This must be accompanied, according to *SR*, by hairs standing on end (*SR* 7.462; *NŚSaṃ* 623). *SR* combines Kuñcita with Saromāñca in the VDP.

(3) **Kṣāma** : The cheeks are depressed (*NŚ* 8.137; *VDP* 3.25.58; *SUS* 5.50; *Mānas* 16.4.1093; *SR* 7.464; *NŚSaṃ* 624).

(4) **Pūrṇa** : To blow the cheeks enough to make them rounded (*NŚ* 8.138; *VDP* 3.25.59; *SUS* 5.50; *Mānas* 16.4.1094; SR 7.463; *NŚSaṃ* 625). The G.O.S. edition of the *NŚ* prefers Ghūrṇa while all other texts and M.M. Ghosh's edition have Pūrṇa.

(5) **Phulla** : The cheeks are blown out (*NŚ* 8.137; *VDP* 3.25.58; *SUS* 5.50; *SR* 7.464; *NŚSaṃ* 625). *Mānas* Utphulla (*Mānas* 16.1093).

(6) **Sama** : The cheeks are kept naturally (*NŚ* 8.138; *SUS* 5.50; *Mānas* 16.4.1095; *SR* 7.465; *NŚSaṃ* 626). *VDP* Prākṛta : (*VDP* 3.25.60).

(7) **Saromāñca** : The cheeks are exercised with the hairs standing on end (*VDP* 3.25.59). The only other mention of the term occurs in one ms. of the NŚ which, however, has been rejected by the G.O.S. edition of the NŚ (*NŚ* vol. II, p.19).

Movements of the Mukha

Mukha, the mouth, is considered to be a Pratyaṅga by the *NŚ SR* includes Mukha in the list of Upāṅgas. Mukharāga is discussed in many texts.

(1) **Udvāhi** : The mouth is turned up to show a woman's pride (*NŚ* 8.155; *SR* 7.515; *NŚSaṃ* 678).

(2) **Ṛju** : The mouth is kept normally (*VDP* 3.24.22).

(3) **Kaluṣa** : Not explained (*AP* 341.12).

(4) **Nirbhugna** : The face is lowered (*NŚ* 8.155; *VDP* 3.24.21).

(5) **Bhugna** : The mouth is slightly open (*NŚ* 8.155). It is also written as Vyābhugna in the *NŚ VDP*; *SR* : A downcast face (*VDP* 3.24.21; *SR* 7.515; *NŚSam* 678).

(6) **Vinivṛtta :** The face is turned aside (*NŚ* 8.154; *SR* 7.517; *NŚSaṃ* 680). *VDP*; described as Nivṛtta also (*VDP* 3.24.20).

(7) **Vidhuta :** The mouh is obliquely open (*NŚ* 8.154; *SR* 7.156; *NŚSaṃ* 680).

(8) **Viruddha :** The face is turned aside (*VDP*. 3.24.20). In the *NŚ* the description of Vinivṛtta is the same as Viruddha in the *VDP*, but the application of Viruddha is like Vidhuta in the *NŚ*.

(9) **Vivṛta :** The lips are kept apart (*NŚ*. 8.155; *SR*. 7.516; *NŚSaṃ* 679). *VDP* : Also as Vivṛta (*VDP* 3.24.21; 24).

(10) **Vyābhugna :** To pull a long face. (*SR* 7.514; *NŚSaṃ* 677).

The Mukharāgas

(1) **Asahaja :** An unnatural face (*SDar* 42b).

(2) **Isaddhāsya :** A smiling face (*SDar* 42b.).

(3) **Kāntibhūṣita :** A graceful face (*SDar* 42b.).

(4) **Prasanna :** Glad (*NŚ* 8.163; *SR* 7.529; *Mānas* 16.1127; *NŚSaṃ* 691; *SDar* 42b; *NN* 17b).

(5) **Rakta :** A reddened face (*NŚ* 164; *SR* 7.529; *Mānas* 16.4.1128; *NŚSaṃ* 692; *SDar* 43b; *NN* 17b).

(6) **Śyāma :** A dark face (*NŚ* 8.164; *SR*. 7.530; *Mānas* 16.4.1128; *NŚSaṃ*. 692; *SDar* 44a; *NN*. 17b).

(7) **Sahaja :** A natural face (*Mānas* 166.4.1127; *SDar* 42b).

(8) **Svābhāvika :** The same as Sahaja (*NŚ* 8.164; *SR*; 7.528; *NŚSaṃ* 691; *SDar* 42b; *NN* 17b).

Movements of the Adhara

These are movements of the lips which are considered to be Upāṅgas. *AP*, which does not consider Upāṅga as a class, places Adhara among Pratyaṇgas.

(1) **Āyata :** The upper lip is stretched (*SR* 7.495; *NŚSaṃ* 658). *Mānas* : The lips are joined and stretched. (*Mānas* 16.4.1100).

(2) **Udvṛtta :** To thrust out the lower lip (*SR* 7.494; *NŚSaṃ*. 657; *Mānas*. 16.4.1096).

(3) **Kampana :** To make the lower lip tremble (*NŚ* 8.142; *VDP* 3.25.71; *Mānas* 16.4.1096; *SR* 7.490; *NŚSaṃ* 652). *SUS* : Vepita (*SUS* 5.49).

(4) **Kūṇita :** The Mukula lip is contracted obliquely. (*Mānas* 16.4.1099).

(5) **Parivartita :** Not explained (*SUS* 5.49).

(6) **Prasārita :** The lips are stretched (*Mānas* 16.4.1103).

(7) **Mukula :** To purse the lower lip (*Mānas* 16.4.1098). The application of Mukula seems to be the same as Samudgaka.

(8) **Recita :** The lower lip moves sideways. (*SR* 7.496; *NŚSaṃ* 658; *Mānas* 16.4.1096).

(9) **Vikāśi :** To show the upper teeth a little (*SR* 7.496; *NŚSaṃ* 657; *Mānas* 16.4.1102).

(10) **Vinigūhana :** The lower lip is drawn in. (*NŚ* 8.146; *SR* 7.492; *NŚSaṃ* (654). *VDP:* Vigūhita (*VDP* 3.25.72). *Mānas* : Nigūhita (*Mānas* 16.4.1104).

(11) **Vivartana :** Contraction of the lower lip (*NŚ* 8.142; *VDP* 3.25.70; *SR* 7.489; *NŚSaṃ* 651).

(12) **Visarga :** The lower lip is opened away from the upper. (*NŚ* 8.143; *VDP* 3.25.71). *SR, NŚSaṃ* : Vistṛta. (*SR* 7.491; *NŚSaṃ* 653). *Mānas* : Prasārita (*Mānas* 16.4.1103 *SUS* : Nisarga. (*SUS* 5.49).

(13) **Śliṣṭa :** Not explained (*SUS* 5.49).

(14) **Sandaṣṭaka :** The lower lip is pressed by the teeth. (*NŚ* 8.143; *VPD* 3.25.72; *SUS* 5.49l; *Mānas* 16.4.1101; *SR* 7.493; *NŚSaṃ* 655).

(15) **Samudgaka :** Pouting with the lower lip (*NŚ* 8.146; *VDP* 3.25.73; *SR* 7.493; *NŚSaṃ* 656.

Movements of the Danta

These are movements of the teeth which are thought to be Upāṅgas.

(1) **Kuṭṭana :** To grind the teeth (*SR* 7.498; *NŚSaṃ* 660). *Mānas* : Kartana (*Mānas* 16.4.1117).

(2) **Khaṇḍana :** To touch and separate the teeth repeatedly (SR. 7.498; *NŚSaṃ* 661).

(3) **Grahaṇa :** To hold something between the teeth (*SR* 7.501; *NŚSaṃ* 663). *Mānas* : Dhārana (*Mānas* 16.4.1119).

(4) **Cukkita :** The teeth are kept apart (*SR* 7.500; *NŚSaṃ* 663).

(5) **Chinna :** The teeth are firmly pressed together (*SR* 7.499; *NŚSaṃ* 662). *Mānas* : Khaṇḍana (*Mānas* 16.4.1116).

(6) **Daṣṭa :** To press the lower lip by the teeth (*SR* 7.502; *NŚSaṃ* 664).

(7) **Niṣkarṣaṇa :** To thrust the teeth forward (*SR* 7.502; *Mānas* 16.4.1118; *NŚSaṃ* 665).

(8) **Mardana :** To munch. (*Mānas* 16.4.1115).

(9) **Sama :** Slight contact of the teeth (*SR* 7.501; *NŚSaṃ* 664).

Movements of the Jihvā

These are movements of the tongue, an Upāṅgas

(1) **Unnatā :** The mouth is wide open while the tongue is fully turned up (*SR* 7.505; *NŚSaṃ* 669). *Mānas* 16.4.1125).

(2) **Ṛjvī :** The tongue is stretched out in an open mouth. (*SR* 504; *Mānas* 16.4.1121; *NŚSaṃ* 667).

(3) **Natā** : The tongue touches the chin (*Mānas* 16.4.1123).

(4) **Lehinī** : The tongue licks the teeth and the lips (*SR* 7.506. *NŚSaṃ* 670).

(5) **Lolā** : The tongue moves in a slightly open mouth. (*SR* 7.506; *Mānas* 16.4.1124; *NŚSaṃ* 669).

(6) **Vakrā** : The mouth is slightly open and the tip of the tongue is turned up (*SR* 7.505; *NŚSaṃ* 668).

(7) **Sṛkkānugā** : To lick the corners of the mouth (*SR* 7.504; *NŚSaṃ* 667). *Mānas* : Sṛkkalehā (*Mānas* 16.4.1122).

Movements of the Cibuka

Cibuka, an Upāṅga, is the chin. Many of the following actions and positions of the chin are due to the movement of the lips, the teeth or the jaws.

(1) **Kuṭṭana** : The action of the chin upon grinding the teeth (*NŚ* 8.148; *VDP* 3.25.67; *ND* p. 189; *SUS* 5.52).

(2) **Khaṇḍana** : The action of the chin upon pressing the teeth together (*NŚ* 8.148; *VDP* 3.25.67; *ND* p. 189; *SUS* 5.52).

(3) **Calasaṃhata** : The chin moves with the lips closed. (*SR* 7.511; *NŚSaṃ* 674).

(4) **Calita** : To open and close the jaws (*SR* 7.512; *NŚSaṃ* 675).

(5) **Cukkita** : The position of the chin when the mouth is wide open. (*NŚ* 8.149; *VDP* 3.25.68; *SUS* 5.5.2). *SR* : Vyādīrṇa (*SR* 7.509; *NŚSaṃ* 672).

(6) **Chinna** : The teeth are finally pressed together (*NŚ* 8.149; *VDP* 3.25.68; *SUS* 5.52.).

(7) **Daṣṭa** : The lower lip is pressed by the teeth (*NŚ* 8.150; *SUS* 5.52).

(8) **Lehita** : To lick the teeth or the lips *NŚ* 8.149; *SUS* 5.52).

(9) **Lola** : To move the chin obliquely (*SR* 7.512; *NŚSaṃ* 675).

(10) **Vakra** : The chin is pushed aside (*SR* 7.510; *NŚSaṃ* 675).

(11) **Śvasita** : The chin is lowered by half an inch (one aṅgula) (*SR* 7.509; *NŚSaṃ* 672).

(12) **Sama** : The lips are lightly joined (*NŚ* 8.149; *VDP* 3.25.69; *SUS* 5.52).

(13) **Samhata** : The chin is kept motionless with the mouth closed (*SR* 7.510; *NŚSaṃ* 673).

(14) **Sphurita** : The chin trembles (*SR* 7.511; *NŚSaṃ* 674).

These actions are described under Danta-Karma in the *VDP* which has no separate section under Ċibuka. *SR* describes both Cibuka and Danta. The *NŚ* combines the two and gives Cibuka-karma.

Movements of the Grīvā

These are the movements of the neck, a Pratyaṅga.

(1) **Añcitā** : The neck is moved back. According to *SR* the neck is stretched and moved. *VDP*. Bending the neck to one side (*NŚ* 8.174; *VDP* 3.24.15; *SR* 333; *NŚSaṃ* 492).

(2) **Unnatā** : The neck is raised (*NŚ* 8.172; *SR* 7.335; *NŚSaṃ* 494).

(3) **Kuñcitā** : The neck is curved (*NŚ* 8.174; *SR* 7.333; *NŚSaṃ* 492).

(4) **Caturā** : It is described as "Madhuraṃ Caturaṃ" which is not an explanation (*VDP* 3.24.16).

(5) **Tiraściña** : Moving the neck up on both the sides to suggest the gliding of a snake. (*ADar* 82).

(6) **Tryaśrā** : The neck is slanted sideways (*NŚ* 8.173; *SR* 7.334; *NŚSaṃ* 493).

(7) **Natā** : The neck is bent down (*NŚ* 8.172; *ND* p. 189; *SR* 7.334; *NŚSaṃ* 496).

(8) **Nivṛttā** : The neck is returned to the position in which it was before bending forward. Another name for this movement is Vivṛttā (*NŚ* 8.175; *VDP* 3.24.16; *SR* 7.331; *NŚSaṃ* 490).

(9) **Parivartitā** : The neck is moved from the right to the left like a half-moon (*ADar* 83).

(10) **Prakampitā** : The neck is moved forward and backward like the neck of a she-pigeon (*ADar* 85).

(11) **Prasāritā** : The neck is stretched. (*VDP* 3.24.16).

(12) **Muktā** : Recitā becomes Muktā by revolving the neck. (*VDP* 3.24.16).

(13) **Recitā** : The neck is shaken and moved. *VDP* : A circular motion of the neck (*NŚ* 8.173; *VDP* 3.24.15; *SR*. 7.332; *NŚSaṃ* 491).

(14) **Valitā** : The neck is turned sideways. The reading accepted in M.M. *NŚ* is Vāhitā. The action is the same (*NŚ* 8.175; *SR* 7.332; *NŚSaṃ* 491).

(15) **Samā** : To keep the neck naturally (*NŚ* 8.171; *ND* p. 189; *SR* 7.330; *NŚSaṃ* 489).

(16) **Sundarī** : The neck move obliquely (*ADar* 80).

(17) **Stabdhā** : The neck is stiff (*VDP* 3.24.17).

Movements of the Skandha

These are the movements of the shoulder. *Mānas* consider Skandha as a Pratyaṅga while *SR* discusses it as an Aṅga, following, it is remarked, the practice of others.

(1) **Ucchrita** : The shoulders are raised in pride (*SR* 7.328; *Mānas* 16.4.1001; *NŚSaṃ* 487).

(2) **Ekānta** : The shoulders are raised in anger (*Mānas* 16.4.1002).

(3) **Ekocca :** One shoulder is raised (*SR* 7.326; *NŚSaṃ* 486).

(4) **Karṇalagna :** The shoulder touches the ear (*SR* 7.327; *NŚSaṃ* 486).

(5) **Saṁlagna :** This seems to be the same as Karṇalagna (*Mānas* 16.4.1000).

(6) **Lola :** The shoulders are moved (*Mānas* 16.4.1002). *SR.* : Lolita (*SR* 7.326; *NŚSaṃ* 485).

(7) **Srasta :** The shoulders are relaxed (*SR* 7.326; *NŚSaṃ* 485; *Mānas* 16.4.1001).

Movements of the Bāhū

Bāhū, a Pratyaṅga, is the arm.

(1) **Añcita :** The arms move out from the chest and come back. (*NŚ* 9.220; *SUS* 5.64; *SSam* 6.105; *SR* 7.340; *NŚSaṃ* 499; *NN* 18a).

(2) **Adhomukha :** The arms point to the ground. *NŚ* 9.220; *SUS.* 5.64; *SSam* 6.105; *SR* 7.338; *NN* 18a *NŚSaṃ* 497). *Mānas* : Nyañca (*Mānas* 16.4.1134). *SSam* : Adhaḥ.

(3) **Apaviddha :** The arms move away from the chest in a circular way (*NŚ* 9.220; *SUS* 5.64; *SR.* 7.339; *NŚSaṃ* 498; *NN* 18a).

(4) **Āndolita :** A swinging movement of the arm (*SR* 7.347; *NŚSam* 508). *Mānas* : Lolita (*Mānas* 16.4.1136).

(5) **Āviddha :** The arms move inwards (*SR* 7.344; *NŚSam* 504; *NN* 18a).

(6) **Utsārita :** To place the arm where it was, before moving it to the other side (*SR* 7.347; *NŚSam* 509; *NN* 18a).

(7) **Udveṣṭita :** The arms move out from the wrist in Vartanā movement (*NŚ* 9.221; *SR* 7.342; *NŚSam* 502; *NN* 18a).

(8) **Ūrddhvastha :** The arm is raised above the head (*SR* 7.338; *NŚSam* 497; *NN* 18a). *NŚ* : Ūrdhvasaṃstha. (*NŚ*. 9.220). *SUS* : *SSam* : Ūrdhva. (*SUS* 5.64; *SSam* 6.105). *Mānas* : Pronnata. (*Mānas* 16.4.1133).

(9) **Kuñcita :** The arm is bent till the elbow is pointed. *Mānas* says that the arms should also tremble (*SR* 7.344; *NŚSam* 504; *SSam* 6.105; *Mānas* 16.4.1135).

(10) **Calita :** The arm is moved up to the elbow (*Mānas* 16.4.1138). *SUS* : Cañcalā (*SUS* 5.64).

(11) **Tiryak :** The arms move to sides (*NŚ* 9.220; *SUS* 5.64; *SSam* 6.105). *SR NN* : Tiryaggata (*SR* 7.338; *NŚSam* 498; *NN* 18a).

(12) **Namra :** The arms are slightly bent (*SR* 7.345; *NŚSam* 506).

(13) **Parāvṛtta :** To move the arm backwards (*Mānas* 16.4.1139).

(14) **Pārsvānuga :** Not explained (*SUS* 5.64).

(15) **Pṛṣṭhānusārī :** The arms moves to the back (*NŚ* 9.220; *SR* 7.343; *NŚSam*. 503). *SUS* : *Pṛṣṭhānuga* (*SUS* 5.64). *SSam* : Pṛṣṭhaga (*SSam* 6.105) (*NN* 18a).

(16) **Prasārita :** The arm is extended to the front (*NŚ* 8.221; *SUS* 5.64; *SR* 7.339; *NŚSam* 499; *NN* 18a).

(17) **Maṇḍalagati :** The arm moves round in all directions. (*NŚ*. 9.220; *SR* 7.340-1; *NŚSam* 500). *SSam* *Maṇḍala* (*SSam* 6.105).

(18) **Lalita :** The arm is slightly bent (*Mānas* 16.4.1136).

(19) **Sarala :** The arm is extended to the front or to the side. (*Mānas* 16.4.1132). *SR* says that the arms should also be stretched downwards (*SR* 7.346; *NŚSam* 507; *NN* 18a).

(20) **Svastika :** The arms cross each other (*NŚ* 9.220; *SSam* 6.105; *SR* 7.341-2; *NŚSaṃ* 501; *NN* 18a).

(21) **Sthira :** Not explained (*SUS* 5.64).

Cālaka and Vartanā

Kallināha, in his commentary on *SR*, quotes Kohala to describe Cālaka and Vartanā which are said to be two types of movements of the arms. These have not been included in the present account as there is no direct textual evidence relating to them. The names, however, are given below.

The names of the Cālakas

(1) Viśliṣṭavartita; (2) Vepathuvyañjaka; (3) Apaviddha ; (4) Laharīcakrasundara; (5) Vartanāsvastika; (6) Sanmukhīnarathānga; (7) Purodaṇḍabhrama; (8) Tribhangivarṇasaraka; (9) Dola; (10) Nirājita; (11) Svastikāśleṣacālana; (12) Mithosaṁvikṣyabāhya; (13) Vāmavakṣavilāsita; (14) Maulirecitaka; (15) Vartanābharaṇa; (16) Kūrmāvatāra; (17) Aṁsavartanaka; (18) Maṇibandhāsīkarṣa; (19) Kalaviṅgavinoda; (20) Catuṣpatrābja; (21) Maṇḍalāgra; (22) Vālavyājanacālana; (23) Viruddhabandhana; (24) Śṛṅgāṭakabandhana; (25) Kuṇḍalīcara; (26) Murujāḍambara; (27) Dvāradāmavilāsaka; (28) Dhanurākarṣaṇa; (29) Sādhāraṇa; (30) Samaprakoṣṭhavalana; (31) Devopahāraka; (32) Tiryaggatasvastikāgra; (33) Maṅibandhagātagata; (34) Alātacakra; (35) Vyastoplutanivartaka; (36) Urabhrasaṁbādha; (37) Triyaktāṇḍavacālana; (38) Dhanurvallīvināmaka; (39) Tārkṣyapakṣavilāsaka; (40) Kararecakaratna; (41) Śarasandhāna; (42) Maṇḍalabharaṇa; (43) Aṁsaparyāyanirgata; (44) Aṣṭabandhavihāra; (45) Karṇayugmaprakirṇaka; (46) Paryāyagajadanta; (47) Rathanemi; (48) Svastikatrikoṇa; (49) Latāveṣṭita; (50) Navaratnaṁukha.

The names of the Vartanās

(1) Patākā ; (2) Arāla; (3) Śukatuṇḍa; (4) Alapadma; (5) Khaṭakāmukha; (6) Makara; (7) Ūrdhva; (8) Āviddha; (9) Recita; (10) Nitamba; (11) Keśabandha; (12) Phāla; (13) Kakṣa; (14) Ura; (15) Khaḍga; (16) Padma; (17) Daṇḍa; (18) Pallava; (19) Ardhamaṇḍala, (20) Ghaṭa; (21) Lalita; (22) Valita; (23) Gātra; (24) Prativartanikā.

Movements of the Hasta

These are gestures of the hand, an Aṅga. The following are the types of the movements and positions of the hand i.e. Asaṁyuktahasta, Saṁyukta-hasta, Nṛtta-hasta, Hasta-karaṇa, Hasta-karma, Hasta-kṣetra and Hasta-Pracāra. *ADar* describes a few more types of movements, called Deva-hasta, Bāndhava-hasta, Daśāvatāra-hasta, Jātīya-hasta and Navagrahahasta. *NŚSaṃ* mentions all these, including those in *ADar*, and adds to them three of its own, as follows : Nakṣatrābhinaya-hasta, Rāśyabhinaya-hasta and Rāgaraginyabhinayahasta.

The Asaṁyukta -hasta

(1) **Aṅkuṣa :** Not explained (*SDām* p. 162; *HR* p. 202).

(2) **Ardhacandra :** The fingers and the thumb are bent resembling the form of a crescent moon or a bow. (*NŚ* 9.43; *AP* 341.14; *VDP* 3.26.22; *SSam* 6.44; *SUS.* 5.71; *SDām* p. 62; *HR* p. 202). *ADar* : The thumb of the Patākā hand is stretched out (*ADar* 111). *Mānas*: The thumb of the Ahiphaṇa hand is stretched out (*Mānas* 16.4.1169). *SR* : All the fingers are closed together on one side while the thumb remain on the other, resembling the crescent moon (*SR* 7.117). *NN* : The fingers of the Pañcāsya hand are closed together while the thumb is separated (*NN.* 19b).

(3) **Ardhapatākā :** The little finger of the Tripatākā hand is bent (*ADar* 103; *NŚSaṃ* 178).

(4) **Ardhasūcī** *:* The forefinger of the Kapittha hand is raised (*ADar* 167).

(5) **Arāla :** The forefinger is bent down to form a bow, the thumb is bent. The rest of the fingers are separated and raised (and also bent a little : *SR*) (*NŚ* 9.46; *VDP* 3.26.24; *SR* 7.122-3; *SDām* p. 62). *ADar* : The forefinger of the Patākā hand is bent. (*ADar* 114).

Māṇas : The forefinger of the Patākā hand is extended (*Mānas* 16.4.1176). *SSam*: The forefinger of the Sarparśirṣa hand is curved. (*SSaṃ* 6.47). *SUS* : The forefinger and the thumb are bent to touch each other (*SUS* 5.72). *NN* : The Catura hand is curved and the forefinger is bent (*NN* 20a).

(6) **Alapadma :** Alapallava is reversed (*NN* 20a).

(7) **Alapallava :** The fingers are separated and moved sideways along the palm (*NŚ* 9.91 *VDP* : Kolapadma (*VDP* 3.26.39). *Mānas* : Alapadma (*Mānas* 16.4.1182-3). *ADar* : The fingers are bent and separted beginning from the little finger (*ADar* 146). *AP* : Alapadma (*AP* 341.15). *SR* says that after moving the hand in the Vyāvartita Karaṇa the fingers move sideways over the palm (*SR* 7.144). *SSam* : The fingers of the Padmakośa hand move along the palm. Alapadma (*SSam* 6.54). *SUS* : Alapadma : The fingers move along the palm. (*SUS* 5.77). *SDām* : Alapadma (*SDām* p. 61). *HR* : Alapadma (*HR* p. 202). It seems that all the texts except *NN,* think Alapallava and Alapadma are the same (*NN.* 20a).

(8) **Utkarāla** : Not explained (*AP* 341.14). It seems to be a scribal error, and Arāla is a possible reading.

(9) **Ūrṇanābha :** The fingers of the Padmakośa hand are bent (*NŚ* 9.120; *AP* 341.16; *SR* 7.173; *SSam* 6.53; *SR* 7. 173; *SUS.* 5.81; *SDām* p. 62; *HR* p. 202). *Mānas* and *NN* say that the thumb is bent as well. (*Mānas* 16.4.1184-5; *NN* 20a).

(10) **Kaṭaka :** The text is not complete. The middle and the ring finger are joined together (*ADar* 168-9).

(11) **Kapittha :** The forefinger of the Śikhara hand is curved and pressed by the thumb (*NŚ* 9.59; *AP* 341.14; *Mānas* 16.4.1204-5; *SR* 7.132; *SSam* 6.60; *SDām* p. 62; *HR* p. 202). *VDP* : The thumb is kept

inside the first (*VDP* 3.26.30). *SUS* : The definition is not quite explicit as the editor points out. It seems that the intended meaning is to touch the thumb with the fingers of the Śikhara hand (*SUS* 5.74). *ADar* : The forefinger of the Śikhara hand is bent to touch the tip of the thumb (*ADar* 121). *NN.* agrees with the *NŚ* (*NN* 20b).

(12) **Kadamba :** Not explained (*SDām* p. 62; *HR* p. 202).

(13) **Kartarīmukha :** The forefinger of the Tripatāka hand is bent back (*NŚ* 9.39; *VDP* 3.26.21; *SUS* 5.71; *Mānas* 16.4.1145; *SDām* p. 61). *ADar* : The forefinger and the little finger of the Ardhapatāka hand are stretched out (*ADar* 105). *SR* : The forefinger of the Tripātakā hand is separated from the middle one and kept behind it (*SR* 7.119-20). *SSam* : Kartarī (*SSam* 6.41). *NN* : Kartarī : The forefinger and the middle finger of the Tripatākā hand are separated (*NN* 20a). *HR* : The ring finger is bent as well. The rest agrees with the *NŚ*. (*HR* p. 202).

(14) **Kākatuṇḍa :** The thumb and the forefinger of the Kapittha hand are separated (*NN* 20b).

(15) **Kāṅgula :** The middle, the forefinger and the thumb are held in a traingular position like that of the three sacrificial fires. The ring finger is bent and the little finger is raised (*NŚ* 9.88; *VDP* 3.26.37-8; *SR* 7.140; *SDām* p. 62; *HR* p. 202). *ADar* : The ring finger of the Padmakośa hand is bent (*ADar* 144). *SSam* : A part of the text is corrupt. So the actions of the three fingers are not clear while on the action of the little and the ring finger *SSam* agrees with the *NŚ* (*SSam* 6.57). *Mānas* : It agrees with the *NŚ* and directs the dancer to keep the thumb, the middle and the forefingers separated (*Mānas* 16.4.1180-1). *SUS* : The middle and the forefinger are held like a flag with the thumb (*SUS* 5.77). *NN* : The thumb of the Mayūra hand is raised (*NN* 20b).

(16) **Kāmūlaka :** Not explained (*AP* 341.15).

(17) **Kuvala :** The dancer moves to the left with the hand in Patākā (*SMak* 2.4.15).

(18) **Kṛṣṇasāramukha :** The middle finger, the ring finger and the thumb are closed together. The other two are slightly curved and raised (*HR* p. 202; *SDām* p. 62).

(19) **Khaṭakāmukha :** The ring finger and the little finger of the Kapittha hand are raised and bent (*NŚ* 9.220; *VDP* 3.26.31; *SR* 7.134; *SDām* p. 62; *HR* p. 202). *AP*: Kaṭakāmukha (*AP* 341.14). *ADar* : Kaṭakāmukha : The forefinger, middle and the thumb of the Kapittha hand are raised (*ADar* 124). *Mānas* : Khaṭikāmukha (*Mānas* 16.4.1206-7). *SSam* : Kaṭakāmukha : The little finger of the Kapittha hand is raised and curved (*SSam* 6.61). SUS : Khaṭikāmukha (*SUS* 5.74). *NN* agrees with the *NŚ* but does not direct the dancer to bend the fingers (*NN* 20b).

(20) **Khaḍgāsya :** The ring finger is added to the Haṁsāya hand (*NN* 20a).

(21) **Gomukha :** The thumb of the Haṁsapakṣa hand is raised (*NN* 19b).

(22) **Caturmukha :** The thumb of the Pañcāsya hand touhes the root of the forefinger (*NN* 19b).

(23) **Catura :** The fingers are extended and the little finger is raised. The thumb is placed between the fingers (*NŚ* 9.93; *AP* 341.15; *VDP* 3.26.40-1; *SDām* p. 62; *HR* p. 202). *ADar* : The thumb touches the root of the ring finger obliquely and the forefinger is kept close to the other fingers while the little finger is raised (*ADar* 149-50). *SMak* : The Kamala hand is raised on the right side (*SMak* 2.4.15). *SR* : The thumb of the Sarpaśirṣa hand touches the middle joint of the middle finger and the little finger is

raised (*SR* 7.154). *Mānas* : The thumb of the Haṁsapakṣa hand bends and touches the root of the middle finger (*Mānas* 16.4.1164). *SSam* : The thumb of the Patākā hand touches the root of the ring finger and the little finger is bent back (*SSam* 6.42). *SUS* : says nothing about the thumb and agrees with the *NŚ*. in describing the rest of the action (*SUS* 5.78). *NN* : The thumb of the Gomukha hand touches the root of the middle finger (*NN* 19b).

(24) **Candrakalā :** The thumb of the Sūcī hand is released. (*ADar* 132; *NŚSaṃ* 183).

(25) **Tantrīmukha :** The ring and the middle finger are bent while the other three are separated (*HR* p. 202; *SDām* p. 62).

(26) **Tāmracūḍa :** The middle finger touches the thumb. The forefinger is bent and the rest of the fingers touch the palm (*NŚ* p. 9.122; *AP* 341.16; *SDām* p. 62; *HR* p. 202). *ADar* : The forefinger of the Mukula hand is raised and curved (*ADar* 163). *Mānas* : The forefinger of the Mukula hand is raised and curved while the little and the ring fingers touch the palm. (*Mānas* 16.4.1197-8). *SR* : The ring and the little fingers of the Bhramara hand touch the palm (*SR* 7.181). *SSam* : The little finger of the Bhramara hand touches the palm (*SSam,* 6.63). *NN* : The forefinger of the Sūcīmukha hand is bent (*NN* 20a).

(27) **Tripatākā :** The ring finger of the Pātakā hand should be bent (*NŚ* 9.28; *AP* 341.13; *VDP* 3.26.17; *ADar* 100; *SR* 7.109; *SSam* 6.40; *Mānas* 16.4.1144; *SUS* 5.70; *SDām* p. 61; *HR* p. 202).

(28) **Trimukha :** The little finger and the thumb of the Caturmukha hand are joined (*NN* 19b).

(29) **Triśulā :** The little finger and the thumb are bent and joined (*ADar* 165; *NŚSaṃ* 184).

(30) **Dvimukha :** The ring finger, little finger and the thumb of the Trimukha hand are joined together, (*NN* 19b).

(31) **Dhṛtahastaka :** The little finger is raised and moved round (*SMak* 2.4.16).

(32) **Nikuñcaka :** The little finger of the Catura hand is kept close to the other fingers (*NN* 19b). *SR* : The thumb of the Patākā hand touches the root of the middle finger (*SR* 7.283). *NŚSaṃ*. does not mention this as a single-hand-gesture.

(33) **Pakṣiruta :** The middle finger and the thumb are pressed together and the rest are bent (*SUS* 5.81).

(34) **Pañcāsya :** Described as Pañcānana also. All the fingers, including the thumb, are raised and separated (*NN* 19b).

(35) **Patākā :** The thumb is bent to touch the root of the forefinger and the rest of the fingers are kept close together and extended (*NŚ* 9.18; *AP* 341.13; *Mānas* 16.4.11-58; *SR* 7.102; *SDām* p. 61; *NN* 19b). *ADar* : The thumb is bent to touch the fingers which are extended (*ADar* 93). *VDP* : The thumb is bent and the fingers are simultaneously extended (*VDP* 3.26.14). *SUS* : All the fingers are extended including the thumb (*SUS* 5.70). *SSam* : and *HR* do not advise touching the forefinger with the thumb. The rest is the same as in the *NŚ*. (*SSam* 6.39; *HR* p. 202).

(36) **Padmakośa :** All the fingers, including the thumb, are bent, keeping them separated from each other without the tips touching (*NŚ* 9.79); *Mānas* 16.4.1174-5; *AP* 341.15; *SR* 7.142; *SSam* 6.52; *SDām* p. 61; *HR* p. 202). *VDP* : The fingers of the Sūcīmukha hand are kept apart and curved with

the thumb, and raised upwards like the tail of a swan (*VDP* 3.26.34). *ADar* : The palm is hollowed while the fingers are separated and bent a little. (*ADar* 134). *SUS* : (The palm) is slightly bent and the fingers are kept close to the thumb (*SUS* 5.75). *NN*: (The palm) is bent like a bow while the fingers are separated including the thumb (*NN* 20a).

(37) **Parikrama** : The hand is moved round on the left while the forefinger and the thumb are joined to form a ring (*SMak* 2.4.18).

(38) **Pallī** : The middle finger of the Mayūra hand touches the back of the forefinger (*ADar* 170).

(39) **Poṇika** : Not explained (*SDām* p. 62). *HR* : Ghoṇika (*HR* p. 202).

(40) **Bhramara** : The tip of the middle finger and of the thumb touch each other. The forefinger is bent while the two other fingers are raised and separated (*NŚ* 9.101; *AP* 341.15; *VDP* 3.26.44; *ADar* 152-3; *SR* 7.167-8; *SDām* p. 62). *Mānas* : The ring and the little fingers of the Mukula hand are extended while the forefinger is curved and raised upwards. (*Mānas* 16.4.1190-1). *SSaṁ* discusses only the middle finger and the thumb (*SSam* 6.51). *SUS* : It gives directions for the middle finger, forefinger and the thumb (*SUS* 5.78). Both these texts agree with the *NŚ*. *NN* : The little and the ring finger of the Tāmracūḍa hand are separated. (*NN* 20b). *HR*: The middle finger and the thumb touch each other while the other three are raised and separated (*HR* p. 202).

(41) **Manuraṇa** : Too obscure to explain (*SMak* 2.4.17).

(42) **Mayūra** : The ring finger and the thumb of the Kartarīmukha hand are joined and the rest are extended (*ADar* 108; *NN* 20b; *NŚSam* 180).

(43) **Mukula :** The fingers of the Haṁsamukha hands are bent and close. The tips touch one another (*NŚ* 9.117; *AP* 341.16; *SDām* p. 62; *SUS*. 5.80; *HṘ* p. 202). *VDP*; *SSam* : The tips of the Padmakośa hand touch each other (*VDP* 3.26.52; *SSam* 6.55). *ADar* All five fingers are joined (*ADar* 161). *SR* : All the fingers are closed and raised. (*SR* 7.1 69-70). *Mānas*: The finger tips, including the tip of the thumb, touch each other to form a Kadalīpuṣpa. (*Mānas*. 16.4.1186-7). *NN* : The fingers shut like a bud (*NN* 20a).

(44) **Muṣṭi :** The finger tips touch the palm and the thumb is placed on them (*NŚ* 9.55; 16.4.119-1200; *AP* 341.14; *VDP* 3.26.27; *ADar* 116-7; *Mānas*. 16.4.1199-1200; *SSam* 6.58; *SUS* 5.73; *SDām* p. 61; *HR* p. 202). *SR* : It prescribes placing the thumb on the middle finger (*SR* 7.128-9; *NN* 20b).

(45) **Mṛgaśīrṣa :** The thumb and the little finger are raised. The rest of the fingers are bent down together (*NŚ* 9.86; *VDP* 3.26.36; *AP* 341.15; *SDām* p. 62). *ADar*; *Mānas* : The little finger and the thumb of the Sarpaśīrṣa hand are extended. (*ADar* 139; *Mānas* : Mṛgaśira 16.4.1172). *SR; SSam* and *SUS* also agree with *ADar* (*SR* 7.159; *SSam* 6.46; *SUS* 5.76). *NN* The forefinger of the Khaḍgāsya hand is raised (*NN* 20a). *HR* : Does not require the bending down of three fingers but agrees with the *NŚ*. in describing the rest of the action (*HR* p. 202).

(46) **Raṇagṛdhraka :** The thumb of the Haṃsavaktra hand is extended sideways (*NN* 20a).

(47) **Valgula :** The middle finger of the Śukatuṇḍa hand is curved while the thumb is slackened (*NN* 20a).

(48) **Varāhamukha :** The little finger of the Muṣṭi hand is extended (*NN* 20b).

(49) **Vālacandra :** The Kākatuṇḍa hand is fully extended (*NN* 20b).

(50) **Vyāghra :** The little finger and the thumb of the Mṛgaśīrṣa hand are bent forward (*ADar* 166).

(51) **Śikhara :** The thumb of the Muṣṭi hand is raised (*NŚ* 9.57; *VDP* 3.26.29; *AP* 341.14; *ADar* 118; *Mānas.* 16.4). 1202-3; *SR* 7.130; *SSam* 6.59; SUS 5.73; *SDām* p. 61; *HR* p. 202; *NN* 20b).

(52) **Śukatuṇḍa :** The ring finger of the Arāla hand is bent. (*NŚ* 9.53; *AP* 341.14; *VDP* 3.26.26; *ADar* 115; *Mānas* 16.3.1178; *SSam* 6.48; *SUS* 5.72; *SDām* p. 62; *HR* p. 202). *SR :* Both the ring and the forefingers of the Arāla hand are very much bent (*SR* 7.137). *NN* suggests that the forefinger is also bent (*NN* 20a).

(53) **Saṁdaṃśa :** The palm of the Arāla hand is slightly hollowed and the forefinger touches the thumb. There are three types of Saṁdaṃśa : Agraga (in front), Mukhaja (near the mouth) and Pārśvagata (one on side) (*NŚ* 9.110-1; *AP* 341-16; *VDP* 3.26.49-50; *Mānas* 16.4.1192-3; *SR* 7.175-6; *SDām* p. 62; *HR* p. 202). *ADar:* The fingers of the Padmakośa hand are joined and separated repeatedly (*ADar* 159). *SSam* agrees with the *NŚ* but does not say anything about the palm (*SSam* 6.50). *SUS* also does not say anything about the palm and is silent about the kinds of Saṁdaṃśa (*SUS* 5.80). *NN* : The forefinger and the thumb of the Pañcāsya hand touch each other (*NN* 20a).

(54) **Sarpaśīrṣa :** All the fingers, including the thumb, are close to one another and the palm is hollowed. (*NŚ* 9.84; *SSam* 6.45; *SDām* P. 62; *HR* p. 202). *VDP* : Ahiśira (*VDP* 3.26.35). *ADar :* The tips of the fingers of the Patākā hand are bent (*ADar* 137). *SR.*; *Mānas* : The palm of the Patākā hand is hollowed (*SR* 7.152; *Mānas* : Ahiphaṇa 16.4.1166). *AP*: Ahiśira (*AP* 341.15). *SUS* does not say anything about the palm (*SUS.* 5.76). *NN* agrees with the *NŚ* (*NN* 19b).

(55) **Siṃhāsya :** The middle and the ring finger touch the thumb while the last two fingers are extended. (*ADar* 142-3; *SDam* p. 62; *NŚSaṃ* : Siṃhamukha. 185). *HR* : The little finger and the thumb are separated while the others are slightly raised and joined at their sides, (*HR* p. 202).

(56) **Sūcīmukha :** The forefinger of the Khaṭakāmukha hand is raised (*NŚ* 9.64; *NN* 20a). *VDP* 3.26.33; *SR*. 7.147; *SUS* 5.75). *AP; SSam; SDām; HR* Sūcyāsya. (*AP* 341.15; *SSam* 6.6.2; *SDām* p. 62; *HR* p. 202). *ADar* : Sūcī (*ADar* 12). *Mānas* : The forefinger of the Muṣṭi hand is stretched out (*Mānas* 16.4.1208-9).

(57) **Haṃsapakṣa :** Three fingers are extended, the little is raised and the thumb is bent (*NŚ* 9.106; *AP* 341.16; *SDām* p. 62; *HR* p. 202; *NN* 19b). *VDP* : The little finger is raised and curved. The thumb is bent. (*VDP* 3.26.47). *ADar.* : The little finger of the Sarpaśira hand is extended. (*ADar* 157). *Mānas* : The little finger of the Patākā hand is raised. (*Mānas* 16.4.1162). *SR* : The three fingers, beginning from the forefinger, of the Patākā hand are slightly bent at their wrists. (*SR* 7.163). *SSam* : The little finger of the Patākā hand is bent back. (*SSam* 6.43). *SUS* : The little finger is raised while the others are slightly bent (*SUS* 5.79).

(58) **Haṃsāsya :** The forefinger, the middle finger and the thumb are closely joined in a triangular position like the three sacrificial fires. The two other fingers are extended (*NŚ* 9.104; *AP* 341.16; *SDāṃ* p. 61). *VDP* : Haṃsavaktra (*VDP* 3.26.45-6). *ADar* : The forefinger touches the thumb while the three fingers, beginning from the middle one, are separated and extended (*ADar* 154). *Mānas* : Haṃsamukha : The little finger of the Mukula hand is raised upwards and the ring finger is bent.

(*Mānas* 16.4.1188-9) *SR* says that the two fingers that are extended should be separated as well. The rest of the action agrees with the *NŚ* (*SR* 7.161). *SSam* : The fingers of the Mukula hand are extended (*SSam* 6.56). *SUS* : Haṃsavaktra : The forefinger, the middle finger and the thumb touch each other at their tips (*SUS* 5.79). *NN* : The fingers join the middle finger (*NN* 20a). *HR* : The forefinger, the middle finger and the thumb are joined to form the bill of a duck (*HR* p. 202).

The Saṃyuktahastas

(1) **Añjali :** The Patākā hands are put together (*NŚ* 9.128; *AP* 341.17; *VDP* 3.26.54; *ADar* 176; *SDām* p. 62; *SUS* 5.91; *SSam* 6.66; *NN* 20b). *Mānas* : The thumb and the whole palm of the Sarpaśira hand joins the other (*Mānas* 16.4.1211-2). *SR* : The palms of the Patākā hands are joined (*SR* 7.185). *HR* : two Patākā hands are joined on one of their sides. The palms are slightly curved (*HR* p. 202).

(2) **Arekhā :** The hands should be joined in Saṁpuṭa and the dancer should look forward (*SMak* 2.4.11).

(3) **Avahittha :** The Śukatuṇḍa hands are bent and placed on the chest and then slowly lowered down (*NŚ* 9.156; *VDP* 3.26.67; *NN* 21a; *SDām* p. 62; *SSam* 6.74; *Mānas* 16.4.1234-5; *SR* 7.208). *HR* : The Śukatuṇḍa hands are placed obliquely on the chest and they are slightly raised (*HR* p. 202).

(4) **Āsaṅga :** Not explained (*AP* 341.18).

(5) **Utsaṅga :** The Arāla hands are kept in reverse position. They face upwards and are bent (*NŚ* 9.139; *SDām* p. 62). *VDP* : The Arāla hands are kept in reverse position with their palms upwards and then changed into Vardhamāna (*VDP* 3.26.60). *ADar* : The Mṛgaśirṣa hands are placed on the

opposite arms (*ADar* 184). *Mānas* : The Sarpaśira hands are crossed in Svastika (*Mānas* 16.4.1221-2). *SR* : The Arāla hands are crossed in Svastika on the opposite shoulders (*SR* 7.198). *SSam* : The text is incomplete. The sense seems to be the same as in the *NŚ* (*SSam* 6.75). *NN* : The Arāla hands are placed on the opposite shoulders, (*NN* 21a). *HR* : The palms of the Arāla hands are either turned upwards or the hands are raised and extended facing the front. (*HR* p. 202). The hands are at the haunches (*SUS* 5.93).

(6) **Kaṭakāvardhana :** The Khaṭakāmukha hands cross at their wrists in Svastika (*ADar* 187).

(7) **Kapota :** The hands are joined on one of their sides in Patākā (*NŚ* 9.130; *AP* 341.17; *VDP* 3.26.55; *ADar* 177; *SDām* p. 62; *SR.* 7.186; *NN.* 20b). *Mānas* : The palms of the Patākā hands are joined. (*Mānas* 16.4.1213-4). *SSam* : The Sarpaśirṣa hands are joined. (*SSam* 6.67). *SUS* : The hands are joined to form a hollow between themselves (*SUS* 5.91). *HR* : The hands in Patākā are joined forming a hollow between themselves. (*HR* p. 202).

(8) **Karkaṭa :** The fingers are interlocked (*NŚ* 9.133; *AP* 341.17; *VDP* 3.26.56; *ADar* 178-9; *Mānas* 16.4.1215-6; *SDam* p. 62; *SUS* p.92; *SR* 7.188-9; *HR* p. 202; *NN* 20b). *SSam* : It suggests Padmakośa for the hands and agrees with the *NŚ* in describing the rest of the action. (*SSam.* 6.68).

(9) **Kartarīsvastika :** The Kartarī hands are crossed in Svastika (*ADar* 188; *NŚSaṃ* 218).

(10) **Kalaśa :** The hands face each other in Ardhacandra (*NŚSaṃ* 222).

(11) **Kīlaka :** The little fingers of the Mṛgaśīrṣa hands are bent and joined (*ADar* 195; *NŚSaṃ* 301).

(12) **Kūrma** : The finger tips of the Cakra hands are curved (*NŚSaṃ* 306). According to *ADar*, the thumbs and the little fingers should not be curved. (*ADar* 197). *SR* thinks that Kapota and Kūrma are the same (*SR* 7.186).

(13) **Kaivala** : The hands are placed on the right breast to show the nipples (*SMak* 2.4.13).

(14) **Khaṭakāvardhamānaka** : One Khaṭaka hand is placed on another Khaṭaka hand (*NŚ* 9.137; *VDP* 3.26.59; *SDām* p. 62; *Mānas* 16.4.1219; *SR* 7.202). *AP; SSam*: Katakāvardhamāna (*AP* 341.18; *SSam* 6.70). *SUS* : Khatikāvardhamāna (*SUS*. 5.93) (*NN* 21a; *HR* p. 202).

(15) **Khaṭikāsana** : The same as Svastika (*SUS* 5.92).

(16) **Khaṭvā** : One Catura hand is placed on another Catura hand. Their thumbs and forefingers are released (*ADar* 202; *NŚSaṃ* 311).

(17) **Gajadanta** : The hands touch the opposite arms between the shoulders and elbows (*NŚ* 9.154; *AP* 341.19; *SDām* p. 62; *NN* 21a). *VDP* and *SR* direct the dancer to move the hands in Sarpaśārṣa and agrees with the *NŚ* in describing the rest of the action (*VDP* 3.26.66; *SR* 7.204-5). *Mānas* : The elbows are curved evenly and joined at the sides. The hands are in Sarpaśīrṣa. (*Mānas* 16.4.1232-3). *SSam* : The Sarpaśīrṣa hands are put forward with the palms turned upward a litte. (*SSam* 6.72). *SUS* : The Patākā hands cross at their wrists (*SUS*. 5.96) *HR* agrees with *VDP* and *SR* (*HR* p. 202).

(18) **Garuḍa** : The Ardhacandra hands are placed obliquely to touch the thumbs (*ADar* 200; *NŚSaṃ* 309).

(19) **Cakra** : The Ardhacandra hands are placed to touch the palms. This is done obliquely (*ADar* 192; *NŚSaṃ* 299).

(20) **Tilaka :** The hands are in Tripatāka. One of them is placed on the forehead while the other is placed on the chest. They face each other (*NŚSaṃ* 223).

(21) **Dardura :** Described as Dardura in the description. The Ardhacandra hands are firmly joined with their palms placed obliquely (*NN* 21a).

(22) **Dola :** The shoulders are slackened and the hands are let down in Patākā (*NŚ* 9.148; *AP* 341.18; *Mānas* 16.4.1225-6; *SDām* p. 62; *NN.* 20b-21a; *HR* p. 202). *ADar* : The Patākā hands are placed on the thighs. (*ADar* 181). *VDP*; *SSam* : They say nothing about the shoulders (*VDP* 3.26.62; *SSam* 6.73). *SUS* : The hands are joined (*SUS* 5.94). *SR* : Dola. (*SR* 7.195).

(23) **Dviśikhara :** The hands are in Śikhara (*NN* 21a; *SR* 7.285).

(24) **Nāgabandha :** The Sarpaśīrṣa hands are crossed in Svastika (*ADar* 201; *NŚSaṃ* 310).

(25) **Niṣadha :** One hand in Kapittha is placed on the other in Mukula (*NS* 9.141; *AP* 341.18; *VDP* 326.61; *SDām* p. 62; *Mānas* 16.4.1223-4; *SR* 7.209; *NN* 21a). *SSam* : The text is incomplete (*SSam* 6.76). *SUS* : Padmakośa hands are joined. (*SUS* 5.94). The G.O.S. edition of the *NŚ* gives three more descriptions of this hand gesture : (i) Mṛgaśīrṣa hand is placed on the Śikhara hand. (ii) The left hand holds the right arm above the elbow and the right hand does the same with the left. (iii) The hands in Haṃsapakṣa are placed in opposite directions (*NŚ* 9.143-7). *HR* agrees with the second view (*HR* p. 202).

(26) **Patākāsvastika :** The hands cross in Patākā with one palm turned up and the other turned down (*NŚSaṃ* 220).

(27) **Pāśa :** The forefingers of the Sūcī hands are bent and joined (*ADar* 194; *NŚSaṃ* 300).

(28) **Puṣpapuṭa :** The Sarpaśīrṣa hands, with their fingers close to one another, meet on one side closely (*NŚ* 9.150; *AP* 341.18; *VDP* 3.26.63; *ADar* 182; *SDām* p. 62; *SR* 7.196; *NN* 21a). *SSam* : Directs the dancer to join the sides of the little fingers (*SSam* 6.77). *SUS* : The hands are bent down. (*SUS* 5.95). *Mānas.* agrees with *SSam* (*Mānas* 16.4.1227-8). *HR* agrees with both the *NŚ* and *SSaṃ* (*HR* p. 202).

(29) **Bahistambha :** Not explained (*AP* 341.19).

(30) **Bheruṇḍa :** The hands are joined at the wrists in Kapittha (*ADar* 203).

(31) **Makara :** The Patākā hands are placed on each other with the thumbs raised and curved (*NŚ* 9.152; *AP* 341.18; *SR* 7.212; *SDām* p. 62). *VDP* : The Patākā hands are placed, one upon the other, on the head and turned down. (*VDP* 3.26.64). *Mānas* : The Patākā hands are joined at their wrists facing the opposite directions (*Mānas* 16.4.1229-30). *SSam* : The Patākā hands are stretched and joined at the wrists with the palms upward (*SSam* 6.78). *SUS* : The Patākā hands are bent downwards with the thumbs raised (*SUS* 5.95). *NN* : The (Ardha) candra hands are upturned and placed on each other (*NN* 21a). *HR* : It does not prescribe to curve the thumb (*HR* p. 202).

(32) **Matsya :** One hand is placed on the back of the other facing downward. The thumbs and the little fingers of both the hands are slightly extended. (*ADar* 196; *NŚSaṃ* 304).

(33) **Marāla :** The hands are separated and they tremble. *SDām* p. 62; *HR* p. 602).

(34) **Yogamuṣṭika :** The Muṣṭi hands are joined at the tips (*NN* 21a). Described as Adhomuṣṭika in the direction.

(35) **Vardhamāna** : The hands are placed in opposite directions in Hamapakṣa. (*NŚ* 9.158; *AP* 341.19; *VDP* 3.26. 68; *SDām* p. 62; *SUS* 5.96; *SR* 7.214). *Mānas* : It prescribes Mṛgaśīrṣa for Haṃsapakṣa and agrees with the *NŚ* in describing the rest of the action. (*Mānas* 16.4.1236). *SSam* : The same as Niṣadha. (*SSam* 6.69). *NN* : The Haṃsapakṣa hands are crossed (*NN* 21a). *HR* : The Mṛgaśīrṣa hands are joined and placed forward. (*HR*. p. 202). Sarpaśīrṣa is also suggested by *SR*.

(36) **Varāha** : One hand in Mṛgaśīrṣa is placed on the other Mṛgaśīrṣa hand. The thumbs join the little fingers (*ADar* 198-9; *NŚSaṃ* 307).

(37) **Vaiṣṇava** : The thumbs of the Patākā hands are locked together (*NŚSaṃ* 225).

(38) **Śakata** : The middle fingers and the thumbs are extended in Bhramara (*ADar* 189; *NŚSaṃ* 296).

(39) **Śaṅkha** : The thumbs of the Śikhara hand joins the other thumb and the forefinger clins round it (*ADar* 190; *NŚSaṃ* 297).

(40) **Śivaliṅga** : The left hand is in Ardhacandra while the right hand is placed on it in Śikhara. (*ADar* 186; *NŚSaṃ* 303).

(41) **Śrṅkhalā** : The Tāmracūḍa hands are joined to form a chain (*NN* 21a).

(42) **Sampuṭa** : The fingers of the Cakra hands are bent down (*ADar* 193; *NŚSaṃ* 302).

(43) **Samprasārī** : Too obscure to explain (*SMak* 2.4.12).

(44) **Samgaika** : The hands are placed on the left breast (*SMak* 2.4.13).

(45) **Sāriṇī** : The hands are quickly placed on the right arm (*SMak* 2.4.11).

(46) **Sunanda** : The hands are joined at the wrists in Śukatuṇḍa (*SUS* 5.97).

(47) **Svastika :** The hands are turned up and joined at the wrists on the left in Arāla (*NŚ* 9.135; *AP* 341.17; *SDām* p. 62; *Manas* 16.4.1217-8; *SR* 7.192-3; *HR* p.202). *VDP* : The Arāla hands are bent sideways and placed one on the other at the wrists the palms turned up in Vardhamāna. (*VDP* 3.26.57). *ADar* : The Patākā hands are crossed at the wrists. (*ADar* 180). *SSam* agrees with the *NŚ* but does not direct the dancer to join the wrists on her left. It asks her to place the hands side by side. (*NSSam*. 6.71). *NN* : The hands cross at the wrists in Patākā. It agrees with *ADar* (*NN* 20b). *SR* suggests Patākā as well. *NŚSaṃ* suggests Tripatākā as well (*NŚSaṃ* 214).

The Nṛttahastas

(1) **Ardharecita :** The left hand is Caturaśra and the right is Recita (*NŚ* 9.194; *VDP* 3.26.78; *SR* 7.237. *SSam* 6.86; *SDām* p. 62; *NN* 21b). *Mānas*: The hands, one in Caturaśra and the other in Recita, are moved in Khaṭakāsya (*Mānas* 16.4.1249-50). *SUS* : The hands are moved in Recita and Udvartita (*SUS*. 5.102).

(2) **Arālakhaṭakāmukha :** The Alapallava hands with their palms turned upwards should be changed to Padmakośa. This is also known as Arālakhaṭaka; or; the hands in Arāla are separated at the wrists (*NŚ* 9.188-9; *SDām* p. 62; *HR* p. 202). *VDP* : Agrees with the second view of the *NŚ* (*VDP* 3.26.74). *Mānas* : One hand is placed on the chest in Khaṭakāsya facing the back while the other is extended obliquely in Arāla (*Mānas* 16.4.1243-5). *SR* : The Patākā hands are crossed in Svastika and moved round. The left hand changed to Arāla and the right hand either assumes Khaṭakāmukha or Caturaśra which points downwards. Finally, they are crossed either in Arāla or Khaṭakāmukha (*SR* 7.224-6). *SSam* ; *SUS*; *NN* : One hand is in

Arāla and the other is in Khaṭaka (*SSam* 6.87; *SUS* 5.100; *NN* 21b).

(3) **Alapadma :** The (Alapallava) hands are raised to the shoulders. (*NN* 22a; *SDām* p. 62; *HR* 202).

(4) **Alapallava :** The Alapallava hands are moved (from the chest to the shoulder) in Udveṣṭita Karaṇa (*NŚ* 9.208; *VDP* 3.26.89; *SR* 7.276-7; *NN* 22a).

(5) **Avahittha :** The Tripatākā hands are slightly bent at the elbows (*VDP* 3.26.79).

(6) **Āviddhavakra :** The hands are moved gracefully with the arms, the elbows and the shoulders. The palms of the hands are turned back (*NŚ* 9.190; *VDP* : Āviddha 3.26.75; *SDām* p. 62; *SR* 7.230; *HR* p. 202). *SSam* : The hands are moved in various ways. (*SSam* 6.86). *Mānas* : The Arāla hands are moved with the elbows, the shoulders and the arms. They point downwards. (*Mānas* 16.4.1246) (*NN* 21b).

(7) **Uttānvañcita :** The shoulders and the elbows are bent. The hands in Tripatākā are moved obliquely (*NŚ*. 9.195; *Mānas* 16.4.1250-1). *SDām HR* : Uttānarecita (*SDām* p. 62; *HR* p. 202). *SSam* : The Tripatākā hands are moved aside. (*SSam* 6.89). *SUS* : The hands touch the cheeks in Tripatākā (*SUS* 5.103). *SR* : The hands are raised to the forehead or the cheek or the shoulders. The Tripatākā hands are extended forward obliquely. The shoulders and the elbows are moved. Some suggest bending of the shoulders (*SR* 7.244). *NN* agrees with *SUS* (*NN* 21b).

(8) **Udvṛtta :** The hands in Haṃsapakṣa are waved like palm leaf fans (*NŚ* 9.185; *SDām* p. 62; *SSam* 6.79; *SUS* 5.98; *Mānas* 16.4.1239; *HR* p. 202). *SR* : It gives two views one of which agrees with the *NŚ* The other one suggests that the Haṃsapakṣa hands are moved in Caturaśra. Then one is raised and placed

near the chest while the other is lowered. (*SR* 7.218). *VDP*; *NŚ* : Also Talāvṛnta (*VDP* 3.26.72). *NN* : This text directs the dancer to perform the action near the chest (*NN* 21a).

(9) **Unnata :** Not explained (*SDām* p. 62).

(10) **Uromaṇḍala :** The hands are moved near the chest, one in Udveṣṭita and the other in Apaveṣṭita (*NŚ* 9.204; *VDP* 3.26.87; *NN* 20a); *Manas* : 16.4.1262; *SSam* 6.96-7). *SDām*; *HR* : Vakṣomaṇḍala (*SDām* p. 62; *HR* p. 202). *SUS* prescribes Arāla for the hands (*SUS* 5.108). *SR* : Agrees with the *NŚ* and quotes two other views one of which directs the dancer to place the hands at her sides after moving it round while the other view suggests Haṃsapakṣa for the hands (*SR* 7.264-5).

(11) **Uraḥpārśvārdhamandala :** The Alapallava and the Arāla hands are moved by turns on the chest and on the sides (*NŚ*.9.205; *Mānas* 16.4.1263-4); *SDām* p. 62; *SUS* 5.109; *SR* 7.267-8; *NN* 22a; *HR* p. 202); *SSam*: It prescribes Arāla for both the hands (*SSam* 6.97-8).

(12) **Ulvaṇa :** The Alapallava hands are raised and moved. (*NŚ* 9.208). *VDP* : The hands are raised, extended and curved (*VDP* 3.26.90). *Mānas* : The Alapallava hands are moved round. (*Mānas* 16.4.1266). *SUS* : The hands are extended upwards (*SUS* 5.111). *SSam :* The Pallava hands are raised and moved in Āveṣṭita and Apaveṣṭita (*SSam* 6.99). *SR* : The hands are raised up to the shoulders are stretched. (*SR* 7.277-8). *NN*: The hands are raised (*NN* 21b).

(13) **Ūrdhvamaṇḍala :** The hands are raised and moved in circles (*NŚ* 9.203; *VDP* 3.26.86; *SDām* p. 62; *HR* p. 202; *NN* 22a). *Mānas* : Prescribes Arāla for the hands which should be moved round over the head. (*Mānas.* 16.4.1260). (*SUS* : Prescribes Arāla

for the hands. *SUS* 5.107). *SR* : The hands are raised up to the forehead and moved round (*SR* 7.260-1).

(14) **Ūrdhvapārśvamaṇḍala** : Ūrdhva and Pārśvamaṇḍalas are done together (*SSam* 6.95-6).

(15) **Karihasta** : One hand is raised in Latā and swung on either side and another hand in Tripatākā is held at the ear (*NŚ* 9.199; *SDām* p. 62; *SSam* 6.90-1; *HR* p. 202). *VDP* : It substitutes Khaṭaka for Tripatākā (*VDP* 3.26.83). *Mānas.* agrees with the *NŚ.* in describing the action of the Tripatākā hand while it directs the dancer to raise and move the other hand which is curved (*Mānas* 16.4.1255-6). *SUS* : The Tripatākā hands are swung on either side. (*SUS* 5.105). *SR* says that Khaṭakāmukha can also be substituted for Tripatākā (*SR* 7.248-9). *NN* agrees with the *VDP* (*NN* 21b).

(16) **Keśabandha** : The hands should move upwards from the two sides to touch the hair and back. This is done repeatedly (*NŚ* 9.197; *SDām* p. 62; *SR* 242; *HR* p. 202; *NN* 21b). *VDP* : The hands move upwards from the sides to the shoulders (*VDP* 3.26.81). *Mānas* : The Tripatākā hands are moved out from the region of hair. (*Mānas* 16.4.1253-4). *SSam* : The hands move out from the region of hair to the sides. (*SSam* 6.88-9).

(17) **Kuñcita** : The Pakṣavañcita hands are moved away from the head (*SUS* 5.106).

(18) **Garuḍapakṣa** : The hands should be placed on the hips with their palms slightly bent and facing downwards (*NŚ* 9.201; *SDām* p. 62; *HR* p. 202; *NN* 22a). *VDP* does not direct the dancer to place the hands on the hips, but agrees with the rest (*VDP* 3.26.85). *Mānas* : The Tripatākā hands are placed obliquely pointing downwards (*Mānas* 16.4.1258).

SSam : The Haṃsapakṣa hands are obliquely stretched facing downwards. (*SSam* 6.93-4). *SUS* : The Patākā hands are waved as fluttering in the wind (*SUS* 5.106). *SR* prescribes. Tripatākā or Patākā for the hands (*SR* 7.259).

(19) **Caturaśra** : The Khaṭakāmukha hands are held forward eight fingers apart from each other on the dancer's breasts. The shoulders are on the same level (*NŚ* 9.184; *VDP* 3.26.71; *Mānas* 16.4.1238-9); *SDām* p. 62; *SR* 7.216;7; *SSam* 6.84; *HR* p. 202; *NN* 21a). *SUS* : The left hand is placed on the right hand and the right is placed on the left (*SUS* 5.98).

(20) **Jñānahasta** : The right hand in Haṃsāsya is placed on the left hand, which is in Patākā (*NŚSaṃ* 291).

(21) **Talamukha** : The hands should be changed from Caturaśra to Haṃsapakṣa and they should be placed obliquely facing each other (*NŚ* 9.186; *SR* 7.221; *SSam* 6.84-5). *Mānas* : The hands are raised and placed obliquely facing the front (*Mānas* 16.4.1240). *SUS* : The hands face each other (*SUS* 5.99). *NN* : It prescribes Udvṛtta for Caturaśra. (*NN* 21b).

(22) **Daṇḍapakṣa** : The Haṃsapakṣa hands move alternately and then stretch out like a staff (*NŚ* 9.202; *SDām* p. 62; *SR* 7.257; *HR* p. 202). *VDP* : The hands are stretched. (*VDP* 3.26.86). *SSam* : *Mānas* : The Haṃsapakṣa hands are extended obliquely and moved round. (*SSam* 6.92-3; *Mānas* : 16.4.1259). *SUS* : The Haṃsapakṣa hands are moved in Vyāvṛtta and Parivartita. (*SUS* 5.107). *NN* : The arms are placed at the sides with the hands in Haṃsapakṣa (*NN* 22a).

(23) **Dviśikhara** : Both the hands are in Śikhara (*NŚSaṃ* 287).

(24) **Nalinīpadmakośa :** The Padmakośa hands are moved in Vyāvṛtta and Parivartita (*NŚ*. 9.207; *SDām* p. 62; *HR* p. 202; *SSam*. 6.98-9; *NN* 22a). *VDP* : Padmakośa : No movement is suggested but the hands should be in Haṃsapakṣa (*VDP* 3.26.89). *SUS* : It suggests no movements but the hands should be in Padmakośa. (*SUS* 5.110). *Mānas* : The Padmakośa hands are moved from the knee to the head with occasional shivers (*Mānas* 16.4.1265). *SR* : (i) The Padmakośa hands face opposite directions. (ii) The Padmakośa hands are joined at the wrists facing each other. (iii) The Padmakośa hands are separated in Vyāvṛtta and Parivartita. (iv). The Padmakośa hands are moved from the knee to the shoulders or the breasts and brought down to the knee in Vyāvṛtta and Parivartita (*SR* 7.272-6).

(25) **Nikuñcaka :** The thumb of the Patākā hand touches the base of the middle finger (*NŚSam* 286).

(26) **Nitamba :** The Patākā hands are moved from the shoulders to the hips (*NŚ* 9.196; *SDām* p. 62; *SUS* : 5.104; *NN* 21b; *HR* p. 202; *SR* 7.238). *VDP* does not prescribe Patākā for the hands and agrees with the rest of the *NŚ* (*VDP* 3.26.80). *Mānas* prescribes Tripatākā for the hands. (*Mānas* 16.4.1252-3). *SSam* : The hands move out from the shoulders and placed at the sides (*SSam* 6.88).

(27) **Pakṣapradyotaka :** Pakṣavañcitaka is reversed. (*NŚ* 9.201; *VDP* 3.26.85; Pakṣadyota : *SDām* p. 62; *HR* p. 202; *NN* 22a; *SSam* 6.92). *Mānas* : The Tripatākā hands are upturned and placed on the waist. (*Mānas* 16.4.1256). *SR* agree with the *NŚ*. and gives another view : The hands are upturned in opposite directions (*SR* 7.255-6).

(28) **Pakṣavañcitaka :** The Tripatākā hands are placed on the top of the hips (*NŚ* 9.200; *VDP* 3.26.84, *SR*

7.255; *Mānas* 16.4.1257-8; *NN* 22a; *HR* p. 202). *SḌām*; Pakṣarañcita (*SDām* p. 62). *SUS* : The hands touch the head (*SUS* 5.105). *SSam* : It prescribes Patākā for the hands. (*SSam* 6.91).

(29) **Pallava :** The Patākā hands are slackened at the wrists, (*NŚ* 9.196; *VDP* 3.26.80; *SDām* p. 62; *SSam* 6.87; *NN* 21bl; *HR* p. 202). *SUS* : The Padmakośa hands are slackened at the wrists (*SUS* 5.103). *Mānas* : It prescribes Padmakośa for Patākā. The hands should point downwards or upwards (*Mānas* 16.4.1251-2). *SR* : (i) The arms are raised in Vyāvartita and the hands are crossed in Svastika. (ii) The Tripatākā hands are slackened. (iii) The Padmakośa hands, one pointing down and other pointing up are slackened at the wrists. (iv) Patākā is substituted for Padmakośa by some theorists (*SR* 7.239-42).

(30) **Pārśvamaṇḍala :** The hands are moved in circles at the sides. (*NŚ* 9.203; *VDP* 3.26.87; *Mānas* 16.4.1251; *SDām* p. 62; *SUS* : 5.108; *HR* p. 202; *NN.* 22a). *SR* gives another view which suggests that the Patākā hands are moved at the sides facing each other (*SR* 7.262-3).

(31) **Pārśvārdhamaṇḍala :** The same as Uraḥpārśvārdha-maṇḍala (*VDP* 3.26.11).

(32) **Prakirṇa :** The same as Viprakīrṇa. The hands are crossed and separated quickly (*VDP* 3.26.88; *NŚSaṃ* 295).

(33) **Mudrā :** The middle fingers and the thumbs are joined while the other fingers are extended. (*NŚSaṃ* 293).

(34) **Muṣṭikasvastika :** The Khaṭakāmukha hands are bent at the wrists and moved round (*NŚ* 9.206; *SDām* p. 62; *SSam,* 6.94; *SUS* 5.109; *Mānas* 16.4.1264-5; *NN* 22a; *HR* p. 202). *VDP* : The lines, describing the

gesture are missing. The editor has quoted the *NŚ*. to explain it (*VDP* 3.26.12, p. 83). Muṣṭasvatika. *SR*: One hand is bent in Arāla and the other is bent in Alapallava alternately. Then the hands assuming Khaṭakāmukha form a Svastika. This Svastika can also be performed with the Muṣṭi, Śikhara or Kapittha hands (*SR* 7.270).

(35) **Recita** : The hands in Haṃsapakṣsa are moved quickly with their palms turned up (*NŚ* 9.193; *VDP* 3.26.77; *Mānas* 16.4.1248-9; *SDām* 62; *SSam* 6.85; *HR* p. 202). *SUS* directs the dancer to move the Haṃsapakṣa hands to the sides (*SUS* 5.102). *SR* says that it can also be performed by stretching the upturned hands (*SR* 7.235). *NN* prescribes Haṃsapakṣa or Patākā for the hands. (*NN* 21b.)

(36) **Laghumukha** : The same as Talamukha (*VDP* 3.26.73).

(37) **Latā** : The hands are extended obliquely at the sides. (*NŚ* 9.198; *VDP*. 3.26.82; *SDām* p. 62; *SSam* 6.90; *HR* p. 202). *SUS, Mānas* and *NN* prescribe Tripatākā for the hands. (*SUS* 5.104; *Mānas* 16.4.1254-5; *NN* 21b). *SR* agree with both views (*SR* 7.246-7).

(38) **Latānana** : Not explained (*HR* p. 202).

(39) **Latānanamukha** : Not explained (*SDām* p. 62).

(40) **Lalita** : The Pallava hands are moved over the head (*NŚ* 9.209; *VDP* 3.26.90; *SSam* 6.100; *NN* 22a). *SUS* : The hands are moved in Āvartita with the palms turned down. (*SUS* 5.101). *SR* agrees with the *NŚ* and quotes two other views. One substitutes Caturaśra for Pallava while the other directs the dancer to join the finger tips over the head (*SR* 7.278-9).

(41) **Varadābhaya** : Both the hands are in Arāla. The right points upwards with the palms facing outwards and

held at the side, while the left hand points downwards with the palms facing outwards and it is held at the same level as the hips. (*SR* 7.285-6). (*NŚSaṃ* 288). *NN* : The hands are placed on the top of the hips in Arāla (*NN* 22a-b).

(42) **Valita :** The Latā hands are crossed at the elbows. (*NŚ* 9.205; *SSam* 6.100; *VDP* 3.26.90; *NN* 22b). *SR* agrees with the *NŚ* and quotes two other views. One directs the dancer to move round the hands in the region of the head in Muṣṭikasvastika while the other says that the dancer should raise her hands touching each other at the finger tips in Khaṭakāmukha and her elbows should be bent backwards (*SR* 7.280-1).

(43) **Viprakīrṇa** : The Svastika hands are separated (*NŚ* 9.187; *VDP* p. 3.26.88; *SDām* p. 62; *SUS* 5.100; *NN* 21b; *HR* p. 202). *Mānas* : Haṃsapakṣa hands are placed on the chest and turned towards the back. They either point downwards or upwards (*Mānas* 16.4.1242-3). *SR* gives both views (*SR* 7.223).

(44) **Śīrṣānuvalita** : The hands in Muṣṭikasvastika are moved above the head (*SUS* 5.110).

(45) **Sūcīmukha :** The Sarpaśirṣa hands, with their thumbs touching the middle fingers, extend their finger tips obliquely; *or* : The Sarpaśīrṣa hands cross each other with their thumbs and middle fingers stretched (*NŚ* 9.191-2. *SDām* p. 62). *VDP* : The Sarpaśīrṣa hands, with their finger tips extended, are crossed in Svastika (*VDP* 3.26.76). *SUS* : Śucyā (Sucyā) sya : The elbows are bent while the thumb and the little fingers are held like the point of a needle. (*SUS* 5.101). *SSam*. The Khaṭakāsya hands face each other (*SSam* 6.84). *Mānas* : The catura hands are extended obliquely with the elbows bent. (*Mānas* 16.4.1247-8). *SR* : The Sarpaśīrṣa hands, with the thumbs touching the middle fingers are

moved to the region of Caturaśra and then they are gradually stretched out with the forefingers extended obliquely. *Or* The Patākā hands are moved first in Vyāvartita and Parivartita. Some direct the dancer to extend the hands assuming Sarpaśīrṣa. Some others prescribe Recita and Svastika for the hands (*SR* 7.232). *NN*: The thumbs and the middle fingers of the Sarpaśīrṣa hands are held like the points of needles. The forefingers are stretched outwards (*NN* 21a).

(46) **Sūcīviddha :** The hands in Sūcīviddha are joined together (*NŚSaṃ* 289).

(47) **Svastika :** The Talamukha hands are crossed at the wrists. (*NŚ* 9.187; *VDP* 3.26.88; *SDām* p. 62; *SSam* 6.79; *HR*. p. 202). *SUS* prescribes Bhramara while *Mānas*; *SR* and *NN* prescribe Haṃsapakṣa for the hands (*SUS* 5.99; *Mānas* 16.4.1241-2; *SR* 7.222; *NN* 21b).

The Devahastas

These are the movements of the hands representing different deities. These are done with both hands.

(1) **Brahmā :** The left hand is in Catura and the right is in Haṃsāsya (*ADar* 205).

(2) **Iśvara :** The left hand is in Mṛgaśīrṣa while the right hand is in Tripatākā (*ADar* 205).

(3) **Viṣṇu :** Both the hands assume Tripatākā (*ADar* 206).

(4) **Sarasvatī :** The right hand is in Sūcī while the left hand, in Kapittha, is raised near the shoulder. (*ADar* 206-7).

(5) **Pārvatī :** The right hand, in Ardhacandra, is raised and the left hand also in Ardhacandra, is lowered. The hands show Abhaya (to dispel fears) and Varada (to grant boons) respectively (*ADar* 207-8).

(6) **Lakṣmī :** The hands, in Kapittha, are placed near the shoulder (*ADar* 208).

(7) **Vināyaka :** The Kapittha hands are placed near the shoulder (*ADar* 208).

(8) **Sanmukha :** The left hand is in Triśūla and the right hand, which is raised, is in Śikhara (*ADar* 209-10).

(9) **Manmatha :** The left hand is in Śikhara and the right hand is in Khaṭakāmukha (*ADar* 210).

(10) **Indra :** Tripatākā hands are crossed in Svastika (*ADar* 211).

(11) **Agni :** The right hand performs Tripatākā while the left hand assumes Kāṅgula (*ADar* 212).

(12) **Yama :** The left hand is in Pāśa and the right hand is in Sūcī (*ADar* 213).

(13) **Nirṛti :** Khaṭṭvā and Śakaṭa to be performed (*ADar* 213).

(14) **Varuṇa :** The right hand is in Patākā and the left hand is in Śikhara (*ADar* 214).

(15) **Vāyu :** The right hand is in Arāla and the left hand is in Aradhapatākā (*ADar* 214-5).

(16) **Kuvera :** The left hand is in Padma while the right hand is in Gadā (*ADar* 215).

The Daśāvatāra-hastas

These are the gestures of the hands signifying the Avatāras. These are done with both hands.

(1) **Matsya :** The hands, after performing Matsya, are placed on the same level with the shoulders (*ADar* 216).

(2) **Kūrma :** Kūrma hands are performed and then the hands are placed on the same level with the shoulders (*ADar* 217).

(3) **Varāha :** The hands are placed by the side of the waist after Varāha is performed (*ADar* 218).

(4) **Nṛsiṃha :** The left hand is in Siṃhamukha and the right hand is in Tripatākā (*ADar* 219).

(5) **Vāmana :** The left hand, in Muṣṭi, is raised and the right hand also in Muṣṭi, is lowered (*ADar* 220).

(6) **Paraśurāma :** The left hand is placed on the waist while the right hand performs Ardhapatākā (*ADar* 221).

(7) **Rāmacandra :** The right hand, in Kapittha, and the left hand, in Śikhara, are raised (*ADar* 222).

(8) **Valarāma :** The right hand is in Patākā while the left hand is in Muṣṭi. (*ADar* 223).

(9) **Kṛṣṇa :** The hands perform Mṛgaśīrṣa together and are placed near the face (*ADar* 224).

(10) **Kalkī :** The left hand is Tripatākā while the right hand is in Patākā (*ADar* 225).

The Jātiya-hastas

These movements of the hands which are joined represent different castes.

(1) **Rākṣasa :** The hands, in Śakaṭa, are brought near the face (*Adar* 226).

(2) **Brāḥmaṇa :** The hands are in Śikhara and the right hand in an oblique position, include the sacred thread (*ADar* 226-7).

(3) **Kṣatriya :** The left hand, in Śikhara, is placed obliquely while the right hand is in Patākā (*ADar* 227-8).

(4) **Vaiśya :** The left hand is in Haṃsāsya while the right hand is in Khaṭakamukha (*ADar* 228-9).

(5) **Śūdra :** The left hand is in Śikhara and the right hand is in Mṛgaśirṣa (*ADar* 229-30).

The Bāndhava-hastas

These joint movements of the hands represent different human relationships.

(1) **Dampatī :** The left hand is in Śikhara while the right hand is in Mṛgaśīrṣa (*ADar* 231-2).

(2) **Mātṛ :** The left hand is in Ardhacandra and the right hand is in Sandaṃśa. Then the left hand is turned round and placed on the belly (*ADar* 232-3).

(3) **Pitṛ :** The right hand of the Mātṛ-hasta assumes Śikhara (*ADar* 234-5).

(4) **Śvaśru :** The right hand in Haṃsāsya is placed near the throat. Then the right hand assumes Sandaṃśa while the left hand touches the belly (*ADar* 236).

(5) **Śvaśūra :** The right hand of the Śvaśruhasta is in Śikhara (*ADar* 237).

(6) **Bhatṛbhrātṛ :** The left hand is in Śikhara while the right hand is in Kartarīmukha and the hands are placed on the sides (*ADar* 238-9).

(7) **Nanāndṛ :** At the end of the Bhartṛbhrātṛ-hasta, the right hand shows a feminine gesture (*ADar* 239-40).

(8) **Jyeṣṭhakaniṣṭhabhrātṛ :** Mayūra hands are shown in front and on two sides (*ADar* 240-1).

(9) **Putra :** The Sandaṃśa hand is placed on the belly and then moved round. The left hand is in Śikhara (*ADar* 241-2).

(10) **Snuṣā :** After showing the Putra-hasta, the right hand shows the gesture of a woman (*ADar* 242-3).

(11) **Saptanī :** After performing the Pāśahasta, both the hands make a feminine gesture (*ADar* 243-4).

The Navagraha-hastas

These are the movements done by both the hands. They represent different planets.

(1) **Sūrya :** The hands are placed near the shoulder in Alapadma and Kapittha (*ADar* 250).

(2) **Candra :** The left hand is in Alapadma and the right hand is in Patākā (*ADar* 251).

(3) **Kuja :** The left hand shows Sūcī and the right hand is in Patākā (*ADar* 252).

(4) **Budha :** Muṣṭi is shown in an oblique position by the left hand while the right hand is in Patākā (*ADar* 253).

(5) **Guru :** The sacred thread is indicated by the Śikhara hands. This gesture can also represent a Ṛsi or a Brāhmin (*ADar* 254).

(6) **Śukra :** Both the hands are in Muṣṭi and the left hand is raised while the right hand is lowered (*ADar* 255).

(7) **Śani :** The left hand is in Śikhara while the right hand is in Triśūla (*ADar* 256).

(8) **Rāhu :** The left hand shows Sarpaśīrṣa and the right hand shows Sūcī (*ADar* 257).

(9) **Ketu :** The left hand is in Sūcī and the right hand is in Patākā (*ADar* 258).

The Hastakaraṇas

A Karaṇa of the hand is that action which has to be performed in order to make a gesture. It may, however, not be the only action for the purpose. Karaṇas are of the following four types :

(1) **Āveṣṭita :** The fingers, beginning from the forefinger, are moved inward (*NŚ* 9.215).

(2) **Udveṣṭita :** The fingers, beginning from the forefinger, are moved outward (*NŚ* 9.216).

(3) **Parivartita :** The fingers, beginning from the little finger, are moved outward (*NŚ* 218).

(4) **Vyāvartita** : The fingers, beginning from the little finger, are moved inward (*NŚ* 9.217).

SR; *Mānas*; *SSam*; *SUS* and *NN* give the same list of the Hastakaraṇas. The descriptions also agree with those given by the *NŚ* (*SR* 7.538-40; *Mānas*, 16.4.1272-6; *SSam* 6.102-3; *SUS*. 5.63; *NN* 23a).

The Hastakarmas

(1) **Āhvāna** : To invite (*NŚ* 9.166; *SR* 7.545; *NN* 23b).

(2) **Utkarṣaṇa** : To draw up (*NŚ* 9.166; *NN* 23b). *SR* : Utkrṣṭa : (*SR* 7.544).

(3) **Udvṛtti** : To raise (*SUS* 5.60).

(4) **Chedana** : The motion of cutting (*NŚ* 9.166; *SUS* 5.59; *SR* 7.544; *NN* 23b).

(5) **Tarjana** : To threaten (*NŚ* 9.167; *SUS* 5.60; *SR* 7.545).

(6) **Tāḍana** : To strike (*NŚ* 9.168; *SR* 7.544; *NN* 23b).

(7) **Todana** : To push (*NŚ* 9.166).

(8) **Tolana** : To lift up (*SR* 7.544).

(9) **Dolana** : To swing (*SUS* 5.59).

(10) **Dhūnana** : To shake (*NŚ* 9.167; *SUS* 5.59; *SR* 7.543; *NN* 23b).

(11) **Dhruva** : To keep still (*SUS* 5.60).

(12) **Nigraha** : To lower (*NŚ* 9.166; *SR* 7.544; *NN* 23b).

(13) **Parigraha** : To enfold. (*NŚ* 9.166; *SR* 7.544; *NN* 23b).

(14) **Pravṛtti** : To move onwards. (*SUS* 5.60).

(15) **Bheda** : The motion of splitting (*NŚ* 9.168; *SR* 7.544; *NN* 23b).

(16) **Bhrama** : A circular movement (*SUS* 5.60).

(17) **Mokṣana** : The motion of releasing (*NŚ* 9.167; *SR* 7.543; *NN* 23b).

(18) **Moṭana** : The motion of crushing (*NŚ* 9.168; *SR* 7.544; *NN* 23b.).

(19) **Yāna :** To lead (*SUS* 5.60).

(20) **Rakṣaṇa :** To protect (*NŚ* 9.167; *SR* 7.543; *NN* 23b). *SUS* Rakṣā : (*SUS* 5.59).

(21) **Vikarṣaṇa :** To remove (*NŚ* 9.166; *NN* 23b). *SR* : Vikṛṣṭi: (*SR* 7.544).

(22) **Vikṣepa :** To throw (*NŚ* 9.167; *SUS* 5.59; *NN* 23b). *SR* Kṣepa : (*SR* 7.543).

(23) **Virāṭi :** Not explained. (*SUS*. 5.60).

(24) **Viyoga :** To separate (*NŚ* 9.167; *SUS* 5.59; *NN* 23b). *SR* : Viśleṣa (*SR* 7.543).

(25) **Visarga :** To send forth (*NŚ* 9.167); *SR* : *NN* : Visarjana (*SR* 7.545; *NN* 23b).

(26) **Vṛtti :** To roll (*SUS*. 5.60).

(27) **Vyākarṣana :** To pull (*NŚ* 9.166). *SR*; *SUS*; *NN*: Ākṛṣṭi. (*SR* 7.544; *SUS* 5.59; *NN* 23b.)

(28) **Saṃśleṣa :** To join (*NŚ* 9.167; *NN*. 23b). *SR*; *SUS* : Śleṣa (*SR* 7.543; *SUS* 5.59).

(29) **Sphoṭana :** To disengage (*NŚ* 9.168; *SR* 7.544; *SUS*. 5.60; *NN* 23b).

The Hastaksetras

Kṣetra is to be taken in its literal meaning, i.e. a position. There are fourteen Hasta-Kṣetras which are the following :

(1, 2) Pārśvadvaya, (3) PurastātŚiras. (4) PaścātŚiras (5) Ūrdhvaḥ-Śiras, (6) Adhaḥśiras, (7) Lalāṭa, (8) Karṇa, (9) Vakṣas, (10) Nābhi, (11) Katiśīrṣa, (12, 13) Urudvaya, (14) Skandha (*SR* 7.546-7; *NN* 23b).

The Hastapracāras

These are the various directions in which the hands may move.

(1) Adhogata (*SR* 7.536).

(2) Agraga (*SR* 7.533; *NN* 23b).

(3) Adhomukha (*NŚ* 9.181; *SR* 7.532; *NN*. 23b).
(4) Agratastala (*SR* 7.533).
(5) Adhastala (*SR* 7.534).
(6) Uroga. (*SUS* 5.62).
(7) ūrdhvaga (*SR* 7.536).
(8) ūrdhvamukha (*SR* 7.535).
(9) uttāna (*NŚ* 9.181; *SR* 7.532; *NN* 23b).
(10) Tryaśra (*NŚ* 9.182; *NN*: Tiryak (*NN* 23b).
(11) Parāṅmukha (*SR*. 7.535).
(12) Pārśvaga (*NŚ* 9.181; *SR* 7.532; *SUS* 5.62; *NN* 23b).
(13) Pṛṣṭhaga (*SUS* 5.62).
(14) Vartula (*NŚ* 9.182).
(15) Sanmukha (*SR* 7.535).
(16) Svasanmukha (*SR* 7.535).

Movements of the Manibandhas

These are the movements of the wrist, a Pratyaṅga.

(1) **Ākuñcita :** The wrist is bent inward. *Mānas* : The wrist is bent outward (*Mānas* 16.4.1141; *SR* 7.370; *NŚSaṃ* 532).

(2) **Cala :** Nikuñca and Ākuñcita are done one after the other repeatedly. (*SR*. 7.371; *NŚSaṃ*. 532).

(3) **Nikuñca :** The wrist is bent outward (*Mānas* 16.4.1140; *SR* 7.369; *NŚSaṃ* 531). *Mānas* does not explain this.

(4) **Bhramita :** Moving the wrist around. (*Mānas* 16.4.1142; *SR* 7.371; *NŚSaṃ* 533).

(5) **Sama :** To keep the wrist straight. (*Mānas* 16.4.1142; *SR* 7.372; *NŚSaṃ* 534).

Movements of the Karāṅgulīs

These are the movements of the fingers, considered to be Pratyaṅgas. Only *SR* discusses these in detail and *NŚSaṃ* quotes *SR*.

(1) **Saṃyutā :** Joined together.

(2) **Viyutā :** Separated.

(3) **Vakrā :** Curved.

(4) **Valitā :** Moved.

(5) **Patitā :** Fallen.

(6) **Kuñcanmūlā :** Bent at the root.

(7) **Prasṛtā :** Spread out (*SR* 7.50; *NŚSaṃ* 683).

Movements of the Vakṣas

These are the movements of the chest, an Aṅga.

(1) **Ābhunga :** The chest is drawn inward. The back is raised and the shoulder is slightly bent forward and slackened (*NŚ.* 9.224; *AP* 341.19; *SDāṃ* p. 63; *VDP* 3.24.26; *ND* p. 189; *SUS* 5.116). *Mānas* : The back is raised (*Mānas* 16.4.1006). *SR* and *NŚSaṃ.* do not say anything about the shoulder (*SR* 7.298; *NŚSaṃ* 458).

(2) **Udvāhita :** The chest is raised. (*NŚ* 9.231; *VDP.* 3.24.29 *SDām* p. 63; *SCS.* 5.115; *SSam* 6.29). *SR* and *NŚSaṃ.* say that the chest must be raised straight (*SR* 7.302; *NŚSaṃ* 461). *Mānas* : Utprasārī, (*Mānas* 16.4.1010).

(3) **Unnata :** The chest is thrown out to represent a proud man (*SUS* 5.116).

(4) **Nartaka :** Not explained. There is another reading of the term : Nirgūṇa (*AP* 341.19).

(5) **Nirbhugna :** The chest is steady and the back is curved. The shoulder is raised (*NŚ* 9.226; *VDP*

5.24.27; *ND* p. 189; *SDām* p. 63; *SCE* 5.116). *Mānas* The back is curved (*Mānas* 16.1006). *SR* and *NŚSaṃ* do not say anything about the shoulder (*SR* 7.300; *NŚSaṃ* 459). *SSam* : The chest is raised (*SSam* 6.30).

(6) **Prakampita** : The chest incessantly heaves up and down. (*NŚ* 9.229; *VDP* 3.24.28; *SDām* p. 63; *SSam* 6.30; *SR* 7.301; *NŚSaṃ* 460). *Mānas:* Vyākampita (*Mānas* 16.4.1007)

(7) **Sama** : When the limbs are in Caturaśra and Sauṣṭhava, the chest is in Sama. This is the natural position of the chest (*NŚ* 9.232; *VDP* 3.24.30; *SDām* p. 63; *SUS.* 5.116; *SSam* 6.28; *Mānas* 16.4.1010; *SR* 7.297-8; *NŚSaṃ* 457).

Movements of the Pārśva

These are movements of the sides, considered to be Aṅgas.

(1) **Apasṛta** : To move out from the Vivartita position of the sides (*NŚ* 9.238; *VDP* 3.24.34; *SDām* p. 63; *SUS* 5.120; *Mānas* 16.4.1017; *SR* 7.305; *NŚSaṃ* 463). *Mānas* : Prasṛta.

(2) **Nata** : To bend slightly one hip and its corresponding side and to move the shoulder away a little (*NŚ* 9.235; *SDām* 6.108; *Mānas* 16.4.1016; *ND* p. 189; *SR* 7.306; *NŚSaṃ* 464). *VDP* : The hip is bent (*VDP* 3.24.32). *SUS* : To bend one side slightly. (*SUS* 5.120).

(3) **Prasārita** : The sides are stretched (*NŚ* 9.237; *VDP* 3.24.33; *Mānas* 16.4.1019-20; *SR* 7.305; *NŚSaṃ* 464).

(4) **Vivartita** : The hip is turned round. *Mānas* says that the hip should be turned obliquely (*NŚ* 9.237; *VDP* 3.24.33; *Mānas.* 16.4.1016; *SR.* 7.304; *NŚSaṃ.* 463).

SDām : Nivartita (*SDam* p. 63). *SUS* : Vyāvartita. (*SUS*. 5.120). *SSam* : Vyāvṛtta. (*SSam*. 6.109).

(5) **Sama :** The sides are in natural position (*SUS*. 5.120; *SDām* p. 63).

(6) **Samunnata :** This is the opposite of Nata. The other side is raised, so are the hip, the arm and the shoulder (*NŚ*. 9.236; *VDP* 3.26.24.32; *SDām* p. 63; *ND* p. 289; *SSam*. 6.108). *Mānas* : One side is raised. (*Mānas* 16.4.1016). *SR*; *NŚSaṃ* : Unnata (*SR* 7.306; *NŚSaṃ* 465).

Movements of the Kaṭi

These are movements of the hips, classed as Aṅgas.

(1) **Āndolitā :** Slow and oblique movement of the hips (*Mānas*. 16.4.1023).

(2) **Udvāhitā :** To raise both the side of the hips slowly (*NŚ* 9.247; *VDP* 3.24.41; *SSam* 6.113; *Mānas* 16.4.1024; *SR* 7.309; *NŚSaṃ* 468; *SDām* p. 63). *SUS*: To bend the hips slightly. (*SUS* 5.122).

(3) **Unnatā :** To raise the hips. (*SUS*. 5.122).

(4) **Kampitā :** Quick and oblique movement of the hips. (*NŚ* 9.247; *SDām* p. 63; *SSam* 6.112; *SR* 7.308; *NŚSaṃ* 467). *VDP* : Prakampitā (*VDP* 3.24.39).

(5) **Chinnā :** To turn the middle of the hips around (*NŚ* 9.245; *SDām* p. 63; *VDP* 3.24.39; *SUS* 5.122; *SSam* 6.112; *Mānas* 16.4.1002; *SR* 7.310; *NŚSaṃ* 469). *Mānas, SSam, SR* and *NŚSaṃ* however remarks that this is done obliquely.

(6) **Nivṛttā :** To turn the hips in order to face the audience. In the preceding position the dancer had her back towards the audience. (*NŚ* 9.246; *VDP* 3.24.40). *SSam* : To turn the hips either to face the audience or to have the back towards the auidence. (*SSam* 6.111). (*ND* p. 189).

(7) **Recitā :** To move the hips in all directions. (*NŚ* 9.246; *SDām* p. 63; *VDP* 3.24.40; *SUS* 5.121; *SSam* 6.111; *SR* 7.312; *NŚSaṃ* 471).

(8) **Vivṛttā :** To move the hips (*Mānas* 16.4.1022). *SR NŚSaṃ* : The same as Nivṛttā. (*SR* 7.311; *NŚSam* 470). (*SDām* p. 63).

(9) **Samā :** To keep the hips in a natural position (*SDām.* p. 63; *SUS* 5.122). *NN* says that the hips should be motionless as well. (*NN* 24a).

Movements of the Udara

These are the movements of the belly, a Pratyaṅga.

(1) **Anatikṣāma :** Not explained (*AP* 341.20).

(2) **Atikṣāma :** Not explained. (*SDām* p. 63).

(3) **Āvartita :** The belly is moved. (*SUS* 5.118).

(4) **Kṣāma :** To flatten the belly. (*NŚ* 9.241; *VDP* 3.24.36; *SDam* p. 63; *SUS* 5.118; *Mānas* 16.4.1011; *SR* 7.354; *NŚSaṃ* 515).

(5) **Khaṇḍa :** Not explained (*AP* 341.20).

(6) **Khalva :** To flatten the belly (*NŚ* 9.241; *AP* 341.20; *SUS* 5.117: *Mānas* 16.4.1011; *SR* 7.355; *NŚSaṃ* 516).

(7) **Nimna :** The same as Khalva (*VDP* 3.4.39).

(8) **Pūrṇa :** To distend the belly (*NŚ* 9.241; *AP* 341.20; *VDP.* 3.24.37; *SDām.* p. 63; *Mānas* 16.4.1013; *SR* 7.356; *NŚSaṃ.* 517). *SUS* : Prauḍha (*SUS* 5.118). Pūrṇa and Prauḍha seem to mean the same action.

(9) **Riktapūrṇa :** The belly is first down in, than distended. (*SDām* p. 63; *Mānas* 16.4.1014). *SR* 7.356; *NŚSaṃ* 517).

(10) **Sama :** Not explained. (*NŚ* 9.243; *SDām* p. 63).

(11) **Sahaja :** To place the belly naturally. (*SUS* 5.118). Sama may be same as Sahaja.

Movements of the ūru

These are the movements of the thigh, a Pratyaṅga.

(1) **Udvartana** : Circular and swinging movement (*NŚ* 9.253; *VDP* 3.24.46; *SUS* 5.124; *SR* 7.359; *NŚSaṃ* 520).

(2) **Kampana** : This is to shake the thighs and this is done by moving the heels up and down (*NŚ* 9.251; *VDP* 3.24.44; *ND* p. 189; *SUS* 5.124; *SR* 7.358; *NŚSaṃ* 519).

(3) **Calita** : The thighs are moved (*SUS*. 5.124).

(4) **Valana** : To turn the thighs, to do which, the knees must be turned inwards. (*NŚ* 9.252; *VDP* 3.24.45; *SR* 7.358; *ND* p. 189; *NŚSaṃ* 519).

(5) **Vivartana** : To turn round by drawing the heels inward. It is also described as Nivartana. (*NŚ*. 9.253; *VDP* 3.24.47; *SUS* 5.124; *SR* 7.360; *NŚSaṃ* 521).

(6) **Stabdha** : The same as Stambhana (*SR* 7.359; *NŚSaṃ* 520).

(7) **Stambhana** : The thighs are motionless (*NŚ* 9.252; *VDP* 3.24.46; *SUS* 5.124).

Movements of the Jānu

These are the movements of the knee, a Pratyaṅga.

(1) **Ardhakuñcita** : The hips are lowered (*Mānas* 16.4.1278; *SR* 7.374; *NŚSaṃ* 536).

(2) **Unnata** : The knees are raised to the height of the breasts (*Mānas* 16.4.1277; *SR* 7.375; *NŚSaṃ* 537).

(3) **Kuñcita** : The shanks and the thighs touch each other. (*Mānas* 16.4.1278; *SR* 7.374; *NŚSaṃ* 535).

(4) **Nata** : To kneel to the ground. (*Mānas* 64.1277; *SR* 7.375; *NŚSaṃ* 536).

(5) **Vivṛta** : The knees are stretched out. In *Mānas*, in the list of the terms the word is Vistṛta, but while

describing the action, it is Vivṛta. The action is the same as in *SR* (*Mānas* 16.4.1279; *SR* 7.376; *NŚSaṃ*. 537).

(6) **Saṃhata :** The knees touch each other. (*Mānas*. 16.4.1279); *SR* 7.373; *NŚSaṃ* 535).

(7) **Sama :** The knees are kept normally. (*Mānas*. 16.4.1280; *SR* 7.376; *NŚSaṃ* 538).

Movements of the Jaṅghā

These are the movements of the shanks, considered to be Pratyaṅgas.

(1) **Āvartitā :** To move the shanks in Āvartitā, the left foot is moved to the left repeatedly. (*NŚ* 9.258; *VDP* 3.24.51; *ND* p. 189; *SUS* 5.125; *SR* 7.363; *NŚSaṃ* 5.24).

(2) **Udvartitā :** Not explained (*SUS*. 5.125).

(3) **Udvāhitā :** The shanks are raised. *VDP* adds that as a result of the raising of the shanks, the thighs are also raised (*NŚ* 9.261; *VDP* 3.24.52; *SUS* 5.125; *SR* 7.365; (*NŚSaṃ* 526).

(4) **Kampitā :** To shake the shanks. *Mānas*: To shake the shanks in Recita (*Mānas* 16.4.1288; *SR* 1.3687; *NŚSaṃ* 529).

(5) **Kṣiptā :** The shanks are thrown outwards. (*NŚ* 9.260; *VDP* 3.25.52; *SR* 7.364; *NŚSaṃ* 525).

(6) **Tiraścīnā :** The shanks just touch the ground *Mānas* : The shanks move sideways (*Mānas* 16.4.1284; *SR* 7.367; *NŚSaṃ* 528).

(7) **Natā :** The knees are bent so that the shanks may be bent (*NŚ* 9.260; *VDP* 3.24.51; *ND* p. 189; *SR* 7.364; *NŚSaṃ* 525; *SUS* 5.125.)

(8) **Niḥsṛtā :** The shanks assume this position upon moving the knees forward (*Mānas* 16.4.1285; *SR* 7.366; *NŚSaṃ* 526).

(9) **Parāvṛttā** : The same as Parivṛttā (*Mānas* 16.4.1285; *SR* 7.366; *NŚSaṃ* 527).

(10) **Parivartitā** : The shank's are moved back from the position in which they had been (*SR* 7.365; *NŚSaṃ* 526).

(11) **Parivṛttā** : To turn back the shanks. *VDP* : The knees touch the ground with the shanks behind them (*NŚ* 9.262; *VDP* 3.24.53).

(12) **Bhramitā** : Not explained (*SUS* 5.125).

(13) **Recitā** : Not explained (*SUS* 5.125).

(14) **Bahiḥkrāntā** : The shanks are moved outward (*Mānas* 16.4.1288).

(15) **Bahirgatā** : The shanks are stretched sideways (*SR* 7.368; *NŚSaṃ* 528).

(16) **Samā** : Not explained (*SUS* 5.125).

(17) **Sthirā** : Not explained (*SUS* 5.125).

Movements of the Pāda

These are the movements of the feet, considered to be Aṅgas.

(1) **Añcita** : The dancer touches the ground with her heels and the foreparts of her feet while her toes are contracted. The śloka in the *NŚ* that describes Añcita, recommends the contraction of the toes, but the commentator *Abhg,* tells us that the toes must, in fact, be taken as Prasṛta, and the toes must be stretched out. (*NŚ* 3.275-6; *SUS* 5.126-7; *NN* 29b). *VDP* : The forepart of the foot is raised. (*VDP* 3.24.61). *SSam* : The dancer contracts and raises her toes (*SSam* 6.116). *SR* and *NŚSaṃ*. agree with *Abhg* (*SR* 7.316; *NŚSaṃ* 475).

(2) **Agraga** : The dancer steps forward quickly (*Mānas.* 16.4.1294; *SR* 7.324; *NN* 24b; *NŚSaṃ* 483).

(3) **Agratalasañcara :** The dancer raises her heels, putting her big toes forward and contracting the rest of her toes. (*NŚ* 9.274; *SR* 7.319-20; *NŚSaṃ* 478). *VDP* has Pārṣṇirecitasañcara in the list which however, is deṣcribed as Agratalasañcara. It suggests raising of the heels. (*VDP* 3.24.59). *SSam* : The dancer stands in Sama. raises her heels and moves about. (*SSam* 6.117). *NN* does not direct the dancer to contract her toes (*NN* 24b).

(4) **Aticitra :** The dancer revolves in the centre of the stage bending her toes (*SMak* 2.4.40).

(5) **Udghaṭṭita :** The dancer stands on her toes and touches the ground with her heels (*NŚ* 9.266; *SSam* 6.114-5; *SR* 7.321; *NN*: The dancer touches the ground standing on her toes (*NN* 24b).

(6) **Udghāṭita :** The same as Udghaṭṭita (*VDP* 3.24.57; *SUS* 5.128).

(7) **Kuñcita :** The dancer raises her heels, contracting her toes and arching her insteps. (*NŚ* 9.277; *VDP* 3.24.62; *SUS* 5.126; *SR* 7.317; *NN* 24b; *NŚSaṃ* 476). *SSam* : The dancer places her heel on the ground in Sama and contracts the forepart of her foot. (*SSam* 6.115-6).

(8) **Ghaṭṭita :** The dancer strikes the ground with her heels (*SR* 7.323; *NN* 24b; *NŚSaṃ* 482).

(9) **Ghāṭita :** The same as Ghaṭṭita (*Mānas* 16.4.1290)

(10) **Ghaṭṭitotsedha :** The dancer repeatedly strikes the ground with her heels and toes (*SR* 7.323; *NN* 24b; *NŚSaṃ* 482). *Mānas* : The dancer strikes the ground with her heels and raises her toes (*Mānas* 16.4.1291). *Mānas* and *SR* have Ghaṭitotsedha.

(11) **Citra :** To move up and down bending the toe gracefully (*SMak* 2.4.39).

(12) **Trāṭita :** With the heels remaining on the ground, to beat the ground with the toes. (*Mānas* 16.4.1293; *SR* (*Ad Lib ed.*) 7.322; *NN* 24b; *NŚSaṃ* 481). *Mānas*: Tāḍita.

(13) **Tryaśra :** The dancer rests her feet in Sama with the heels inward and the big toes stretched out (*NŚ* 9.270, 72).

(14) **Nija :** The toes touch the ground and the feet are motionless. (*Mānas* 16.4.1298).

(15) **Pārśvaga :** The dancer moves her feet sideways or stands at the side of the stage. (*Mānas* 16.4.1296; *SR* 7.325; *NN* 25a; *NŚSaṃ* 484).

(16) **Pārṣṇiga :** To move backwards on the heels. (*Mānas.* 16.4.1295; *SR* 7.325; *NN* 24b; *NŚSaṃ* 484).

(17) **Mardita :** The sole, of which the side is at an angle to the floor, rubs it. (*Mānas.* 16.4.1292; *SR* 7.324; *NN* 24b; *NŚSaṃ* 483).

(18) **Recita :** The dancer moves on her toes raising her heels. The feet must be at an angle to the ground (*SUS* 5.127).

(19) **Vindanti :** Too obscure to explain (*SMak.* 2.4.41).

(20) **Sama :** The dancer rests her feet in a natural position (*NŚ* 9.269; *VDP.* 3.24.58; *SSam* 6.114; *SMak* 2.4.42; *SR* 7.315; *NN* 24b; *NŚSaṃ* 474; *ND* p. 189).

(21) **Sūcī :** The dancer rests her left foot in Sama, raises the heel of her right foot and touches the ground with the tip of the big toe. (*NŚ* 9.279; *SR* 7.318; *NN* 24b; *NŚSaṃ* 477). *Mānas* : The dancer stands on her big toes. (*Mānas.* 16.4.1279).

The Pādakarmas, given only in SUS

(1) **Ardhaghaṭṭita :** The dancer strikes the ground with her heels and big toes (*SUS* 5.131).

(2) **Ūrdhvāṅguṣṭha :** The dancer strikes the ground with her big toes (*SUS* 5.131).

(3) **Kuṇḍala :** The dancer moves forward on her heels (*SUS* 5.134).

(4) **Ghaṭṭita :** The dancer strikes the ground with her heels (*SUS* 5.132).

(5) **Pariveṣa :** The dancer moves around her toes (*SUS* 5.133).

(6) **Recitaghaṭṭita :** The dancer strikes one of her feet with the other (*SUS* 5.133).

(7) **Sthānu :** The feet are at rest (*SUS* 5.132).

Movements of the Ankles

These are Upāṅgas.

(1) **Aṅguṣṭhasaṃśliṣṭa :** touching the big toe.

(2) **Antargata :** turned inward.

(3) **Bahirmukha :** turned outward.

(4) **Mithoyuta :** joined together.

(5) **Viyukta :** separated.

(*SR* 7.519; *NŚSaṃ* 682).

Movements of the Heels

These are Upāṅgas.

(1) **Utkṣipta :** raised.

(2) **Patita :** fallen.

(3) **Utkṣiptapatita :** raising and falling.

(4) **Antargata :** turned inward.

(5) **Bahirgata :** turned outward.

(6) **Mithoyuta :** joined together.

(7) **Viyukta :** separated.

(8) **Aṅgulisaṃśliṣṭa :** meeting the toes.

(*SR* 7.517; *NŚSaṃ* 681).

Movements of the Caraṇāṅgulī

These are movements of the toes, which are Pratyaṅgas.

(1) **Adhaḥkṣipta :** To bend the toes repeatedly. *Mānas* : Avakṣipta (*Mānas* 16.4.1300; *SR* 7.522; *NŚSaṃ* 685).

(2) **Utkṣipta :** To raise the toes repeatedly. (*Mānas* 16.4.1301; *SR* 7.523; *NŚSaṃ* 685).

(3) **Kuñcita :** The toes are curved. (*Mānas* 16.4.1302; *SR* 7.523; *NŚSaṃ* 686).

(4) **Prasārita :** The toes are straight and motionless. (*Mānas* 16.4.1303; *SR.* 7.524; *NŚSaṃ* 686).

(5) **Saṃlagna :** The toes are joined together (*Mānas.* 16.4.1305; *SR* 7.525; *NŚSaṃ* 687).

The first four movements are performed by the big toes by themselves and also with the rest of the toes (*Mānas* 16.4.1304; *SR* 7.524).

CHAPTER FOUR

More Complicated Movements : Cāri, Maṇḍala, Sthāna, Gati, Recaka

The *NŚ* describes the Cārīs as delicate movements of one leg or the coordination of movements of the feet, shanks and thighs. It is said to be one form of exercise known as Vyāyāma which is of four kinds : Cārī, Karaṇa, Khaṇḍa and Maṇḍala. These Karaṇas are different from the Nṛttakaraṇas and indicate movements of both the legs. Khaṇḍa is the combination of Karaṇas while Maṇḍala is a series of three or four Khaṇḍas. The *NŚ* also describes the Cārī and Mahācārī as parts of the preliminaries. The Cārīs, according to the *NŚ*, are of two kinds : Ākāśikī and Bhūmi. Sixteen varieties of each kind are known.[1]

The *VDP* simply describes the Cārīs as graceful movements and the Mahācārīs as vigorous movements without discussing them in detail.[2] *ADar* describes the Cārīs without defining the term. These Cārīs represent a different tradition and there are eight of them.[3]

SMak refers to Samacārī without any detail.[4] *Mānas* discusses twenty-six Bhūmicārīs and sixteen Vyomacārīs. These belong to dances of the Deśī style.[5] *SR* follows the *NŚ* in describing the Cārīs but adds some Desī Cārīs. Thirty-five Bhūmicārīs and nineteen Ākāśacārīs of the Deśī type are described in this text. It says that as the gestures of the hands are meant for Abhinaya, so the Cārīs are suitable for Gatis.[6]

SUS defines the Cārīs as the bending of the hips. It describes Bhūmi and Ākāśacārīs of thirty-two varieties but gives no details. The definitions and names given here vary considerably from those found in the *NŚ*.[7] *SDām* describes the Cārī following the *NŚ* and gives the same list of thirty-two Cārīs without discussing them in detail. It also gives the list of the Deśī Cārīs, but says that these are taken as Cārīs by other scholars.[8] *NŚSaṃ* merely copies the *NŚ* on the Mārga and *SR* on the Deśī Cārīs.[9] *NN* follows the *NŚ* and *SR* on the Cārīs and describes eighty-two of which fifty-one are Bhūmi and thirty-one are Ākāśacārīs.[10]

The Cārīs are of the greatest importance in the whole procedure of dancing. The *NŚ* clearly states, followed closely by *NN*, that without a Cārī no dramatic representation may be perfect.[11] It also states that they are to be performed in the preliminaries of a play.[12] *SDām* tells us that a dance is incomplete without the Cārīs, which make the dancing graceful.[13]

The Sthāna is a static posture which is assumed at the beginning and at the end of a long movement, and since a long movement is necessarily a Cārī, the two are closely connected. The *NŚ* discusses after the Cārīs, six Sthānas for men while the other postures, that is, three Sthānas for women, the sitting and reclining postures, are discussed in the chapter on Gatis. Since the sitting and reclining postures are not parts of the Karaṇas and Aṅgahāras and this do not belong to dancing proper they are left out from this study.[14]

The *VDP* describes after the *NŚ*, the four classes of the Sthānas.[15] *ADar* describes six of the Deśī Sthānas described in *SR*, *Mānas*, *SSam*, *SDām*, and *NŚSaṃ*.[16] *Mānas* discusses twenty-one Deśī which are the same as those found in *SR*.[17] *SR* discusses the four Sthānas which are the same as those found in *SR*[17] *SR* discusses the four classes of Sthānas following the *NŚ* and adds four more to the postures for women. It also describes twenty-three Deśī Sthānas.[18]

SSam discusses twenty Deśī Sthānas.[19] *SUS* discusses the postures for men and women following the *NŚ*. The numbers and the descriptions of these postures are the same but the postures for women are called Shānakas.[20] *SDam* gives thirty-three Deśī Sthānas without mentioning details.[21] *NN* discusses twenty-seven Deśī and Mārga Sthānas.[22] *NŚSaṃ* follows *SR* and discusses both the Mārga and the Deśī Sthānas.[23]

Another type of figure, asssociated with the Cārī, is Maṇḍala which is a combination of several Cārīs. Very few texts have discussed Maṇḍalas.

The *NŚ* lists twenty, of which ten are Bhauma while the rest are Ākāśa.[24] The *VDP* gives the similar list of twenty with a few variations in names, but does not discuss them.[25] *ADar* discusses ten Maṇḍalas about none of which it agrees with the *NŚ* nor does it recognise the classification into Bhauma and Ākāśa.[26] *SR* discusses after the *NŚ* twenty Manḍalas.[27] *SDām* speaks of ten Bhauma and ten Ākāsa Maṇḍalas but it gives the names of nine Bhauma Maṇḍalas.[28] The names are generally the same as those in the *NŚ*, though some new names occur. None is discussed.

The *NŚ*, the *VDP* and *ADar* prescribes that certain gaits should be employed in drama and dance. While, however, the *NŚ* and the *VDP* confine the description to general remarks about how one ought to walk without associating the gaits with the Karaṇas or Aṅgaharas,[29] that is, with dancing. *ADar* describes ten that may also be so used while *NN* and *SDar* discuss the gaits that a dancer should have.[30] We shall therefore consider here only the suggestions of *ADar, NN* and *SDar*.

Certain other movements that are generally applicable to the neck, the hips, the hands and the legs, are the Recakas.[31] No Karaṇa is complete without these movements which will therefore be discussed in this chapter.

The Mārga Bhūmicaris

(1) **Añcitā :** Not explained (*SUS* 6.124).

(2) **Aḍḍitā :** One foot in Agratalasañcara rubs its forepart or the back against the other. (*NŚ* 10.23; *SR* 7.934; *NN* 28b).

(3) **Adhyardhikā :** The left foot rests on the back (heel) of the right foot and then it is drawn away. (*NŚ* 9.17; *SDām* p. 65). *SR* agrees with the first part of the description given by the *NŚ*. and suggests that the right foot should be drawn away to its own side and placed obliquely at a distance of one Tāla and a half. Then in the same way the right foot (should be placed) on the heel of the left foot (and after being moved away) it should be placed obliquely. (*SR* 7.923-4). *NN* agrees with the *NŚ*. in describing the first part of the action and says that the right foot should be moved away to its own side (*NN* 28a).

(4) **Apasyanditā :** It is Syanditā done with the other foot. (*NŚ* 10.26; *NN* 28b). *SDām* : Apaspanditā (*SDām* p. 65). *SR* : Avaspanditā (*SR* 7.936).

(5) **Ācchanditā :** Not explained (*SDām* p. 65).

(6) **Ucchanditā :** Not explained (*SDām* p. 65).

(7) **Utspanditā :** The feet are slowly moved inwards and outwards in Recaka (*NŚ* 10.24). According to *SR*, the dancer touches the ground with her little and big toes alternately while she moves her feet slowly in and out. (*SR* 7.931-3). *SUS* : Utsanditā. (*SUS* 6.124). In one ms. of the *NŚ* the term Utsanditā can be found. (*NŚ* vol. II, p. 95). The *ASS* ed. of *SR* has Utsanditā. (*SR* 7.940-1). *ASS* ed. p. 759). *NN*. prescribes a Recaka movement but agrees with *SR* in describing the rest of the action. (*NN* 28b).

(8) **Urdhikā :** Not explained (*SUS* 6.124).

(9) **Udveṣṭitā :** Not explained (*SUS* 6.125).

(10) **Ūrudvṛttā :** The heel of a (Agra) talasañcara foot is raised outwards. One shank is a little bent while (the other) is raised (*NŚ* 10.22; *SUS* 6.124; *NN* 28b). *SDām* : Uruvṛttā. (*SDām* p. 65). *SR* : The heel of the Talasañcara foot is placed facing the back of the other foot, or the reverse is done. One of the shanks with the knee, drawn in, faces the other. (*SR* 7.939-40).

(11) **Elakākrīḍitā :** The dancer jumps alternately up and down with her feet in (Agra) talasañcara (*NŚ* 10.20; *SUS* 6.124; *NN* 28a; *SR* 7.927). *SDām* : Eḍakā (Elakā) krīḍitā. (*SDām* p. 65).

(12) **Cāṣagati :** The right foot is extended and then drawn away. The left foot is also drawn away (*NŚ* 10.18). *SR* : The right foot is put forward by one tāla and then drawn back by two tālas. Then the dancer jumps with both the feet. She first brings them together and separates them, then she separates them and brings them together, the whole action being done alternately. (*SR* 4.925-6). *NN* agrees with the first part of the action described in the *NŚ* The action of the other foot is not very clear. (*NN* 28a).

(13) **Janitā :** One hand is placed on the chest in Muṣṭi while the other is moved round. One foot is moved round. The other is in (Agra) talasañcara (*NŚ* 10.25; *SDām* p. 65; *SUS* 6.125; *SR* 4.938-9). *NN* does not say anything about the movements of the hands and agrees with the *NŚ*. in describing the action of the foot. (*NN* 28b).

(14) **Tāḍitā :** Not explained (*SDām* p. 65).

(15) **Baddhā :** The shanks are crossed in Svastika and the thighs are moved in Valana (*NŚ* 10.21; *SDām* p. 65; *NN* 28b). *SUS* : Viddhā. (*SUS* 6.125). *SR* agrees

with the *NŚ* but gives another description as well : The dancer separates (her feet) from Svastika, makes circular movements and brings each foot to its own side (*SR* 7.936-7).

(16) **Bhramatallī** : Not explained (*SUS* 6.124). (It is a curious word. The form Bhramamattallī might give some sense).

(17) **Mattallī** : The dancer moves backward in a circular movement with both feet. Her hands move in Udveṣṭita and are then thrown out (*NŚ* 10.28). *SR* : The entire sole touches the ground, the legs cross in Svastika at the shanks and they are slightly oblique. Then with circular movement, they either come together or move away from each other (*SR* 7.930-1). *NN* does not say anything about the movements of the hands (*NN* 28b).

(18) **Recikā :** Not explained (*SUS* 6.124).

(19) **Vicyavā :** The feet are separated from Samapādā and they pound the ground with their toes (*NŚ* 10.19; *SR* 7.922; *NN*. 28a). *SUS* : Vicyatā (Vicyavā). (*SUS* 6.124).

(20) **Vivyādhā :** Not explained (*SDām* p. 65).

(21) **Vīcī :** Not explained (*SUS* 6.125).

(22) **Śakaṭāsyā** : The body is straight, one foot is put forward in Agratalasañcara and the chest is raised in Udvāhitā (*NŚ* 10.16; *SUS* 6.125; *NN* 28a). *SDām* : Śakaṭa. (*SDām* p. 65). *SR* : The body is held with effort. The rest of the description agrees with the *NŚ* (*SR* 7.920-1).

(23) **Saṃśliṣṭā :** Not explained (*SUS* 6.125).

(24) **Samatanvī :** Not expalined. (*SDām* p. 65).

(25) **Samapādā :** The dancer stands with her feet together in Samanakhā (*NŚ* 10.14; *SDām* p. 65; *SR* 7.917-8; *NN* 28a).

(26) **Samotsāritamaḍḍikā :** Not explained (*SDām* p. 65).

(27) **Samotsāritamattalī :** The dancer goes backward in a circular movement with her feet in (Agra) talasañcara (*NŚ* 10.27; *NN* 28b). *SR* : One foot is kept behind the other in Agratalasañcara while the shanks are crossed in Svastika. The other foot assumes Agratalasañcara. Then the dancer makes circular movements with both the feet, moving them away and then bringing them together (*SR* 7.928-9).

(28) **Subāhukā :** Not explained (*SUS* 6.125).

(29) **Spanditā :** One foot is put forward five tālas apart from the other (*NŚ* 10.26; *SDām* p. 65). *NN*; *SR* : According to *SR* and *NN* this action is done by the right foot and it is placed obliquely. The left foot is in sama while the thigh is motionless. (*SR* 7.935; *NN* 28b). The GOS ed. of the *NŚ* has Syanditā though it suggests another reading, i.e. Spanditā. (*NŚ* vol. II, p. 100).

(30) **Sthitāvartā :** One foot rubs against the ground and moves inwards. The other foot is moved away (*NŚ* 10.15; *SDām* p. 65; *SUS* 6.124). *SR; NN* : One foot in Agratalasañcara moves across the outer side of the other foot to form a Svastika with the knee drawn in; similarly, the other foot is separated and brought to its own side (*SR* 7.919-20; *NN* 28a).

The Mārga Ākāśacārīs

(1) **Atikrāntā :** The dancer raises one foot in Kuñcita. She extends it forward and places it on the ground. (*NŚ* 10.30; *NN* 30b; *SDām* p. 65; *SUS.* 6.126). *SR* : The dancer raises her Kuñcita foot to the region of the ankle of the other foot and extends it a little. Then she raises it normally and throws it forward on the ground at a distance of four tālas (*SR* 7.942-3).

(2) **Apakrāntā :** The thighs are moved in Valana, one foot is raised and thrown sideways in Kuñcita (*NŚ* 10.31; *SDām* p. 65; *NN* 30b). *SR* directs the dancer to perform the Baddhā Cārī. The movement of the foot agrees with the *NŚ* (*SR* 7.127).

(3) **Alagasaṃsthānā :** *Not* explained (*SUS* 6.127).

(4) **Alatā :** One foot is extended backwards. Then it is moved and put inwards. Finally, it is thrown down on its heel (*NŚ* 10.41; *SUS* 6.126; *NN* 31a). *SR* : One foot is stretched backwards with its sole facing the other thigh. Then its heel is brought down to the ground at its own side. (*SR* 7.950).

(5) **Aviddhatālā :** Not explained (*SDām* p. 65). This seems to be scribal error and Āviddhā and Alātā are possible readings.

(6) **Ākṣiptā :** The Kuñcita foot is thrown up and then placed on the Añcita foot. The shanks are crossed in Svastika. (*NŚ* 10.37; *SUS* 6.126; *NN* 31b). *SDām* : The editors of this text think that the term should be Ksiptā. But Ākṣiptā is likelier as this is the form found in all other texts (*SDām* p. 65) *SR* directs the dancer to raise the Kuñcita foot to the height of three tālas and to bring it to the other side. The shanks are to be crossed in Svastika and then the foot is to be brought sharply down to the ground on its heel. (*SR* 7.961-2).

(7) **Āviddhā :** One Kuñcita foot is moved out from Svastika and stretched. Then it falls on the ground in Añcita (*NŚ* 10.38; *NN* 31b). *SR* : One Kuñcita foot is moved out obliquely from a Svastika made without the shanks touching each other. Then it is brought to its own side and placed with its heel on the other heel. (*SR*. 7.963).

(8) **Utplutā :** Not explained (*SUS* 6.127).

(9) **Udvṛttā :** The foot of the Āviddhā (Cārī) surrounds the other. Then the dancer jumps up and after moving round, places it on the ground. The action is repeated by the other foot. (*NŚ* 10.39; *NN* 31b). *SR* : One foot is in Āviddhā and its heel kept in the region of the other thigh. The dancer jumps and turns round. Then she placed it on the ground. Similarly, the dancer raises her other foot (and performs the rest of the action) (*SR* 7.964-5).

(10) **Unmattā :** Not explained (*SUS* 6.127).

(11) **Ūrdhvajānū :** One foot is raised in Kuñcita and the knee is brought to the level of the breast. The other foot is kept motionless. The same action is repeated by the other foot (*NŚ* 10.33; *SDām* p. 65; *SUS* 6.126; *SR* 7.949). *NN* does not say anything about repeating the action. (*NN* 31a).

(12) **Ghūrṇitā :** Not explained (*SUS* 6.127).

(13) **Tiryagañcitā :** Not explained (*SUS* 6.126).

(14) **Daṇḍā :** Not explained (*SUS* 6.126).

(15) **Daṇḍapādā :** One foot performs Nūpura and stretches out. Then it is stretched forward quickly (*NŚ* 10.44; *SDām* p. 65). *SR* : One foot is placed on the heel of the other as in Nūpura. Then it is stretched forward quickly with the tip of the knee facing the body (*SR* 7.955-6). *NN* suggests that the foot can either be stretched out in Nūpura or it can cross the other obliquely in Svastika. The rest agrees with the *NŚ* (*NN* 31a).

(16) **Dolapādā :** The dancer raises her Kuñcita foot and swings it sideways. Then she places it on the ground as in Añcita. (*NŚ* 10.36; *SUS* 6.126; *SDām* p. 65; *NN* 31a). *SR* : Ḍolāpāda. The first part of the action agrees with the *NŚ*. The dancer places her foot on the heel at its own side (*SR* 7.954).

(17) **Nūpurapādikā :** The dancer moves one Añcita foot backwards. Then she quickly touches the ground with her toes (*NŚ* 10.35; *SUS* 6.126; *SDām* p. 65; *NN* 31a). *SR* directs the dancer to move her Añcita foot back and to touch the hips with it as well. She should bend one of her shanks and touch the ground with the toes of that foot (*SR* 7.953).

(18) **Pārśvakrāntā :** One foot in Kuñcita is raised and the knee is brought up to the level of the breast. Finally, the foot is moved in Udghaṭṭita, (*NŚ* 10.32; *SDām* p. 65). *SR* : One Kuñcita foot is raised on its own side and then it is brought down to the ground on its heel. This is well known to the people as Pārśvadaṇḍapādā. According to the other view, one foot is raised near the other thigh and then brought down on the ground in Udghaṭṭita. (*SR* 7.945-7). *NN*: It does not direct the dancer to bring the knee upto the level of the breast, but agrees with the *NŚ* in describing the rest of the action (*NN* 30b).

(19) **Bhujaṅgatrāsitā :** One Kuñcita foot is raised, the thigh is moved round obliquely. The hips and the knees are also moved round (*NŚ* 10.42; *NN* 31b). *SDām* : Bhujaṅgatrāsikā. (*SDām* p. 65). *SUS* : Bhujaṅgā. (*SUS* 6.127). *SR* : One Kuñcita foot is raised to the groin and the heel is turned to the hips. The knee moves to the right if it is the right knee and to the left if it is the left. The sole is turned up by moving round the hips and the knee (*SR* 7.959-60).

(20) **Bhramarī :** The dancer performs the Atikrāntā Cārī and turns her hips round. She moves round her other foot (*NŚ* 10.45; *NN.* 31b). *SDām* : Bhramarikā (*SDām* p. 65). *SR* : One foot is moved in Atikrāntā. The thigh is moved round obliquely. The body is moved round by turning the sole of the other foot (*SR* 7.958-9).

(21) **Vidyudbhrāntā :** One foot is moved round backwards and then extended to touch the head. The dancer moves it round in all directions (*NŚ* 10.40; *SDām* p. 65; *SUS* 6.126; *SR.* 7.957). *NN* suggests that the foot can also be moved round forward and after moving it round in all directions it is brought down and placed on the ground (*NN.* 31a).

(22) **Vibhrāntā :** Not explained (*SDām* p. 65).

(23) **Vṛttā :** Not explained (*SUS* 6.127).

(24) **Saṃkṣiptā :** Not explained (*SUṢ* 6.127).

(25) **Sūcī :** One foot in Kuñcita is raised and the knee is extended upward. Then it touches (the ground) with its forepart (*NŚ* 10.34; *NN.* 31a). *SDām*; *SUS* : Sucikā. (*SDām* p. 65; *SUS* 6.126). *SR* : The dancer stretches her shanks bringing them up to the knee or the thigh and she does not extend her knee. The rest of the action is the same as in the *NŚ* (*SR* 7.951-2).

(26) **Hariṇaplutā :** One foot performs the Atikrāntā Cārī.The dancer jumps up and then she places it on the ground. The (other) shank is bent and thrown backward (*NŚ* 10.43; *NN* 31a). *SR* : Mṛgaplutā : The dancer raises her Kuñcita foot, jumps up and places it on the ground. The other shank of the Añcita foot is thrown backward (*SR* 7.948).

The Deśī Bhūmicārīs

(1) **Apakuñcitā :** The dancer gradually moves backward with her feet bent (*SR* 7.992; *NN* 30a). *Mānas* : The same action is performed, but with one foot only (*Mānas* 16.4.1361).

(2) **Ardhamaṇḍalikā :** The dancer moves her feet outward dragging them against the ground one by one slowly in a circular way (*SR* 7.985; *NN* 29b). *Mānas* : It suggests moving backward and agrees with *SR* in describing the rest of the action (*Mānas* 16.4.1349).

(3) **Ardhapurāṭī** : The dancer makes Nikuṭṭa on the Udvṛtta[32] foot with the other which is in Udvṛtta and Nikuṭṭa (*SR* 7.996-7; *NN* 30b).

(4) **Aḍḍaskhalitikā** : The dancer stamps one foot obliquely (*SR* 7.1000; *NN* 30b).

(5) **Utkuñcitā** : The dancer throws up her Kuñcita feet and places them forward one by one (*SR* 7.989; *NN* 30a; *Mānas* 16.4.1359).

(6) **Ūrutāḍitā** : The dancer stands in the Ekapāda Sthāna and strikes the ground with one thigh and the foot (*SR* 7.981; *NN* 29b; *Mānas* 16.4.1348).

(7) **Ūruveṇī** : The dancer crosses her thighs and rubs the ground with the sides of her feet (*SR* 7.982; *Mānas* 16.4.1352; *NN* 29b).

(8) **Karihastā** : The dancer stands in Saṁhata Sthāna and rubs the ground with the sides of her feet (*SR* 7.977; *NN.* 29a; *Mānas* 16.4.1346).

(9) **Kātarā** : The dancer stands in the Nandyāvarta Sthāna and steps backward (*SR* 7.979; *NN* 29a; *Mānas* 16.4.1340).

(10) **Kukīrikā** : The dancer stands in the Nandyāvarta Sthāna and then moves obliquely (*SR* 7.978; *NN* 29a; *Mānas* 16.4.1341).

(11) **Khuttā** : The dancer strikes the ground with her toes. (*SR* 7.994; *NN* 30a).

(12) **Taladarśinī** : The dancer stands in the Saṁhasta Sthāna and moves her feet separately and obliquely touching the ground with their outer sides (*SR* 7.995; *NN* 30a; *Mānas* 16.4.1345).

(13) **Talodvṛttā** : The dancer quickly moves the forepart of her feet forward with the back of her toes touching the ground (*SR* 7.983; *NN.* 29b; *Mānas* 16.4.1353).

(14) **Tiryakkuncitā** : The dancer bends one foot and repeatedly throws it down obliquely (*SR* 7.986; *NN* 29b; *Mānas* 16.4.1360).

(15) **Tiryaṅmukhā :** The dancer stands in the Vardhamāna Sthāna and then slides her feet quickly to the left and the sides (*SR* 7.975; *NN* 29a; *Mānas.* 16.4.1338).

(16) **Nikuṭṭakā :** The dancer stands on bent toes (*SR* 7.998; *NN* 30b).

(17) **Nūpuraviddhikā :** The dancer stands with her legs crossed in Svastika and then performs Recita with her heels and toes (*SR* 7.974; *NN* 29a; *Mānas* 16.4.1337).

(18) **Paravṛttatalā :** The dancer raises one foot, its sole, facing her back, and stretches it outwards (*SR* 7.973; *NN* 29a; *Mānas* 16.4.1347).

(19) **Pārṣṇirecitā :** The dancer stands in the Pārṣṇipārś-vagata Sthāna and performs Recita with one heel. (*SR* 7.980; *NN* 29a-b; *Mānas* 16.4.1334).

(20) **Purāṭikā :** The dancer performs Nikuṭṭana with both feet with their soles turned up (*SR* 7.996; *NN* 30a-b).

(21) **Madālasā :** The dancer places her feet unsteadily here and there as in intoxication (*SR* 7.987; *NN* 29b; *Mānas* 16.4.1358).

(22) **Marālā :** The dancer stands in the Nandyāvarta Sthāna. Then she moves her heels and toes in Recita and stretches the feet forward (*SR* 7.976; *NN* 29a; *Mānas* 16.4.1339).

(23) **Rathacakrā :** The dancer stands in the Caturaśra Sthāna and slides her feet forward and backward touching the ground (*SR* 7.971-2; *NN* 28b-29a; *Mānas* 16.4.1342).

(24) **Laṅghitajaṅghikā :** The dancer stands in the Khaṇḍasūcī Sthāna and drags one foot quickly and crosses it with the other (*SR* 7.991; *NN* 30a; *Mānas*

16.4.1356).

(25) **Latākṣepā :** The dancer places one foot forward after placing it at her back and makes Nikuṭṭa on the ground (*SR* 7.999; *NN* 30b).

(26) **Viśliṣtā :** The dancer stands in the Pārṣṇividdha Sthāna and separates the feet. Then the feet appoach each other or move away from each other (*SR* 7.978-9; *NN* 29a; *Mānas* 16.4.1343).

(27) **Sañcāritā :** The dancer bends one foot, throws it up repeatedly and brings it down obliquely to touch the other (*SR* 7.988; *NN* 29b-30a; *Mānas* 16.4.1354).

(28) **Samanakhā :** The dancer stands in Sama and exends her feet obliquley (*Mānas* 16.4.1356).

(29) **Samaskhalitikā :** The dancer stamps with her feet obliquely and simultaneously forward and backward (*SR* 7.1001; *NN* 30b).

(30) **Saṅghaṭṭitā :** The dancer stands in the Viṣamasūcī Sthāna, jumps up and when she comes down she stamps on the ground with her feet (*SR* 7.993; *NN* 30a). *Mānas* : Saṅghaṭṭana (*Mānas* 16.4.1357).

(31) **Sārikā :** The dancer glides one foot forward (*SR* 7.997; *NN* 30b).

(32) **Sphurikā :** The dancer glides forward with both feet, placed in the Sama Sthāna (*SR* 7.998; *NN* 30b).

(33) **Sphuritā :** The dancer quickly moves her feet forward touching the ground with their sides (*SR* 7.992; *NN* 30a; *Mānas* 16.4.1355).

(34) **Stambhakriḍanikā :** The dancer extends one of her feet obliquely and touches its side with the sole of the other foot repeatedly (*SR* 7.990; *NN* 30a; *Mānas* 16.4.1350).

(35) **Svastikā :** The dancer performs Svastika with her feet (*SR* 7.994; *NN* 30a).

(36) **Hariṇatrāsikā :** The dancer crosses her Kuñcita feet in Svastikā and curves the foreparts of the soles. Then she jumps up and comes down (*SR* 7.984; *Mānas* 16.4.1351; *NN* 29b).[33]

The Deśī Ākaśacāris

(1) **Aṅghritāḍitā :** The dancer stretches her feet, jumps up and claps them. (*SR* 7.1007-8; *Mānas* 16.4.1364; *NN* 32a).

(2) **Apakṣepā :** The dancer touches one of her thighs with the outer side of the other foot which is then moved near the hips (*SR* 7.1005; *Mānas* 16.4.1367; *NN* 31b).

(3) **Alātā :** The dancer places one of her feet backwards and crosses it quickly with the other (*SR* 7.1009; *Mānas* 16.4.1375). *NN* : Also written as Lattā (*NN* 32a).

(4) **Udveṣṭanā :** The dancer performs Veṣṭana at the back and stretches her feet in front (*SR* 7.102; *NN* 32a).

(5) **Utkṣepā :** The dancer throws up one foot which is bent, forward and backward upto the knee (*SR* 7.1012-3; *NN* 32a).

(6) **Ūrdhvajānū :** The dancer raises her Kuñcita foot to touch the breast with the knee and shakes it. (*Mānas* 16.4.1369). This seem to be the same as Ūrdhvajānu described in the *NŚ* as a Mārga Ākāśacārī.

(7) **Ullolā :** The dancer waves her feet one by one in the air. (*SR.* 7.1017; *NN.* 32a-b).

(8) **Jaṅghāvartā :** The dancer throws up one foot, the sole of which is turned inwards, at the back of the knee, while she places at its side, the other foot, the sole of which is turned inwards (*SR* 7.1010; *Mānas* 16.4.1368; *NN* 32a).

(9) **Jaṅghālaṅghanikā** : The dancer kicks up one of her feet by the other which is slightly bent. (*SR* 7.1008-9; *NN* 32a). *Mānas* : Jaṅghālaṅghanacārikā : It says that the foot which is bent should also be oblique. (*Manas* 16.4.1373).

(10) **Ḍamarī** : The dancer makes circualr movements at the right and the left sides with one foot which is bent. (*SR* 7.1006; *Mānas* 16.4.1363; *NN* 31b-32a).

(11) **Daṇḍapādā** : The dancer crosses her feet in Svastika and throws them up obliquely (*SR* 7.1006-7; *Mānas* 16.4.1377).

(12) **Purahkṣepā** : The dancer throws up her Kuñcita foot and stretches it forward quickly. Then she places it on the ground (*SR* 7.1002-3; *NN* 31b). *Mānas* : The dancer raises her Kuñcita foot to touch her breast with the knee. (*Mānas.* 16.4.1365).

(13) **Pṛṣṭhotkṣepā** : The dancer performs Utkṣepā only at her back (*SR* 7.1013; *NN* 32a).

(14) **Prāvṛtā** : The dancer turns round herself delicately with her foot in Udvṛtta (*SR* 7.1016; *NN* 32a).

(15) **Bhramarī** : The dancer stretches her foot and moves round quickly (*Mānas* 16.4.1365).

(16) **Vikṣepā** : The dancer extends one foot in front and bends it repeatedly (*SR* 7.1003-4; *Mānas* 16.4.1362; *NN* 31b).

(17) **Viddhā** : The dancer crosses her feet in Svastika and then swings one of them to the front and assumes Kuñcita with the other (*SR* 7.1015; *Mānas* 16.4.1372; *NN* 32a).

(18) **Vidyudbhrāntā** : The dancer throws up one of her feet in front and moves it round quickly over her forehead. Then she places it on the ground (*SR* 7.1001-2; *Mānas* 16.4.1374).

(19) **Veṣṭanā :** The dancer encircles one of her feet with the other. This is also known as Valana (*SR* 7.1011; *NN* 32a).

(20) **Sandolitā :** The dancer swings her Kuñcita foot at her back (*Mānas* 16.4.1371).

(21) **Sūcī :** The dancer places one foot by the side of her thigh and then extends it forward pointing her toes (*SR* 7. 1014; *Mānas* 16.4.1370; *NN* 92503).

(22) **Hariṇaplutā :** The dancer jumps up with one foot bent and lets it fall down repeatedly (*SR* 7.1004; *Mānas* 16.4.1376).[34]

The Cārīs described in ADar

(1) **Kuṭṭana :** The dancer stamps the ground with the heels or the foreparts or the soles of her feet (*ADar* 305-6).

(2) **Caṅkramaṇa :** The dancer moves in jumps with the outer sides of her feet (*ADar* 301-2).

(3) **Calana :** The dancer walks (*ADar* 301).

(4) **Luṭhita :** The dancer stands in Svastika and stamps the ground with the foreparts of her feet (*ADar* 306).

(5) **Lolita :** The dancer stamps the ground slowly and moves without touching the ground (*ADar*. 307).

(6) **Viṣamasañcara :** The left foot is encircled by the right and the right foot is encircled by the left (*ADar* 308).

(7) **Veginī :** The dancer moves quickly with the forepart or the heel of one foot. The hands assume Alapadma and Tripatākā. (*ADar*. 304-5).

(8) **Saraṇa :** One foot is brought down to the ground with the heel of the other foot. The hands assume Patākā (*ADar* 302-3).

The Mārga Sthānas for men

(1) **Ālīḍha** : The Mandala Sthāna is performed with the right foot extended by five tālas from the other foot (*NŚ* 10.678; *VDP* 3.23.11). *SR* : The left thigh is still. *NN* : 4.4.22-23. The rest agrees with the *NŚ* (*SR* 7.1049-51). *SUS* : Pratyāliḍha is reversed and the feet are placed five tālas apart (*SUS* 5.140). (*SDām* 64; *NN*. 25b).

(2) **Pratyāliḍha** : The Āliḍha Sthāna is reversed by extending the left foot and bending the right (*NŚ* 10.70-1; *VDP*. 3.23.15-6; *SR* 7.1052-4). *SUS* : The right foot is extended in Kuñcita (*SUS* 5.140) (*SDām* p. 64; *NN*. 26a).

(3) **Maṇḍala** : The feet are placed obliquely four tālas apart and they are turned sideways. The knees and the hips are kept normally. (*NŚ* 10.65-6). *VDP* prescribes three tālas and agrees with the *NŚ*. in describing the rest of the action. (*VDP* 3.23.9). *SUS* : It prescribes one tāla and the rest is the same as in the *NŚ* (*SUS* 5.139). *SR* : The feet are placed obliquely on the ground and kept one tāla apart. They are turned sideways. The hips and the knees are kept naturally. Then the feet are raised in the air and kept two tālas and a half apart. The thighs are motionless (*SR* 7.1046-8).

(4) **Vaiśākha** : The feet are placed obliquely three tālas and a half apart. They are turned sideways. The thighs are motionless. (*NŚ* 10.62; *VDP* 3.23.6-7). *SR*. does not direct the dancer to keep the thigh motionless. Its says also that the feet and the thighs are placed at the same distance (*SR* 7.1043-5). *SUS* gives the first part of the action which agrees with the description of the *NŚ* (*SUS* 5.139).

(5) **Vaiṣṇava** : The feet are placed two tālas and a half apart. One of them is raised while the other is

placed obliquely with the toes pointing sideways. The shank is slightly bent. Sauṣṭhava is observed (*NŚ* 10.52-3). *VDP* says that one foot is placed naturally which, according to the *NŚ* is raised (*NN* 4.420-21 *VDP* 3.23.2). *SR* agrees with *VDP* in prescribing Sama for the foot. The rest agrees with the *NŚ*. (*SR*. 7.1039-40). *SUS* : It directs the dancer to place the feet two tālas and a half apart (*SUS* 5.138).

(6) **Samapāda :** The feet are in Sama and placed one tāla apart. Sauṣṭhava is observed (*NŚ* 10.58-9); *VDP* 3.23.3-4.; *SR* 7.1041-2; *SUS* 5.138).

The Mārga Sthānas for women

(1) **Avahittha :** The left foot is in Sama while the other is placed obliquely. The left hip is raised. An alternative direction is to move one foot forward obliquely while the other is drawn away in Sama and they are placed one tāla apart. The hip is slightly raised. One hand is in Latā while the other is placed on the hip (*NŚ* 12.163-4, 167-9). *VDP* does not say anything about the hands and agrees with the *NŚ* in describing the rest of the action. (*VDP* 3.23.21-2). *SUS* : The dancer performs Aśvapluta. (*SUS* 5.135). *SR* : The Āyata Sthāna is reversed (*SR* 7.1063-4). *NN* agrees with *SR* (*NN* 25b).

(2) **Aśvakrānta :** One foot is in Sama while the toes of the other foot are curved. Then one foot in Sūcī may be either placed on the heel of the other which is in Sama or kept apart (*NŚ* 12.173; *VDP* 3.23.23-4 : Hayakrānta). *SR* : One foot in Sūcī may be either placed on the heel of the other which is in Sama, or placed on its own side in Sama at a distance of one tāla. (*SR* 7.1065-8). *NN* : It does not direct the dancer to curve her toes and agrees with the rest of the action described in the *NŚ*. (*NN*. 25b).

(3) **Āyata :** The left foot is placed normally in Sama while the other is placed obliquely one tāla apart. The chest is raised and the hands in Latā are placed on the hips. The dancer has a pleasing expression. Alternatively, the right foot is placed in Sama while the left is placed obliquely. The left hip is raised. (*NŚ* 12.161-4; *VDP* 3.23.18-20). *SUS*: The right foot is in Sama while the left is placed obliquely. (*SUS* 5.136). *SR* : The left foot is placed obliquely at a distance of one tāla while the right foot is in Sama. The dancer has a pleasing expression. The chest is raised while the hips are not. The right hand is placed on the hips while the other is in Latā. (*SR* 7.1055-6). *NN* gives the first part of the action given in the *NŚ*. (*NN* 25b).

(4) **Gatāgata :** The dancer, after raising one of her feet hesitates to move. (*SR*. 7.1069).

(5) **Motita :** One foot is in Sama while the other is in Kuñcita with the toes touching the ground. The hands are raised at the front in Karkaṭa (*SR* 7.1071-2).

(6) **Lalita :** One foot in Sūci either strikes the other or it is kept apart (*SUS* 5.136).

(7) **Valita :** The body is slightly twisted round while the foot of that side, towards which the body is moved, touches the ground with the little toe. The other foot touches the ground with the big toe (*SR* 7.1070).

(8) **Vinivartana :** It is Moṭita performed turning backwards (*SR* 7.1073).

The Deśī Sthānas

(1) **Antarapadmāsana :** The dancer jumps and extends her feet. Then she joins their soles in Padmāsana. (*SSam* 6.149).

(2) **Ardhamaṇḍala :** Not explained (*SDām* p. 64).

(3) **Ūrdhvāsana :** Not explained (*SDām* p. 64).

(4) **Ekajānunata :** One foot is in Sama while the other foot is kept obliquely with the knee bent and placed at a distance of four aṅgulas from the Sama foot. (*SR* 7.1083; *Sdām* p. 64). *Mānas* : Ekajānugata. (*Mānas* 16.4.1319).

(5) **Ekapāda :** One leg is in Sama with the knee raised. The other foot touches the outer side of the knee with its own outer side (*SR* 7.1078; *Mānas* 16.4.1322; *SDām* p. 64; *NN* 25b). *SSam* : The text is corrupt (*SSam* 6.143).

(6) **Ekapārśvagata :** One foot is placed obliquely touching the ground with its outer edge in front of the other foot which is in Sama (*SR* 7.10.82). *Mānas* gives Ekapārśva while describing the action (*Mānas* 16.4.1318). *SSam* : Ekapārṣṇi (*SSam* 6.142).

(7) **Utkaṭa :** The dancer stands in Samanakha with her feet either in Sama or in Kuñcita (*NN*. 25b). *SR* describes Utkaṭa as an Upaviṣṭa Sthāna. (*SR* 7.1.100-1).

(8) **Kamalāsana :** Not explained (*SDām* p.64).

(9) **Kuṇḍala :** Not explained (*SDām* p. 64).

(10) **Kūrmāsana :** The right leg touches the ground with the knee and the outer side of the ankle. The left foot is in Sama (*SR* 7.1092; *NN* 26b). *SSam* : The left repeats the action of the right. (*SSam* 6.150).

(11) **Khaṇḍasūcī :** One leg is in Kuñcita. The other is stretched obliquely touching the ground with its knee and heel. (*SR* 7.1087; *SSam* 6.139; *SDām* p. 64). *Mānas* : Khaḍgasūcī in the list of the terms. (*Mānas* : 16.4.1310, 1330).

(12) **Garuḍa :** The left leg bends forward slightly while the other touches the ground at the back with the

knee. (*SR* 7.1091; *SDām* p. 64; *Mānas* 16.4.1326; *SSam* 6.138; *NN* 26b).

(13) **Caturaśra :** It is Nandyāvarta with the feet placed eighteen aṅgulas apart (*SR* 7. 1080; *SDām* p. 64). *Mānas* directs the dancer to keep her feet three vitasti apart (3 x 12 = 36) aṅgulas) (*Mānas* 16.4.1616). *SSam* : Acording to it, the dancer keeps her feet one and a half tāla apart: Caturaśra (*SSam* 6.144). *NN* prescribes two tālas (*NN* 25b).

(14) **Jāta :** Not explained (*SDām.* p.64).

(15) **Jānunivartaka :** Not explained (*SDām* p. 64).

(16) **Tribhaṅgika :** The text is not very clear. It seems that the direction is to dance gracefully by placing the right foot obliquely and the left foot in Sama. The left hip is extended. (*SSam* 6.141).

(17) **Dārdura :** Not explained (*SDām* p. 64).

(18) **Nandyāvarta :** It is Vardhamāna with the feet placed six or twelve angulas apart (Vitasti = twelve aṅgulas) (*SR* 7.1075; *SDām* p. 64). *Mānas* : prescribes twelve aṅgulas. (*Mānas* 16.4.1615). *SSam.* prescribes six aṅgulas (*SSam* 6.131) while *NN* prescribes eight aṅgulas (*NN* 25b).

(19) **Nāgabandha :** The dancer sits and places her right shank on her left thigh (*SR* 7.1093; *NN* 26b). *SSām* : Some letters are missing. It seems to give the same description (*SSam* 6.14).

(20) **Padmāsana :** The full description of the action can not be found as parts of the text are missing. From what is left it appears that the dancer stands in Samasūcī and performs some other action (*SSam* 6.146).

(21) **Parāvṛtta :** The big toe and the little toes are kept at the same level as the heel (of the other foot) (*SR* 7.1084); *SDām* p. 64; *Mānas* 16.4.1320; *SSam.* 6.137).

(22) **Pārṣṇipārśpagata** : One heel is placed on the inner side of the other (*SR*. 7.1081; *SDām*. p. 64). *Mānas* gives Pārsnipārśva while describing the action (*Mānas* 16.4.1317). *SSam* : Pārṣṇipārśvaka (*SSam* 6.136).

(23) **Pārṣṇividdha** : The heel touches the big toe (*SR* 7.1081); *SDām* p. 64; *Mānas* 16.4.1317; *SSām* 6.136; *NN* 25a).

(24) **Pṛṣthottānatala** : One foot is moved back touching the ground with the back of the toes, while the other is put forward in Sama. (*SR* 7.1079; *Mānas* 16.4.1321; *NN* 25b). *SDām* : Pṛṣṭhottānadalana. (*SDām* p. 64).

(25) **Brahmā** : One foot is in Sama while the other is moved back in Kuñcita and then thrown up keeping the knee joint straight (*SR* 7.1088; *SDām* p. 64; *NN*. 26a). *Mānas* does not direct the dancer to throw up her leg though it agrees with the rest of the action described by *SR* (*Mānas* 16.4.1326).

(26) **Maṇḍuka** : Not explained (*SDām*. p. 64).

(27) **Vardhamāna** : The feet are placed obliquely with the heels touching each other (*SR* 7.1074; *SDām* p. 64; *Mānas* 16.4.1314; *SSam* 6.132; *NN* 25b).

(28) **Viśākhaka** : Not explained (*SDām* p. 64). It may be the same as the Vaiśākha described in *NN*.

(29) **Viṣamapadmāsana** : Too obscure to explain (*SSam* 6.148).

(30) **Viṣamasūcī** : The Sūcī feet are stretched apart simultaneously, one forward and the other backward. According to some, the knees and the ankles of these legs must touch the ground (*SR* 7.1085-6; *SDām* p. 64). *Mānas* gives both views together (*Mānas* 16.4.1329). *SSam* and *NN* give the first view. (*SSam* 6.145; *NN* 26a-b)

(31) **Vṛṣabhāsana :** The knees are placed on the ground together or separated. This is done with Sauṣṭhava (*SR* 7.1094); *SDām* p. 64; *Mānas* 16.4.1327; *NN* 26b).

(32) **Vaitānasa :** Not explained (*SDām* p. 64).

(33) **Vaisākha :** Vardhamana is performed with the feet placed three tālas and a half apart (*NN* 25b).

(34) **Vaiṣṇava :** One foot is in Sama and the other after being slightly bent is extended to the front obliquely (*SR* 7.1089; *SDām* p. 64; *Mānas* 16.4.1324; *SSam* 6.135). *NN* says that the feet are placed two tālas apart and agree with the rest of the description given by *SR* (*NN* 26a).

(35) **Śaiva :** The left foot is in Sama while the other is raised to the level of the knee-cap (of the other foot) in Kuñcita (*SR* 7.1090; *SDām* p. 64; *Mānas* 16.4.1325; *NN* 26a).

(36) **Samapāda :** The body is kept normally while the feet are straight and placed twelve aṅgulas apart (*SR* 7.1077); *SDām* p. 64; *Mānas* 16.4.1312). *SSām.* : The text is corrupt. (*SSam* 6.133). *NN* agrees with *SR* (*NN* 25a).

(37) **Samasūcī :** The heels, the shanks and the things touch the ground and the legs are extended obliquely (*SR* 7.1084-5; *Mānas* 16.4.1328; *SSam* 6.140; *NN.* 26a). *SDām* : Samasūcī (*SDām* p. 64).

(38) **Saṁhata :** The body is kept normaly. The soles are joined together and so are the ankles. (*SR* 7.1076; *SDām* p. 64). *Mānas, NN.* : The feet are in Nūpura with the little toes and the rest of the toes are closed together (*Mānas* 16.4.1311; *NN* 25b).

(39) **Svastika :** The dancer stands in Saṁhata with her feet in Kuñciṭa. Then the feet cross in Svastika with their little toes touching each other (*SR* 7.1073-4; *SDām* p. 64). *Mānas* : The feet are in Nūpura with

the little toes touching each other and the soles are raised a little. (*Mānas* 16.4.1313). *SSaṃ* directs the dancer to perform the Mañjarīsthāna and agrees with *SR* in describing the rest of the action. (*SSam* 6.134). *NN* agrees with *SR* in describing the second part of the action (*NN* 25a).

The Ākāśamaṇḍalas

(1) **Atikrānta :** The right foot performs Janita. Udvāhita follows. The left foot performs Alāta and then the right foot performs Pārśvakrānta. (The left foot performs Sūcī while the right foot again performs Pārśvakrānta. The left foot again performs Sūcī and Apakrānta is performed by the right foot). The left foot repeats Sūcī and the dancer turns round her hips. Then the right foot performs Udvṛtta while the left foot performs Alāta again. Paricchinna is performed with Bāhyabhramaraka. Again the left foot performs Atikrānta and finally Daṇḍapāda is performed by the right foot. (*NŚ* 11.7-10; *VDP* 3.20.24). *SR* prescribes Śakaṭāsyā Cārī after Janita. Recita is to be done by the left side of the body after performing Bāhyabharamaraka. The rest agrees with the description in the *NŚ*[35] (*SR* 7.1174-6).

(2) **Alāta :** The right foot performs Sūcī and the left foot performs Apakrānta. The right foot again performs Pārśvakrānta while the left foot performs Alāta. These Cāris are repeated gracefully in a series for six or seven times. (The right and the left foot perform Apakrānta and Abhikrānta). Apakrānta is again performed by the right foot while the left foot performs Atikrānta and Bhramara (*NŚ* 11.29-32; *VDP* 3.20.24). *SDām* : Ālābha. (*SDām* p. 68). *SR* : The left foot performs Sūcī and Bhramarī while the right foot performs Bhujaṅgatrāsita. The left foot performs Alāta. These are repeated six or seven

times and the dancer moves round quickly in four directions. The right foot does Apakrānta and the left foot performs Atikrānta and Bhramarikā. These are done gracefully (*SR* 7.1199-1201).

(3) **Krānta** : The right performs Sūcī and Pārśvakrānta while the left foot performs Apakrānta and Pārśvakrānta. The dancer moves round performing these Cārīs alternately. Then she performs Sūcī with her left foot and Apakrānta with her right foot (*NŚ* 10.40-3; *VDP* 3.20-25; *SR* 7.1180-1).

(4) **Janita** : Not explained (*SDām* p. 68).

(5) **Daṇḍapāda** : The right foot performs Janita and Daṇḍapāda successively while the left foot performs Sūcī. The hips are turned round. Then the right foot performs Udvṛtta, Pārśvakrānta. Bhujaṅgatrāsita and Daṇḍapāda successively and the left foot performs Alāta, Atikrānta and Sūcī successively. The hips are turned round (*NŚ* 11.22-4; *VDP* 3.20.24; *SDām* p. 68; *SR* 7.1177-9).

(6) **Lalita** : The right foot performs Sūcī, Pārśvakrānta, Bhujaṅgatrāsita, (Ākṣipta), Pārśvakrānta and Apakrānta successively while Apakrānta (Atikrānta), Atikrānta, Ūrudvṛtta, Alāta, Sūcī and Atikrānta are performed by the left foot. These movements are to be performed gracefully. (*NŚ* 11.36-40; *VDP* 3.20.25; *SDām* p. 68; *SR* .1202-5).

(7) **Lalitasañcara** : The right foot performs Ūrdhvajānu and Sūcī successively. The left foot performs Apakrānta and the right foot is moved to the side. Again the left foot performs Sūcī and the hips are turned round. Then the right foot performs Pārśvakrānta, Sūcī and again Pārśvakrānta while the left foot does Atikrānta, Apakrānta and again Atikrānta, one after the other. Paricchinna is performed with Bāhyabhramaraka. (*NŚ* 11.16-9; *VDP* 3.20.24; *SR* 7.1182-5).

(8) **Līna :** Not explained (*SDām* p. 68).

(9) **Vāmabandha :** Sūcī and Daṇḍapāda are performed by the right foot while Aparkrānta and Sūcī are performed by the left foot. The hips are turned round and the right foot moves in Pārśvakrānta. Ākṣipta and Daṇḍapāda are done simultaneously by the left and the right foot. The right foot performs Ūrudvṛtta and the left foot performs Sūcī. The hips are turned round. Again Alāta and Atikrānta are performed by the left foot while Pārśvakrānta is done by the right foot (*NŚ* 11.32-6; *SR* 7.1188-91). Vāmabaddha (*VDP* 3.20.25). *SDām* : Vāmaviddha (*SDām.* p. 68).

(10) **Vicitra :** The right foot performs Janita first and then moves in Nikuṭṭa. The left foot is moved in Āspandita while Pārśvakrānta is performed by the right foot. Then left foot performs Sūcī and the right foot performs Apakrānta. The left foot performs Bhujaṅgatrāsita, Alāta, Sūcī and Apakrānta successively while in the same manner the right foot performs Atikrānta, ūdvṛtta, Pārśvakrānta and Vikṣepa successively. Finally, Bāhyabhramaraka and Vikṣepa are preformed. (*NŚ* 11.11-5 *VDP* 3.20.24). *SDām* : Vicitrita (*SDām* p. 68). *SR* : The dancer performs Janita, Ūrudvṛtta and Vicyavā with her right foot and then standing in Sama she moves round in Vyavartanā and Āvartana. She performs Syandita, Bhujaṅgatrāsita, Udvṛtta, Pārśvakrānta or Sūcī and finally Apakrānta with her left foot while Pārśvakrānta, Atikrānta, Alāta and Vikṣepa are performed by the right foot. (*SR* 7.1192-4).

(11) **Vihṛta :** The right foot performs Janita and Nikuṭṭaka and the left foot performs Āspandita. Then the right foot performs Udvṛtta, Sūcī and Ākṣipta successively while the left foot performs Alāta and

Pārśvakrānta. The hips are turned round. Daṇḍapāda is performed. Sūcī is performed by the left foot and the hips are again turned round. Finally the right foot performs Bhujaṅgatrāsita while the left foot performs Atikrānta (*NŚ* 11.25-8; *VDP* 3.20.24). *SDām* : Vikṛta, (*SDām* p. 68). *SR* : The right foot performs Vicyavā and Syanditā. Then it performs Pārśvakrānta while the left foot performs Syanditā. Then the right foot performs Udvṛtta, Sūcī and Ākṣipta successively and the left foot performs Alāta and Pārśvakrānta. The dancer then moves round with both the feet and performs Daṇḍapāda. Finally, the left foot performs Sūcī, Bhramarī and then Atikrānta while the right foot performs Bhujaṅgatrāsita (*SR* 7.1195-8).

(12) **Sūcīviddha :** The dancer performs Sūcī with her left foot and turns round her hips. Then she performs Pārśvakrānta, Sūcī and again Pārśvakranta with her right foot while her left foot performs Atikrānta and Apakrānta (*NŚ* 11.20-1; *VDP* 32.20.24; *SDām* p. 68). *SR* : The right foot performs Sūcī and Bhramarī while the left foot performs Pārśvakrānta and Apakrānta. The right assumes Sūcī. Then the left foot performs Apakrānta while the right performs Pārśvakranta (*SR* 7.1186-7).

The Bhaumamaṇḍalas

(1) **Aḍḍita :** The right foot moves in Udghaṭṭita, then turns round and performs Āskandita. The left foot performs Śakaṭāsya. The right foot performs Pṛṣṭhāpasarpī and Cāṣagati while the left foot performs Aḍḍita. Again the right foot performs Apasarpita and the left foot performs Bhramaraka. The right foot performs Āskandita and strikes the ground (*NŚ* 11.58-61; *VDP* 3.20.27; *SDām* p. 67). *SR* the right foot performs Udghaṭtita, Baddha,

Samotsāritamattallī, Ardhamattallī, Apakrānta, Udvṛtta, Vidyudbhrānta, Bhramara and Syanditā. The left foot performs Śakaṭāsya. The right foot performs Cāṣagati twice. The left foot performs Aḍḍita and Adhyardhikā while the right performs Cāṣagati. The left foot performs Samotsaritamattallī, Mattallī and Bhramara and the right foot stamps the ground after doing Syandita (*SR* 7.1160-3).

(2) **Adhyardha** : The right foot performs Janita and Āspandita successively while the left foot performs Apasarpī. Again the right foot performs Śakaṭāsya. The dancer moves round doing these in a series (*NŚ* 11.63-5; *SDām* p. 67). *VDP* Ahya (Adhya) rdha (*VDP.* 3.20.27). *SR* : prescribes four Caris, namely, Adhyardhikā, Cāṣagati, Samotsārita-mattallī, and Mattallī to be performed by the left foot instead of doing Adhyardhikā only. The rest are the same as in the *NŚ* (*SR* 7.1167-8).

(3) **Apagata :** Not explained (*SDām.* p. 67).

(4) **Āvarta :** The right foot performs Janita, Śakaṭāsya and Urudvṛtta while the left performs Nikuṭṭṭaka, Pṛṣṭhāpasarpī and Cāṣagati. Again the right foot performs Āspandita and Bhramara and the left performs Śakaṭāsya. The hips are turned round. The left foot Pṛṣṭhāpasarpī (*NŚ* 11.50-3; *SDām* p. 67). *VDP* : Mārdava (Āvarta ?). (*VDP* 3.20.26). *SR* : The right foot performs Janita while the left performs Sthitāvarta, Śakaṭāsya, Elakākrīḍita. Ūrudvṛtta, Aḍḍita, Janita and Samotsāritamattallī successively. The right foot performs Śakaṭāsya and Ūrudvṛtta and the left foot performs Cāṣagati. The right foot performs Spanditā twice. The left performs Śakaṭāsya while the right performs Bhramara and afterwards the left foot performs Cāṣagati (*SR* 7.1154-7).

(5) **Āspandita** : The right foot performs Bhramara and the left foot performs Aḍḍita. The hips are turned round and the right foot performs Śakaṭāsya and Ūrdudvṛtta while the left foot makes Apasarpita. The hips are turned round. The right foot moves in Spandita and the left foot moves in Śakaṭāsya and then strikes the ground violently. *VDP* (*NŚ* 11.47-50): Āskandita. (*VDP* 3.20.26). *SDām* : Āskandita (*SDām* p. 67). *SR*: Āskandita : The hips are turned round and the Bhramarī Carī is performed. According to *SR* the first Bhramarī is performed by the right foot while the second one is done by the left foot (*SR* 7.1151-3).

(6) **Elakākrīḍita** : The dancer touches the ground with her feet and moves them in Sūcīviddha and Elakākrīḍita. The hips are quickly turned round. Then she moves round in Sūcīviddha and Apaviddha successively (*NŚ* 11.56-8); *SDām* p. 67). *VDP* : Eḍakākrīḍita (*VDP* 3.20.26). *SR* says that the Sūcīviddha Karaṇa is to be performed by doing Sūcī and Viddhā Cārīs. At the end, *SR* prescribes Ākṣipta. The dancer moves round in four directions. (Viddha is the same as Āviddha). (*SR* 7.1169-70).

(7) **Cāṣagata** : The dancer moves round in Caṣagati (*NŚ* 11.67-8; *VDP* 3.20.27; *SR* 7.1173).

(8) **Parārdha** : Not explained (*SDām* p. 67).

(9) **Piṣṭakuṭṭa** : The right foot performs Sūcī while the left foot performs Apakrānta. Then both the feet perform Bhujaṅgatrāsita. The dancer moves round in Bhujaṅgatrāsita (*NŚ* 11.65-7; *VDP* 3.20.27; *SR* 7.1171-2).

(10) **Bhramara** : The right foot performs Janita and Śakaṭāsya while the left foot performs Āspandita and then it is extended. The right foot performs

Bhramara and the hips are turned round. Again the left foot performs Āspandita, Pṛṣṭhāpasarpī and Bhramara while the right foot performs Śakaṭāsya. (*NŚ* 11.44-7; *VDP* 3.20.26; *SDām* p. 67). *SR* : The right foot performs Janita and the left foot performs Spandita. Again the right foot performs either Śakaṭāsya or Bhramara and the left performs either Avaspandita or Spandita. Finally the right foot performs Ṣakaṭāsya and Bhramara while the left foot performs Cāṣagati and Spandita (*SR* 7.1149-50).

(11) **Śakaṭāsya** : The right foot performs Janita first and goes on to Nikuṭṭaka and Śakaṭāsya while the left foot performs Āskandita. The dancer moves round with her feet in Śakaṭāsya (*NŚ* 11.61-3; *VDP* 3.20.27; *SDām* p. 67). *SR* : The dancer performs Janita first and the seven beginning with Sthitāvarta, mentioned in the Āvarta Maṇḍala. (They are : Sthitāvarta, Śakaṭāsya, Elakākrīḍita. Ūrudvṛtta, Aḍḍita, Janita and Samotsaritamattallī). The rest are the same as in the *NŚ* (*SR* 7.1158-9).

(12) **Samotsārita** : The dancer stands in the Samapāda Sthāna, extends her hands with her palms turned upwards and moves them continuously in Udveṣṭita and Āveṣṭita. She places (her left hand) on her hips and moves round her right hand in Āvartita. In the same manner, she moves her left hand in Āvartita and extends it. She moves round doing the Cārī as one in a series (*NŚ* 11.53-6; *SDām* p. 67). *VDP* : Samāsarita. (*VDP* 3.20.26). *SR*. agrees with the first part of the action and says that after moving the hands in Udveṣṭita and Āveṣṭita, the dancer should place both of them on her hips and then to make a circular movement first with the right foot and then with the left. Then the left foot is extended. Thus

she moves in four directions successively (*SR* 7.1164-6).

The Maṇḍalas, given in ADar

(1) **Āyata :** The dancer stands in Caturaśra with her feet placed nine inches apart. (Vitasti = twelve aṅgulas = nine inches). Her knees are a little bent, obliquely (*Adar* 263).

(2) **Āliḍha :** The dancer places her left foot twenty-seven inches apart from the right foot. He left hand is in Śikhara while her right hand is in Kaṭakāmukha (*ADar* 264-5).

(3) **Pārśvasūcī :** The dancer stands on her toes and touches the ground on one side with one knee. (*ADar* 273).

(4) **Prayāliḍha :** The Āliḍha Maṇḍala is reversed (*ADar* 266).

(5) **Preṅkhaṇa :** The dancer places one foot by the side of the heel of the other. Her hands are in Kūrma (*ADar* 266).

(6) **Prerita :** The dancer stamps on the ground at her side with one foot placed at a distnace of twenty-seven inches from the other. Then she stands with her knees slightly and obliquely bent. One of her hands is placed on the chest in Śikhara while the other hand is extended in Patākā (*ADar* 267-8).

(7) **Moṭita :** The dancer stands on her toes and touches the ground with her knees alternately. Her hands are in Tripatākā. (*ADar* 270).

(8) **Samasūcī :** The dancer touches the ground with her toes and knees (*ADar* 272).

(9) **Sthānaka :** The dancer stands in Sama with her body kept straight and places her hands on the hips in Ardhacandra (*ADar* 262).

(10) **Svastika :** The hands and the feet are crossed. (*ADar* 269).

The Gatis

(1) **Kaukkuṭī :** The dancer moves her feet together like an excited cock (*NN* 43a).

(2) **Khañjanī :** The dancer bends her knees with her hands in Tripatākā and moves round quickly with the foreparts of her feet and stops (*NN* 43a).

(3) **Khañjaritā :** The dancer moves like a bird (*SDar* 42a).

(4) **Gajalīlā :** The dancer stands in Samapada and moves slowly with a grave look (*NN* 43a; *SDar* : Gajagāminī 41b). *ADar* : The dancer moves slowly in Samapāda with her hands in Patāka on both sides (*ADar* 314-5).

(5) **Turaṅgiṇī :** The dancer raises her right foot and jumps repeatedly with her left hand in Śikhara and the right in Patākā (*ADar* 315-6). *SDar* : The dancer moves very quickly (*SDar.* 42a). *NN* : Hayalīlā : The dancer moves round quickly touching the ground with the sides of her feet and stops in the middle of the stage (*NN* 42b).

(6) **Bhānavī :** The hands are moved upwards describing a circle (*NN* 42b). *SDar* : The dancer moves like the sun (*SDar* 41b).

(7) **Bhujaṅgī :** The dancer repeats the movement of the Siṁhī Gati with her hands in Tripatākā on both sides (*ADar* 318).

(8) **Mānavi :** The dancer moves in circles and comes forwards repeatedly with her left hand placed on the hips and the right is in Khaṭakāmukha (*ADar* 321).

(9) **Māṇḍukī :** The dancer walks almost like a lion with her hands in Śikhara (*ADar* 319).

(10) **Mayūrī** : The dancer moves her hands gradually upwards and slowly raises her feet (*NN* 42b). *ADar* The dancer stands on her toes with her in Kapittha and shakes both her knees alternately (*ADar* 312).

(11) **Mṛgī** : The dancer looks with straight eyes like a deer and her movements follow the accompanying song. (*NN.* 42b-43a). *SDar* : It gives only the first portion of the action given by *NN* (*SDar* 42b). *ADar* : The dancer moves quickly to the front or sideways like a deer with her hands in Tripatākā (*ADar* 313).

(12) **Mainavī** : The dancer moves her both sides. (*NN.* 42b). *SDar* : The dancer moves without rest like a fish in a well. (*SDar.* 41b).

(13) **Virā** : The dancer comes forward from a distance with her left hand in Śikhara and the right hand in Patāka (*ADar* 320).

(14) **Siṁhī** : The dancer stands on her toes and jumps quickly to the front. Her hands are in Śikhara (*ADar* 317).

(15) **Haṁsī** : The dancer places her foot at a distance of half a cubit from the other and bending her body on both sides alternately walks like a goose with her hands in Kapittha (*ADar* 311). *NN* : Marālī : The dancer moves like a swan with appropriate Bhāvas and Hāvas and casts passionate glances (*NN* 43a). *SDar*: The dancer moves like a goose (*SDar* 42b).

The Recakas

(1) **Pādarecaka** : The dancer moves her feet in various ways from one side to another (*NŚ* 4.248b-c). *SR* : The heels and the toes are repeatedly moved inwards and outwards. They are raised and curved (*SR* 7.893). (*NN* 33b).

(2) **Kaṭirecaka** : The hips are raised, turned round and drawn backwards (*NŚ* 4.248c-d). *SR* : The hips are

turned in all directions with oblique movement of the separated and spread out toes (*SR* 7.895). (*NN* 33b).

(3) **Hastarecaka :** The hands are raised, thrown out, extended, turned round and drawn backwards (*NŚ* 4.248d-e). *SR:* A quick and circular movement of the Haṁsapakṣa hands, done alternately (*SR* 7.894). (*NN.* 33b).

(4) **Grīvārecaka :** The neck is raised, then lowered and then bent sideways (*NŚ* 4.428e-f). *SR* : The neck is moved round (*SR* 7.896). (*NN* 33b).

CHAPTER FIVE

The Movements of the Body as a Whole : Karaṇa

The Karaṇas are the basic dance sequences, made up of the combination of the movements of the hands and the feet. Two karaṇas make up a Mātṛkā. Kalāpaka is the combination of three Karaṇas and Ṣaṇḍaka is made up of four. Five Karaṇas make up a Saṅghātaka while Aṅgahāra can be of six, seven, eight or more Karaṇas.

The *NŚ* has an exhaustive discussion of the Karaṇas. It defines Karaṇa as the coordination of the movements of the hands and the feet,[1] which may be supplemented with the movement of the other limbs as well. Not every movement can make up a Karaṇa, for the constituent movements of a Karaṇa must be beautiful.[2] The *NŚ* discusses a hundred and eight Karaṇas in great detail. But Bhramarī, which is discussed in great detail by *SR* and the other treatises that give an account of the Deśī style and which appear to be the same as Cāri, though not so called, is only briefly mentioned in the *NŚ*. It regards Bhramari as a form of Cārī.[3]

The *VDP* says that there are a hundred and eight Karaṇas but gives ninety names without discussing them in detail.[4] Some names are different from those in the *NŚ*. *ND* speaks of a hundred and eight Karaṇas, but names only one, Talapuṣpaputa.[5] *Mānas* discusses eighteen Karaṇas of the Deśī style. These are found in *SR* as Utplutikaraṇas.[6] *SR* discusses a hundred and eight Karaṇas following the *NŚ* and the interpretation of *Abhg*. It also gives thirty-six Utplutikaraṇas and discusses them. These thirty-six Karaṇas are of the Deśī type and they involve jumping. It also discusses nine Bhramarīs in its account of the Utplutikaraṇas.[7] *SSam* discusses eleven Utplutikaraṇas and five Bhramarīs. Bhramarīs are not defined.[8] *SUS* discusses a hundred and five Karaṇas in detail following the *NŚ*. Some of the names do not agree with those in the *NŚ*. It also gives a list of eight Brahmarīs.[9] *SDām* gives a list of a hundred and eight Karaṇas and differs slightly from the *NŚ*.[10] It also gives a list of thirteen Utplutikaraṇas calling them Viṣama. These can be of two types : Bhauma and Ākāśa of which Ākāśa includes three Bhramarīs.[11] *ADar* gives five Utplavanabhedas and seven Bhramarīs. Some of them represent a different tradition.[12] *NN* says that there are thousands of Karaṇas and describes only those which are necessary for performing the Bandhanṛtta. There are sixteen such Karaṇas and in this *NN* agrees with the *NŚ*. It also describes five Bhramarīs.[13] The other texts do not discuss Karaṇas.

The Mātṛkā, Ṣaṇḍaka and Saṅsghātaka are not discussed by any of the theorists.

The Karaṇas

(1) **Añcita :** Having moved the (Karihasta) hand in Vyāvṛtta and Parivartita, it is arched over the tips of the nose touching it (*NŚ* 4.83-4; *SDām* p. 67). *SUS* agrees with the first part of the action and prescribes the last part of the Ardhasvastika Karaṇa for the rest of that action (*SUS* 6.27). *SR* : The first part of the action agrees with the *NŚ*. The hand which is arched over the tip of the nose should be in Karihasta and then changed to Alapadma (*SR* 7.594).

(2) **Ajapluta :** Not explained *VDP* 3.20.51).

(3) **Atikrānta** : One foot is placed forward after performing the Atikrāntā Cārī. The hands are moved in harmony (*NŚ* 4.126-7; *VDP* 3.20.49; *SR* 7.685-6; *SDām* p. 66). *SUS* agree with the first part of the action and says that the left hand should be brought near the face (*SUS* 6.70).

(4) **Apakrānta** : The thighs are moved in Valita. The Apakrāntā Cārī is performed and the hands are moved in harmony (*NŚ* 4.139-40; *SDām* p. 66). *SR* does not say anything about moving the thighs, which is a part of the Apakrāntā Cārī. (*SR* 7.713), Avakranta (*VDP* 3.20.49).

(5) **Apaviddha** : The right hand describes a circle and is placed on the thigh in Śukatuṇḍa. The left hand should be placed on the breast (*NŚ* 5.64-5; *VDP* 3.20.40). *SUS* prescribes Khaṭikāmukha for the left hand (*SUS* 6.8). *SR*: The right hand is in Caturaśra and it is moved away in Vyāvartanā. The Ākṣiptā Cārī follows. The right hand is placed on the thigh in Śukatuṇḍa. The left hand is placed on the chest in Khaṭakāmukha (*SR* 7.595-7).

(6) **Aṁsāñcita** : The hands are bent over the shoulders and they are moved in Vyāvarta and Parivarta. The feet moves in Nikuṭṭa. The editor of this text compares this Karaṇa with Vṛścika, in which the hands are placed over the shoulders (*SUS* 6.51 p. 125).

(7) **Argala** : One foot is stretched backward and the feet are kept apart by two tālas and a half. The hands are moved in the same manner (*NŚ* 4.117-8; *SUS* 6.6.1). *VDP* 3.20-48). *SR* : The right foot is placed on the little toe of the left foot. The knees are kept apart by two tālas and a half and they are motionless. The left hand in Alapallava is still and the right hand is a little stretched to the front (*SR*

the right hand is a little stretched to the front (*SR* 7.664-6).

(8) **Ardhanikuṭṭa :** The hands, facing each other, are bent between the head and the arms. Thus Ardhanikuṭṭa is the result of doing half of Nikuṭṭa. (*NŚ* 4.70-1; *SR* 6.607; *SDām* p. 67).

(9) **Ardhamattallī :** The feet are drawn away from Skhalita and the left hand moves in Recita. The right hand is placed on the hips (*NŚ* 4.88-9; *VDP* 3.20.44; *SDām*. p. 67). *SR* : The Nitamba and Keśabandha Vartanās are performed with the right hand. The feet are moved in agitation. The left hand assumes partial Recita (*SR* 7.631-2).

(10) **Ardharecita :** The hands move away in Sūcīmukha. The feet move in Nikuṭṭa. One side reposes in Saṅnata (*NŚ* 4.72-3; *VDP* 3.20.41; *SDām* p. 67. *SUS* : The left hand is in Recita while the right is in Khaṭakāmukha. the feet are in Nikuṭṭaka with one side bent (*SUS* 6.16). *SR* : The dancer stands in the Maṇḍalasthāna and changes her hands from Sūcīmukha to Khaṭakāmukha. The feet are in Udghaṭṭita and one side is bent (*SR* 7.628-9).

(11) **Ardhasūcī :** The Alapadma hand is placed on the head and the right foot is in Sūcī. (*NŚ* 4.137-8; *VDP* 3.20.4; *SDām* p. 66). *SUS* : This is Sūcī with the left hand curved and bent (*SUS* 6.80). *SR* : This is Sūcī done with one side of the body (*SR* 7.700).

(12) **Ardhasvastika :** The feet cross each other in Svastika. The right hand is in Karihasta and the left hand is on the chest (*NS* 4.82-3; *VDP* 3.20.43; *SDām* p. 67). *SUS* : The movement of the right hand is as in the *NŚ* but the left hand assumes Śūkatuṇḍa. The hips move in Chinnā (*SUS* 6.26). *SR* : The movements of the hand and the feet are as in the *NŚ* but Khaṭakāmukha is prescribed for the left hand.

According to *SR.* some scholars substitute Pakṣavañcitaka for Karihasta. The hands are placed on the hips in Pakṣapradyotaka and Ardhacandra (*SR* 7.585-7).

(13) **Alātaka :** One foot moves in Alāta the right hand moves down from the shoulder. The Ūrdhvajānu Cārī follows (*NŚ* 4.78-9; *VDP* 3.20.42). *SDām* : Alāta (*SDām* p. 67). *SUS* describes Ūrdhvarecita which is the same as Alāta with the exception that it prescribes Recita for Alāta (*SUS* 6.22). *SR* : The Alātā Cārī is performed. The right hand assumes Nitamba first and then Caturaśra. The left side of the body performs Ūrdhvajānu with the left foot (*SR* 7.615-6).

(14) **Avahittha :** Having performed the Janita Karaṇa, the dancer moves her hands with the palms facing each other. Then she slowly lowers them (*NŚ* 4.155-6; *SDām* p. 66). *SR* agrees with the *NŚ* but describes the hand movements in greater detail. The hands are in Arāla and Alapadma, and are moved gradually over the forehead and the chest, facing each other. Then they are moved in Udveṣṭita at the sides. In the same manner they are moved in Apaveṣṭita and placed on the chest facing each other (*SR* 7.720-3).

(15) **Ahisarpita :** Not explained (*SDām* p. 66).

(16) **Ākrānta :** Not explained (*VDP* 3.20-51).

(17) **Ākṣipta :** The hands and the feet are quickly thrown out in Ākṣipta. (*NŚ.* 4.115-6; *VDP* 3.20.48; *SDām* p. 67). *SUS* : The hands are moved in Ākṣiptarecita. The dancer looks downward with one side bent. (*SUS* 6.590). *SR* : The Ākṣiptā Cārī is performed while the hands in Khaṭakāmukha and Catura are thrown out in Ākṣipta (*SR* 7.663-4).

The right hand moves in Ākṣiptarecita. Finally, this hand is moved away in Recita (*NŚ* 4.80-1; *VDP* 3.20.43; *SDām* p. 67). *SUS* : The left hand is moved in Ākṣiptarecita, so is the right foot (*SUS* 6.24). *SR* : The hands are placed on the chest. They are raised in Vyāvartanā and are thrown down at the sides. Then one hand pointing dowards in Haṁsapakṣa, is brought forward with a quick circular movement to the chest. The other hand is moved in similar manner. The feet are in Añcita and Sūcī (*SR* 7.583-4).

(19) **Āvarta :** One foot in Kuñcita should be put forward and them turned round quickly. The hands should be moved in harmony. (*NŚ* 4.19-20); *SDām* p. 67). *SUS* : Vartita in *SUS* is the same as Āvarta in the *NŚ*. (*SUS* 6.63). *SR* : The Dolā hands are moved in Udveṣṭita and Apaveṣṭita. The Cāṣagati Cārī is performed (*SR* 7.673-4).

(20) **Utsarpita :** Not explained (*SDām* p. 66).

(21) **Udvṛtta :** The hands, the feet and the whole body is stretched out in Ākṣipta. The body performs Udvṛtta (*NŚ* 4.151-2; *SDām* p. 66; *SR* 7.731).

(22) **Udghaṭṭita :** The feet are in Udghaṭṭita, the hands are clapped and one side is bent (*NŚ* 4.163-4; *SDām* p. 66; *SR* 7.740).

(23) **Udghāṭita :** The elbows are moved to the right side of the body with the hands facing each other. The feet are moved to the left side (*SUS* 6.105).

(24) **Unmatta :** The feet are in Añcita and the hands move in Recita (*NŚ* 5.74-5; *VDP* 3.20.42; *SDām* p. 67). *SUS* : One side is bent. The dancer looks downward with her hands in Recita and the moves about in jumps (*SUS* 6.18). *SR* prescribes Āviddhā Cārī to be performed by the Añcitapāda (*SR* 7.599).

(25) **Upasṛta :** One foot is thrown out and the hands are moved in the same manner. The body is bent forward (*NŚ* 4.152-3; *SDām* p. 66). *SUS* : The left hand and the left foot are let down. The right hand is bent (*SUS* 6.94). *SR* : The Ākṣiptā Cārī is performed with the left foot. The hands are moved in Vyāvṛtta and Parivartita and placed in Arāla on the right side of the body which is bent (*SR* 7.727-8).

(26) **Ūruvṛtta :** The thighs move in Vivartita. The feet move in Recita. One hand is in Lalita and the other is in Latā (*SUS* 6.100). This term occurs also in the *VDP*. and *SDām*. which do not explain the action. The editors of *SDām*, however, think that this is a scribal error for ūrudvṛtta, a term that occurs in the *NŚ*. and *SR* (*VDP* 3.20.41; *SDām* p. 66).

(27) **Ūrudvṛtta :** One hand is moved round and then arched over to the back of the thigh. The shanks are bent and raised (*NŚ* 4.158-9). *SR* : The Arāla and Khaṭaka hands are moved in Vyāvṛtta while doing the ūrudvṛttā Cārī. Then they are placed on the thighs (*SR* 7.742-3).

(28) **Uromaṇḍala :** The feet are moved out of Svastika and they perform Apaviddha. The hands are in Uromaṇḍala (*NŚ* 4.114-5; *VDP* 3.20.48; *SDām* p. 67). *SR* : The dancer performs the Baddhā and Sthitāvartā Cārīs with her hands in Uromaṇḍala. (*SR* 7.672).

(29) **Ūruśliṣṭa :** The thighs and the feet touch each other. One side is a little bent and the left arm is raised (*SUS* 6.98).

(30) **Ūrdhvajānu :** The Kuñcitapāda is thrown up and the knee is raised to the level of the hands while the hands are moved in harmony (*NŚ* 4.85-6; *VDP* 3.20.43; *SDām*. p. 67; *NN*. 33a). *SUS* : The feet are

bent, the left being placed forward. The hands move in Vyāvṛtta and Āvartita (*SUS* 6.29). *SR* : The feet are in Kuñcita and the knees are raised. One hand in Alapadma or Arāla points upward. The knees are raised to the level of the breasts. The other hand assumes Khaṭakāmukha. Finally, the hands assume Pakṣavañcitaka (*SR* 7.626-7).

(31) **Ūrdhvarecita :** See Alātaka (*SUS* 6.22).

(32) **Elakākriḍīta :** The dancer jumps with the feet in Talsañcara and while she comes down to the ground, her body is bent and turned round (*NŚ* 4.157-8; *SDām* p. 66). *SUS* : The dancer jumps and rests her feet (on the ground). The hands are in Kuñcita and Recita (*SUS* 6.99). *SR* agrees with the *NŚ* about the movement of the body but also prescribes the Elakākriḍītā Cārī and Dolā and Khaṭakāmukha hands (*SR* 7.725).

(33) **Kaṭicchinna :** The hips moves in Chinna. The hands are repeatedly placed on the head in Pallava (*NŚ* 4.17-2; *SDām* p. 67). *VDP* : Karichinna. (*VDP* 3.20.41). *SUS* : Kaṭividdha (*SUS* 6.15). *SR* : The dancer stands in the Maṇḍalasthāna and moves her sides round. The rest is the same as in the *NŚ* (*SR* 7.608-9).

(34) **Kaṭinikuṭṭaka :** The hands are arched, one on the chest and the other on the hips, while the dancer looks downward and the rest are in Nikuṭṭa (*SUS* 6.104). The editor of this text compares this Karaṇa with Viṣkambha in the *NŚ* (*SUS* p. 136).

(35) **Kaṭibhrānta :** Having performed the Sūcī, the right foot is placed (on one side of the body after removing the left foot quickly). The hips are moved in Recita (*NŚ* 4.103-4; *SDām* p. 67). *SR* : Having performed Sūcī with the left foot, it is quickly drawn away. The right foot is placed on the right

side of the body. Bhramarī Cārī follows. The hands are moved in Vyāvṛta and Parivartita and then they are placed in Caturaśra (*SR* 7.649-51).

(36) **Kaṭirecita :** The feet are moved in Nikuṭṭa while the hands are in Latā. The hips are moved round (*SUS* 6.47).

(37) **Kaṭisama :** The feet are separated from Svastika. One hand is placed on the navel and the other on the hips. The side is raised (*NŚ* 4.79-80; *VDP* 3.20.42; *SDām.* p. 67). *SUS* : The feet move in Nikuṭṭaka while one hand is placed on the chest and the other on the hips. (*SUS.* 6.23). *SR* : The dancer performs the Ākṣiptā and Apakrāntā Cārīs and crosses her hands in Svastika. She places her right hand in Khaṭakāmukha on the navel and the left hand in Ardhacandra on the hip. One side is bent and the other side is raised. This is done in the Vaiṣṇava Sthāna (*SR* 7.610-2).

(38) **Karihasta :** One hand is placed on the chest and the other moves in Udveṣṭita. One foot is in Añcita (*NŚ* 4.147-9; *VDP* 3.20.52; *SDām* p. 66). *SUS* : The left foot moves back while the right foot moves forward. The left hand is bent and placed on the hips (*SUS* 6.89). *SR* : According to *SR*, the hand that is placed on the chest should be in Khaṭakāmukha. The other hand is in Tripatākā and it is moved in Udveṣṭita and placed near the ear. The foot in other side should be moved in Añcita (*SR* 7.710-1).

(39) **Kuñcita :** The right foot and the right hand are bent. The same hand is turned upward and placed on the left side (*NŚ* 4.112-3; *VDP* 3.20.47; *SDām* p. 66). *SUS* : The right leg touches the ground while the left leg is bent. The hands are a little bent (*SUS* 65.56). *SR* : The right hand is raised and placed on the left side in Alapadma. The feet are in Agratalasañcara (*SR* 7.674-5).

(40) **Kuṭṭa :** Not explained (*SDām* p. 67).

(41) **Krānta :** One foot is bent back in Kuñcita. Then Atikrānta is performed. The hands are thrown down (*NŚ* 4.111-2; *SDām* p. 66). *SUS* : The hands assume Khaṭikāmukha. One side is bent and the feet are in Recita (*SUS* 6.55). *SR* : One leg is bent on the ground in the Atikrāntā Cārī. One hand is moved away in Vyāvṛtta and then it is again moved away in Parivartita. The same hand is placed on the chest in Khaṭakāmukha. The action is repeated by the other side of the body (*SR* 7.655-6).

(42) **Kṣipra :** Not explained (*VDP* 3.20.43).

(43) **Gangāvataraṇa :** The feet are raised with the soles turned up. The hands are turned down in Tripatākā and the head is bent (*NŚ* 4.168-9; *VDP* 3.20.53; *SR* 7.747; *NN* 32b). *SDām* : This text contains an unexplained term, Aṅgāvabharaṇa, which may be conjectured to be a scribal error for Gaṅgāvataraṇa (*SDām* p. 66). *SUS* : The left leg is raised while the left hand is in Recita. The chest is raised. (*SUS.* 6.110).

(44) **Gajakriḍīta :** The left hand is arched over the ear the right hand is in Latā. Dolapāda is then performed (*NŚ* 4.128-9; *SDām* p. 66). *SUS* : The right leg is placed at the back while the right hand is put forward. The left leg points upward (*SUS* 6.72). *SR* : There is nothing about the right hand. It prescribes Karihasta for the left hand. The rest are the same as in the *NŚ* (*SR.* 7.689-90).

(45) **Gaṇḍasūcī :** The feet are in Sūcī. One side is bent. One hand is placed on the chest and the other touches the cheek in a curve (*NŚ* 4.131-2; *VDP* 3.20.50; *SDām* p. 66). *SUS* : One foot is in Agratalasañcara while the other, the right, is bent. One hand touches the cheeks in a curve (*SUS*

6.74). *SR* prescribes Khaṭakāmukha for the right hand and Alapallava for the left hand. The rest of the action is the same as in the *NŚ*. According to *SR*, some critics advise that one foot should be placed in Sūcī on one cheek. Other critics sąy that it is the hand that should touch the cheek in Sūcīmukha (*SR* 7.690-2).

(46) **Garuḍapluta :** The feet are extended backward. One hand is in Latā and the other is in Recita. The head is raised (*NŚ* 4.130-1; *VDP* 3.20.50; *SDām* p. 66). *SR* : The feet are placed in Vṛścika. The rest is the same as in the *NŚ* (*SR* 7.693).

(47) **Gṛdhrāvalīnaka :** One foot is extended backward. One knee is a little bent while the arms are stretched out (*NŚ* 4.134-5; *VDP* : 3.20.51; *SDām* p. 66). *SUS* : The feet are placed five tālas apart, the hands are left down and the dancer looks to the front (*SUS* 6.77). *SR* : The foot which is extended backward should touch the ground with its big toe and the hands should move in Latā (*SR* 7.697).

(48) **Ghūrṇita :** The right hand is moved round. The left hand is in Dolā. The feet are drawn away from Svastika (*NŚ* 4.92-3; *VDP* 3.20.44; *SDām* p. 67). *SUS* : The right hand, the head and the feet, all move round (*SUS* 6.36). *SR* : The (right) hand moves out from the side and raised in Vyāvartanā. Then it points downward in Parivartanā. The foot of that side assumes the Aparkrāntā Cārī. The left hand is in Dolā (*SR* 7.624-5).

(49) **Catura :** The left hand is in Añcita while the right hand is in Catura. The right foot moves up and down (*NŚ* 4.99-100; *VDP* 3.20.45; *SDam* p. 67). *SUS*; Catura is substituted by Khaṭikāmukha. Nothing is said about the feet (*SUS* 6.43). *SR* prescribes Alapallava for Añcita (*SR* 7.648-9).

(50) **Cakramaṇḍala :** The hands hang down and the body is bent in (*NŚ* 4.113-4; *VDP* 3.20.47; *SDām* p. 66). *SUS* : The hands are placed on the thighs with the right hand bent. The dancer spins like a wheel. (*SUS* 6.57). *SR* : The dancer performs the Additā Cārī and with her hands in Dolā, bends her body to the front and spins like a wheel (*SR* 7.671).

(51) **Candrāvarta :** One foot is raised at the side to touch the ear and the dancer moves slowly in Bhramarikā holding her big toe with her hand (*NN* 33a).

(52) **Chinna :** The hands in Alapadma are placed on the hips which moves repeatedly in Chinna. The action is performed in the Vaiśākha Sthāna (*NŚ* 4.105-6; *VDP* 3.20.46 (twice); *SR* 7.643; *NN* 32b). *SDām* : Chinnaka (*SDām* p. 67). *SUS* : The hands in Tripatākā are moved in Vyāvartanā and Āvartanā. The rest agrees with the *NŚ* (*SUS* 6.49).

(53) **Janita :** With one hand placed on the chest and the other hanging down, the dancer stands on her toes (*NŚ* 4.154-5; *SDām* p. 66; *NN* 33a). *SUS* : The right hand is in Latā while the left hand is in Recita. The legs are bent and so is the neck (*SUS* 6.96). *SR* agrees with the *NŚ* but discusses this Karaṇa in greater detail. The Janitā Cārī is performed with one hand in Muṣṭi placed on the chest and the other hand is in Latā (*SR* 7.726).

(54) **Ḍolāpāda :** One foot in Kuñcita is thrown up and then moved from one side to the other. The hands are moved in harmony (*NŚ* 4.120-1) *VDP*: Dolāpāda (*VDP* 3.20.49, 52). *SDām* : Dolāpāda. (*SDām*. p. 67). *SUS* : Dolāpāda : The feet are first moved in Kuñcita and then they are moved from one side to the other. The palms are shown (*SUS* 6.64). *SR* : The Ūrdhvajānu and Dolāpāda Cārīs are performed successively. The hands are in Dolā (*SR* 7.676).

(55) **Taḍitbhrānta :** Not explained (*VDP* 3.20.44).

(56) **Talapuṣpapuṭa :** One hand should be on the left side in Puṣpapuṭa, one foot should be in Agratalasañcara and one side should be in Saṁnata. (*NŚ* 4.61-2; *SDām* p. 67; *SUS* 6.6; *NN* 33a). *VDP* : Talapuṣpa. (*VDP* 3.20.40). *SR* : The dancer does the Adhyardhikā Cārī and stretches out her right leg. She moves her hands in Vyavartanā and brings them to her right side. Then she moves her hands in Parivartanā and brings them to the left side which is bent in Saṁnata. Then she places them on her breasts in Puṣpapuṭa. The feet are in Agratalasañcara (*SR* 7.568-71).

(57) **Talavilāsita :** One foot is raised and extended at the side with the toe and the sole turned up. The palms are bent (*NŚ* 4.116-7; *SDām* p. 67; *NN*. 33a). *VDP* : The unexplained term Latālasita (Lalālasita in the translation of the text, vol. II. p. 43) in the *VDP* is thought by the editor to be Talavilāsita (*VDP* 3.20.8, p. 51). *SR* : The movemnt of the foot agrees with the description given in the *NŚ* while the hands in Patākā are joined at their tips. The action is repeated on the other side of the body (*SR* 7.667). *SUS* : The Patākā hands are moved round and joined in Añjali. The movement of the foot is the same as in the *NŚ* (*SUS* 6.60).

(58) **Talasaṅghaṭṭita :** Having performed Dolāpāda, the hands are clapped repeatedly. Then the left hand is moved in Recita (*NŚ* 4.153-4; *SDām* p. 66). *SUS* : The feet rub against the ground in Agratalasañcara. One side is in Vivartita (*SUS* 6.95). *SR* : It agrees with the *NŚ*. in describing this Karaṇa but describes some other actions as well. The dancer stands in the Vaiṣṇava Sthāna and moves her Patākā hands in Recita. Then she places her right hand on her hips and the left hand is moved in Recita. These actions

are performed with the actions described in the *NŚ* (*SR* 7.729-30).

(59) **Talasaṁsphoṭita :** A leg is lifted quickly and put forward. The Talasaṁsphoṭita hands are presented simultaneously (*NŚ* 4.129-30; *SDām* p. 66). *SUS* : The movements of the hands agree with the *NŚ* while the feet rub against the ground. The dancer moves in four directions (*SUS* 6.73). The feet are quickly thrown up in the Daṇḍapādā and the Atikrāntā Cārīs and put forward. The hands are clapped (*SR* 7.694-5).

(60) **Daṇḍapakṣa :** Having performed Ūrdhvajānu Latā hands should be plasced on the knees (*NŚ* 4.94-5; *VDP* 3.20.45; *SDām* p. 66; *NN* 33a). *SUS* : It prescribes placing one hand on the knee which is lifted. The other foot is bent (*SUS* 6.38). *SR* prescribes the same action done on both sides (*SR* 7.636-7).

(61) **Daṇḍapāta :** The feet are extended in Daṇḍapāda after performing Nūpura. The Āviddhavakra is performed quickly (*NŚ* 4.142-3; *SDām*; p. 66); *SUS*: Daṇḍapāta : The feet are bent forward and then extended straight like a staff. The hands are in Āviddha. (*SUS* 6.84). *SR* : Agrees with the *NŚ* in prescribing the Nūpurapādikā and Dolāpādā Cārīs. The hands are placed straight like a staff (*SR* 7.704).

(62) **Daṇḍarecita :** The hands and the feet are thrown out in all directions rigidly and they move in Recita. (*NŚ* 4.101-2; *SDām* p. 67). *SUS* : Does not ask the dancer to move her hands and feet in Recita though it agrees with the *NŚ* in describing the rest of the action (*SUS* 6.45). *SR* : The Daṇḍapādā Cārī is performed with the hands in Daṇḍapakṣa (*SR* 7.646-7).

(63) **Diksvastika** : The hands and the feet are placed in Svastika in front or at the sides of the dancer (*NŚ* 4.77-8; *VDP* 3.20.42; *SDām* p. 67). *SUS* directs that the action should be performed at the left side of the dancer. (*SUS* 6.21). *SR* : Svastika is performed at the sides, the front and the back. The hands and the feet move in Recita. The text says that the ancient masters of this art employed this Karaṇa while singing. This can be employed to other forms of Svastika as well (*SR* 7.587-9).

(64) **Nata** : Not explained (*VDP* 3.20.51).

(65) **Nāgaprakiriḍita** : Not explained (*VDP* 3.20.50).

(66) **Nāgarasarapita**: The feet are moved away from Svastika. The head moves in Parivāhita. The hands are moved in Recita (*NŚ* 4.166-7; *SR* 7.745-6). *SUS* : In describing the movements of the feet the *SUS* agrees with the *NŚ* The face rests on the right shoulder while the hands move in Latā and Recita (*SUS* 6.108).

(67) **Nīkuñcita** : One foot moves in Vṛścika. The (left) hand is bent at the side. The right hand is arched over the tip of the nose, barely touching it. (*NŚ* 4.86-7; *SDām*. p. 67). *VDP* : mentions this term twice (*VDP* 3.20.43.49). *SUS* : The hands are in Khaṭikāamukha. The feet are a little bent and the hips are bent. (*SUS* 6.30). *SR* agrees with the *NŚ* differing only in prescribing that one hand in Arāla should be placed near the head and the other hand which is arched over the tip of the nose touching it, should assume Arāla on the chest. Some scholars prescribe Patākā and Sūcyāsya of the hands (*SR* 7.621-3).

(68) **Nikuṭṭaka** : The hands move in Nikuṭṭaka between the head and the arm. The feet are also moved in Nikuṭṭa (*NŚ* 4.69-70; *VDP*. 3.20.41). *SUS* : Nikuṭṭita:

The hands move above the shoulders in Añcita (*SUS* 6.14). *SR* : The dancer stands in the Maṇḍala Sthāna and moves her right hand in the Udveṣṭita Karaṇa assuming Caturaśra near the shoulder and the head. The same hand in Alapadma should move its last two fingers up and down. Then the right hand assuming Caturaśra, is moved in Āviddhavakravartanā and the right foot is moved in Udghaṭṭita. This action is repeated by the left hand and the left foot (*SR* 7.603-6).

(69) **Nikuntaka :** Not explained (*SDām*. p. 67).

(70) **Nitamba :** The arms are raised with the palms facing each other. Then the Baddhā Cārī is performed (*NŚ* 4.145-6; *VDP* 3.20.52; *SDām* p. 66). *SUS* : The arms move in Recita with the palms facing each other. The feet cross in Svastika (*SUS* 6.87). *SR* The Patākā hands, with the fingers pointing down are brought near the head and moved out from the shoulder in Parivṛtta. They are placed in the Nitambavartanā, facing each other and facing the body (*SR* 7.714-5).

(71) **Nitambasvastika :** The hands are bent and placed on the hips. The feet are moved away from Svastika. The right side is bent (*SUS* 6.58).

(72) **Nivṛtta :** See Vivṛtta (*SUS* 6.66; *VDP* 3.20.49).

(73) **Niveśa :** The hands are placed on the chest which is in Nirbhugna. The dancer assumes the Maṇḍala Sthāna (*NŚ* 4.156-7; *SDām* p. 66). *SR* : Prescribes Khaṭakāmukha for the hands. The rest of the action is the same as in the *NŚ* (*SR* 7.724).

(74) **Niśumbhita :** Nistambhita in the GOS edition of the *NŚ*. One foot in Kuñcita, is moved back. The chest is in Samunnata. The hand is placed in Tilaka (*NŚ* 4.124-5; *NN* 33a-b). *SDām* : Niśumbhita (*SDām* p. 66). *SR* : One foot in Kuñcita is placed on the heel

of the other. The chest is raised in Samunnata. The middle finger of the Khaṭaka hand is placed on the forehead in the form of a Tilaka (*SR* 7.682-3). *SUS* : See Pṛṣthakuñcita (*SUS* 6.68).

(75) **Nūpura** : The hips should be turned round gracefully. The hands should move in Latā and Recita. One foot should perform Nūpura (*NŚ* 4.96-7; *VDP* 3.20.45; *SDām* p. 67). *SUS* : The hips and the neck are bent as well (*SUS* 6.40). *SR* prescribes the Bhramarī Cārī. The rest of the action is the same as in the *NŚ* (*SR* 7.639-40).

(76) **Patitotpatita** : The right leg is bent and one foot is moved up and down. The hands follow the movements of the foot (*SUS* 6.97). *SUS* : The editor of this text compares this Karaṇa with the Avahittha Karaṇa in the *NŚ* (*SUS* p. 134).

(77) **Parikṣipta** : Not explained (*VDP* 3.20.50).

(78) **Parivṛtta** : The hands are raised in Apaveṣṭita, the feet are moved round in Sūcī. The hips are turned round (*NŚ* 4.131-2; *VDP* 3.20.49; *SDām* p. 66). *SUS* : The hands move in Añcita and the feet, the hips and the waist are moved round (*SUS* 6.75). *SR* : The hands are in Ūrdhvamaṇḍala. The Baddhā Cārī is performed with feet in Sūcī. The dancer moves round in the Bhramarī Cārī (*SR* 7.703).

(79) **Pādakrānta** : One foot is curved and pointed upward. The other foot is placed forward. The hands are raised in Dolā (*SUS* 6.102). The editor of this text compares it with the Viṣṇukrānta mentioned in the *NŚ* (*SUS* p. 135).

(80) **Pādāpaviddhaka** : The Khaṭakāmukha hands are placed on the navel with palms turned upwards. The feet are in Sūcīviddha and Apakrānta (*NŚ* 4.90-1). *VDP* Pādaviddha (*VDP* 3.20.44). *SDām* : Pādaviddhaka (*SDām*. p. 67). *SUS* prescribes the

Khaṭikāmukha hands to be placed on the navel and says nothing about turning them upward. The rest of the action is the same as in the *NŚ* (*SUS* 6.34). *SR* : The movement of the hands agree with the *NŚ*. One foot in Sūcī is brought to touch the other and the Apakrāntā Cārī is performed with the same foot. The action is repeated by the other foot (*SR* 7.638-9).

(81) **Pārśvakrānta :** (The foot) is put forward after doing Apakrānta. The hands are moved in harmony (*NŚ* 4.123-4; *SDām* p. 66; *SUS* 6.67). *VDP* : Pārśvākrānta. (*VDP*. 3.20.49). *SR* : it substitutes Pārśvakrānta for Apakrānta, the rest being the same as in the *NŚ* (*SR* 7.695-6).

(82) **Pārśvajānu :** One foot is kept normally and the other is placed on the thigh. One hand is placed in Muṣṭi on the chest (*NŚ* 4.133; *SDām* p. 66; *NN* 33a). *VDP* : Pārśvajānuka (*VDP* 3.20.50). *SUS* : The hands should be bent. In describing rest of the action the *SUS* agrees with the *NŚ* (*SUS* 6.76). *SR* prescribes stretching backward the foot which should be placed on the thigh according to the *NŚ*. The *NŚ* prescribes action for one hand only while the other hand, according to *SR*. should be plced on the hips in Ardhacandra (*SR* 7.695-6).

(83) **Pārśvanikuṭṭaka :** The hands are in Svastika and they are placed on one side. The feet are in Nikuṭṭa. (*NŚ*. 4.109-10). *SDām* Pārśvakuṭṭa (*SDām* p. 67). *SUS* : The left foot is slightly bent and the right foot moves in Nikuṭṭa. The face rests on the left shoulder (*SUS* 6.53). *SR* : The hands in Svastika are placed, one pointing up and the other pointing down. The rest of the action is the same as in the *NŚ* (*SR* 7.669-70).

(84) **Pārṣṇisaṅghatṭṭita :** The hands in Kartarimukha are arched over the chest. The heels rub against the thighs (*SUS* 6.93).

(85) **Pṛṣṭhakuñcita** : This seems to be the same as the Niśumbhita Karaṇa. The text prescribes bending the body as well (*SUS* 6.68).

(86) **Pṛṣṭhasvastika** : The hands move in Vikṣiptākṣipta. The feet cross each other in Svastika. Apakrānta and Ardhasūcī are performed (*NŚ* 4.76-7; *VDP* 3.20.42; *SDām* p. 67). *SUS* : The hands move in Vyāvṛtta and Āvartita. Then they are placed on the back. The feet cross in Ākṣipta (*SUS* 6.20). *SR* : The arms are extended in Udveṣṭita. The Apakrāntā Cārī follows. Then Apavestita is perfomed. The other foot is moved in Recita, performing Sūcī. The hands and the feet are crossed in Svastika (*SR* 7.589-91).

(87) **Prasarpitaka** : One hand is in Recita and the other is in Latā. The feet are dragged on the ground, rubbing it (*NŚ* 4.148-9; *SDām.* p. 66). *VDP* : Prasarpitatala (*VDP* 3.20.53). *SUS* : It prescribes Śukatuṇḍa in place of Latā and the feet are to be moved in Nikuṭṭa. (*SUS* 6.90). *SR* : The foot that is on the same side as the hand, is rubbed against the ground and the other foot moves slowly. The rest is the same as in the *NŚ* (*SR* 7.711.2).

(88) **Preṅkholita** : After doing Dolāpāda, the dancer jumps up and on coming down, she moves her hips round (*NŚ* 4.144-5; *VDP* 3.20.52; *SDām* p. 66). *SUS* : The dancer moves her body in half circles, first backward and then forward. The hands are contracted at the end (*SUS* 6.86). *SR* : Prescribes the Bhramarī Cārī which is performed by moving the hips round. The rest is the same as in the *NŚ* (*SR.* 7.706-7).

(89) **Bṛṁhita** : See Mattallī (*SUS* 6.31).

(90) **Bhujaṅgatrastarecita** : First Bhujaṅgatrāsita is to be performed. Then the hands in Recita should be

moved to the left side (of the dancer) (*NŚ* 4.95-6; *VDP* 3.20.45: *SUS* 6.39; *SR* 7.644-5). *SDām* : Bhujañgasra (tra) starecita (*SDām* p. 66).

(91) **Bhujaṅgatrāsita :** One foot in Kuñcita is thrown up and one thigh is moved obliquely. The hips and the knees are also moved (*NŚ* 4.84-5; *VDP* 3.20.43; *SDām* p. 66). *SUS* : The left hand is raised and then bent in Khaṭikāmukha. The right hand points downwards. (*SUS* 6.28). *SR* : Having performed the Bhujañgatrāsitā Cārī, one foot in Kuñcita is thrown up. The thighs, the hips and the knees are moved round obliquely. One hand in Dolā moves in Vyavṛtta and Parivartita (*SR* 7.613-4).

(92) **Bhujañgāñcita :** The right foot is in Bhujañgatrāsita. The right hand is moved in Recita and the left hand is in Latā (*NŚ* 4.100-1; *VDP* 3.20.46; *SDām* p. 66). *SUS* : The right hand is placed on the hips in Añcita. (*SUS* 6.44). *SR*. agrees with the *NŚ* (*SR* 7.645-6).

(93) **Bhramaraka :** The feet are first placed in Ākṣipta and then in Svastika. The hands move in Udveṣtita. The hips are turned round (*NŚ* 4.98-9: *VDP* 3.20.45). *SDām* ; Bhramara. (*SDām* p. 66). *SUS* : The hands are in Recita as well. The feet are only in Svastika (*SUS* 6.42). *SR* : The Ākṣiptā Cārī is performed. The rest is the same as in the *NŚ* (*SR* 7.641-2).

(94) **Bhrāmita :** Not explained (*VDP* 3.20.48).

(95) **Maṇḍalasvastika :** The hands are placed in Svastika with the palms turned up and facing the front. The body should be in the Maṇḍala Sthāna (*NŚ* 4.68-9; *VDP* 3 20.41; *SDām* p. 66; *SUS* 6.12) (*SR* : Having moved the hands in Caturaśra, the Vicyavā Cārī is performed. After performing the Udveṣṭita Karaṇa the hands form Ūrdhvamaṇḍala. Svastika is performed finally. The dancer stands in the Maṇḍala Sthāna (*SR* 7.579-80).

(96) **Mattallī :** The left and the right feet are thrown back with a whirling movement. The hands move in Udveṣṭita and thrown back (*NŚ* 4.87-88; *SDām* p. 66). *VDP* : Mattalli (*VDP* 3.20.44). *SUS* has Bṛṁhita which is the same as Mattaḷḷī with the exception that the hands are moved in Vyāvṛtta and Āvartita (*SUS* 6.31). *SR* agrees with the second part of the action given in the *NŚ*, the first part being to move the ankles in Svastika (*SR* 7.630-1).

(97) **Madaskhalitaka :** The hands are let down, the head is in Parivāhita and the feet are moved round and turned away (*NŚ*. 4.159-60). *SUS* : Madanaskhalitaka. The hands are in Latā while the feet are slack. The head is bent and the face assumes various expressions (*SUS* 6.101). *SR* agrees with the *NŚ* but describes this Karaṇa in greater detail. The Janitā Cārī is performed with one hand in Muṣti placed on the chest and the other hand is in Latā (*SR* 7.734-5).

(98) **Mayūralalita :** Vṛścika is performed by one foot. The hands are moved in Recita. The hips are turned round (*NŚ* 4.140-1; *VDP* 3.20.51; *SDām* p. 67). *SR* directs the dancer to perform the Bhramarī Cārī by moving the hips round (*SR* 7.705-6).

(99) **Maṇḍita :** Not explained (*VDP* 3.20.51).

(100) **Mukula :** Not explained (*SDām* p. 67).

(101) **Recitanikuṭṭita :** The hands move in Recita. The right foot moves in Nikuṭṭa. The left hand moves in Dolā. (*NŚ* 4.89-90; *SUS* 6.33). *VDP* : Recakanikuṭṭaka. (*VDP* 3.20.44). *SR* : Recakanikuṭṭaka. It prescribes Udghaṭṭita of the feet (*SR* 7.633).

(102) **Recita :** The feet move in Nikuñcita while the hands are in Recita. The hips are also moved in Recita (*SUS* 6.13; *VDP* 3.20.45). *SDām* : Recaka (*SDām* p. 67).

(103) **Latākuñcita :** The left hand is in Latā while the right hand is arched. The hips move in Chinnā. The legs are bent (*SUS* 6.103).

(104) **Latālasita :** See Talavīlāsita. (*VDP*. 3.20.48).

(105) **Latāvṛścika :** One foot moves backward in Añcita with the toes curved up. The left hand is in Latā (*NŚ* 4.104-5; *VDP* 3.20.46; *SDām* p. 67; *NN* 33b). *SUS* : The left hand and the left foot are in Vṛścika while the right hand is in Latā (*SUS* 6.48). *SR* : The foot is moved in Vṛścika. The movement of the hand agrees with the *NŚ* (*SR* 7.662).

(106) **Lalaṭatilaka :** One foot moves in Vṛścika and with its big toe a tilaka is marked on the forehead (*NŚ* 4.110-1; *VDP* 3.20.47; *SDām* p. 67; *SR* 7.668; *NN* 33b). *SUS* : The hands move up and down in Vyāvṛtta and Parivartita. The left foot touches the forehead (*SUS* 6.54).

(107) **Lalita :** The left hand is in Karihasta. The right hand is moved round. One foot is repeatedly moved up and down (*NŚ* 4.93-4; *VDP* 3.20.45; *SDām* p. 67). *SUS* : The hands are moved with the left hand in Khaṭikāmukha. The body moves in graceful manner (*SUS* 6.37). *SR* : Prescribes that the right hand be moved in the Nitamba and Kesabandha Vartanās. The rest of the action is the same as in the *NŚ* (*SR* 7.634).

(108) **Līna :** The Patākā hands are replaced on the chest in Añjali. The neck is elongated while the shoulders are bent in Nihañcita (*NŚ* 4.66-71; *SDām* p. 67; *SUS*. 6.10; *VDP* (twice). 3.20.40; 51; *NN* 33a). *SR* : Having moved the hands in Ūrdhvamaṇḍala the dancer places them on the chest in Añjali. The shoulders are in Nihañcita, while the neck is bent (*SR* 7.572-3).

(109) **Lolita :** The hands are arched and moved in Recita. The head is moved in Lolita on all sides (*NŚ* 4.1455-6; *SDām* p. 66). *SUS* prescribes Lolita of the feet as well which is Lolana (*SUS* 6.107). *SR* : One hand is moved in Recitạ and the other hand is placed on the chest in Alapallava. The head moves in all directions in Lolita. The dancer stands in the Vaiṣṇava Sthāna (*SR* 7.733-4).

(110) **Vaktramarecita :** The heels are joined together while the left hand is moved round in Recita (*SUS* 6.32). The editor of this text compares this Karaṇa with Ardhamattallī in which the hands are moved in Recita (*SUS* p. 121).

(111) **Vakṣorecita :** The same as Vyaṁsita (*SUS* 6.52).

(112) **Vakṣaḥsvastika :** The feet cross each other in Svastika. The hands move in Recita near the chest which is arched (*NŚ* 4.73-4; *VDP* 3.20.42, *SDām* p. 67). *SUS* : The feet move in Nikuñcita once. The hands cross in Svastika on the chest. The hips are moved in Valana (*SUS* 6.17). *SR*: Having moved the hands in Caturaśra, the dancer moves them in Recita and after performing Vyāvartanā, places them on the Ābhugna chest. The hands are crossed in Svastika, so are the legs (*SR* 7.581-2).

(113) **Vartita :** Having moved the hands in Vyāvṛtta and Parivartita, the dancer bends them at the wrists. Then she places them on the thighs (*NŚ* 4.62-3). *SDām* : Varjita. (Vartita ?) (*SDām* p. 67). *SUS* : Vartita is the same as Āvarta. (*SUS* 6.63). *SR* : The hands are crossed at the wrists in Svastika facing each other. Then they are separated over the chest. At the same time they are to be moved in Vyāvṛtta and Parivartita. They are raised and then placed on the thighs. (*SR* 7.573-6).

(114) **Valita :** One hand is thrown out while the feet are in Sūcī. The hips are turned round. (*NŚ* 4.91-2; *VDP* 3.20.44; *SDām* p. 67). *SUS* : Prescribes Sūcīmukha for the hands and says nothing about the feet. The face should be charming (*SUS* 6.35). *SR* : One hand in Sūcīmukha is moved away from the body. The feet are drawn away from Sūcī. The Bhramarī Cārī follows. The body is charmingly moved (*SR* 7.635-6).

(115) **Valitoru :** The Śukatuṇḍa hands are moved in Vyavṛtta and Parivartita simultaneously. The thighs are moved VDP 3.20.44; *SDām* p. 67). *SUS* : Prescribes Sūcīmukha to be moved in Vyavṛtta and Parivartita simultaneously and they are brought together by doing Parivartanā in the Ākṣiptā Cārī. Then they are placed on the chest in Śukatuṇḍa, pointing downwards and the dancer stands after doing the Baddhā Cārī. (*SR.* 7.576-8).

(116) **Vānarapluta :** Not explained (*VDP* 3.20.48).

(117) **Vikṣipta :** The hands and the feet are thrown backward and in the same manner they are moved sideways. (*NŚ* 4.118-9; *VDP* 3.20.48; *SDām* p. 67). *SUS* : The left foot in Vṛsścika and the left hand in Latā are thrown forward and sideways (*SUS* 6.62). *SR* : The Vidyudbhrāntā Cārī and the Daṇḍapādā Cārī are performed successively. The hands are moved jointly to the same direction in Udveṣṭita and Apaveṣṭita and are thrown out to the front, at the back and at the sides. (*SR.* 7.686-7).

(118) **Vikṣiptākṣiptaka :** The hands and the feet are thrown up and down (*NŚ* 4.81-2; *SDām* p. 67; *SUS* 6.25). *SR* : One hand is moved in Vyavartanā and thrown outward, one leg is thrown outward. The other hand assuming Caturaśra is moved in Parivartanā and thrown out, the other leg being moved in the same manner (*SR* 7.616-20).

(119) **Viddha :** Not explained (*SDām* p. 67).

(120) **Vidyudbhrānta :** One foot is moved round backward and then it is extended (and arched) to touch the head (*NŚ* 4.125-6; *SDām* p. 66). *SR* does not direct the dancer to touch the head with her foot, but to move round the foot backward near the head. (*SR* 7.684). *NN* : *The* Vidyudbhrāntā Cārī is performed with the hands moved in harmony (*NN* 33a).

(121) **Vinivṛtta :** Sūcīviddha is performed first. The hips are turned round and the hands are moved in Recita. (*NŚ* 4.122-3). *SUS* : The hands move in Recita. One side is in Vivartita while the left foot is in Nivartita. (*SUS*. 6.65). *SR* : One foot in Sūcī is crossed in Svastika touching the heel of the other. The hips are moved round from one side in Vyāvṛtti and Pratyāvṛtti. The Baddhā Cārī is performed. The hands are in Recita (*SR* 7.678-9).

(122) **Vipluta :** Not explained (*VDP* 5.20.50).

(123) **Vilāsa :** Not explained (*VDP* 3.20.48).

(124) **Vilolita :** Apakrānta is performed and the right leg crosses the left in Svastika. The hands are joined at the wrists (*SUS* 6.82). The editor of this text compares this Karaṇa with Apakrānta in the *NŚ* (*SUS* p. 131).

(125) **Vivartitaka :** One hand and one foot are thrown out. The hips are turned round. The other hand is moved in Recita (*NŚ* 4.127-8; *VDP* 3.20.49; *SR* 7.688-9). *SDām* : Vivartaka (*SDām* p. 66). *SUS* : In describing the movements of the hips and the feet the *SUS* agrees with the *NŚ*, but the left hand is in Latā while the right hand is moved to one side (*SUS* 6.71).

(126) **Vivṛtta :** The hands and the feet are thrown out. The hips are moved round. The hands are moved in

Recita. (*NŚ.* 4.121-2). *SDām.* : Vi (ni) vṛtta. (*SDām.* p. 66). *SUS* : Nivṛtta ; The hands and the feet are moved round in Svastika (*SUS* 6.66). *SR* : The feet are thrown out in the Ākṣiptā Cārī. The hands are also thrown out in Vyāvartanā and Parivartanā. Bhramarī is performed while the hands are moved in Recita (*SR* 7.677-8).

(127) **Viṣṇukrānta :** One foot is put forward and bent as if to start walking. The hands are moved in Recita (*NŚ* 4.160-1; *VDP* 3.20.51; *SDām* p. 66; *SR* 7.732).

(128) **Viṣkambha :** One hand, placed in Sūcī, strikes the other while one foot is in Nikuṭṭaka. Then the left hand is placed on the chest (*NŚ* 4.162-3). *SDām* : Vikaṣṭa (Viskambha?) (*SDām* p. 66) *SR* : The right hand in Sūcīmukha strikes the left hand. The (left) foot performs Nikuṭṭa. The left hand is placed on the chest. The action is repeated on the outer side of the body. Then the right foot assumes Sūcī while the right hand assumes Alapadma. The left hand returns to the previous pose. The whole action is performed repeatedly (*SR* 7.737-9).

(129) **Vaiśākharecita :** The hands, the feet, the hips and the neck move in Recita. The action is performed in the Vaiśākha Sthāna (*NŚ* 4.97-8; *SR* 7.657-8; *NN* 33a). *ŚDām* : Viśākharecita. (*SDām* p. 67). *SUS* : The Arāla and the Recita hands are moved in Vyāvartaṇā. The action is done in the Vaiśākha Sthāna (*SUS* 6.41).

(130) **Vṛścika :** The hands are bent over the shoulders and one foot is bent and turned towards the back. The dancer bends her body far back (*NŚ* 4.107-8; *VDP* 3.20.47; *SDām* p. 67). *SR* prescribes Karihasta for the hands and says nothing about the movements. One foot is bent and turned towards the back like the tail of a scorpion (*SR* 7.658-9).

(131) **Vṛścikakuṭṭita :** One foot is moved in Vṛścika and the hands are moved in Nikuṭṭa (*NŚ* 4.102-3; *SDām* p. 67). *SUS* : Vṛścikanikuṭṭita: It prescribes Vṛścika for the right foot while the left foot is kept normally (*SUS* 6.46). *SR* prescribes Alapadma for the hands which are to be moved over the shoulder in Nikuṭṭa (*SR* 7.660).

(132) **Vṛścikarecita :** One foot moves in Vṛścika while the hands cross each other in Svaṣtika. Then they are moved in Recita and Viprakīrṇa. (*NŚ* 4.106-7; *VDP* 3.20.46; (twice); *SDām* p. 67; *SR* 7.661-2;). *SUS* : The right foot is in Vṛścika while the right hand is in Recita. The hips are a little curved (*SUS* 6.50).

(133) Vṛ**ṣabhakriḍīta :** Alāta is performed first. The hands move in Recita and then they are bent and inverted. *NŚ* 4.164-5; *VDP.* 3.20.53; *SDām* p. 66). *SUS* : The feet move in Nikuṭṭa, the hips are bent, the hands are inverted, so are the feet. One side is bent (*SUS* 6.106). *SR* : The Alapadma hands are moved in Vyāvartanā and inverted on the shoulders. The rest is the same as in the *NŚ* (*SR* 7.744).

(134) **Vyaṁsita :** The action is performed in the Ālīḍha Sthāna. The hands move near the chest in Recita. Then they move up and down in Viprakīrṇa (*NŚ* 4.108-9; *VDP* 3.20.47). *SDām* : Vyaṅgita (*Vyaṁsita?*). (*SDām* p. 67). *SUS* has Vakṣorecita which is the same as Vyaṁsita (*SUS* 6.52). *SR* : One hand is spread out below in Udveṣṭita, the other is raised in Viprakīrṇa and brought near the chest. Both hands move in Recita, one palm turned up and the other turned down. The action is performed in the Ālīḍha Sthāna (*SR* 7.652-4).

(135) **Śakaṭāsya :** The body is at rest. One foot is stretched in Talasañcara and the chest is in Udvāhita (*NŚ* 4.167-8; *SDām.* p. 66). *SUS* : The left hand is placed

on the chest and the right hand points downwards and the legs are bent (*SUS* 6.109). *SR* : The Śakaṭāsyā Cārī is performed by stretching one hand and one leg while other hand is plasced on the chest in Khaṭakāmukha (*SR* 7.741).

(136) **Śīrṣāvalita :** The right foot and the head are moved round backwards. The hands are bent and they move up and down (*SUS* 6.69). The editor of this next compares this Karaṇa with Vidyudbhrānta (*SUS* p. 131).

(137) **Saṁnata :** The dancer jumps up and places her feet forward in Svastika. The hands are bent. (*NŚ* 4.135-6). *SUS* : The hands are let down and the dancer looks to the front. (*SUS.* 6.77). *SR* : According to *SR.* the dancer jumps in Mṛgapluta and crosses her legs in Svastika while her hands are bent in Dolā (*SR* 7.707-8).

(138) **Saṁjñita :** Not explained. In the translation of the text, i.e. vol. II, the editor gives the term as Sañcita (*VDP* 3.20.43; vol. II, p. 42, Karaṇa No. 22).

(139) **Sambhrānta :** One hand is moved in Āvartita and it is then arched over the thigh. The thigh is in Āviddha (*NŚ* 4.161-2; *SDām* p. 66). *SR* : The hand that is placed on the thigh should be in Alapadma and is moved in Vyavartanā and Parivartanā. The Āviddhā Cārī is performed (*SR* 7.736).

(140) **Samanakha :** The feet are joined in Samanakha. The hands are let down while the body is kept normally (*NŚ* 4.65-6; *SDām* p. 67; *SUS.* 6.9; *NN* 32b). *SR* prescribes Latā for the hands (*SR* 7.598).

(141) **Samunnata :** Not explained. (*SDām.* p. 66).

(142) **Sarpita :** The feet move away from Añcita. The head moves in Parivāhita. The hands move in Recita (*NŚ* 4.141-2; *VDP* 3.20.52). *SUS* : The feet move in Nikuṭṭa, the right hand is bent while the left is in

Latā (*SUS* 6.83). *SR* prescribes that the head should be moved down to one foot which is stationary and not moved like the other, away from Añcita. The hand on that side should be moved in Recita. The action is repeated on the other side of the body (*SR* 7.708-9).

(143) **Siṁhavikrīḍita :** The dancer performed Alāta and moves quickly. The hands are moved in harmony (*NŚ* 4.149-50; *VDP* 3.20.53). *SUS* : The left foot is quickly placed on the right foot and the dancer looks backward (*SUS* 6.91). *SR* prescribes the Alātā Cārī. The hands are clapped (*SR* 7.717).

(144) **Siṁhākarṣitaka :** One foot is moved backward while the hands are in Nikuñcita. The action must be repeated (*NŚ* 4.150-1). *SDām* : Siṁhākarṣita (*SDām* p. 66). *SUS* : Siṁhākarṣana. The right foot is contracted and the head is bent. The hands are also bent and they must not face each other (*SUS* 6.92). *SR* : One foot is moved in Vṛścika. The hands are in Padmakośa and Ūrṇanābha. The other foot is also moved in Vṛścika. The hands return to their previous poses (*SR* 7.718-9).

(145) **Sūcī :** One foot in Kuñcita is lifted up and then placed forward on the ground. The hands are moved in harmony (*NŚ* 4.136-7; *SDām* p. 66). *SUS* : One big toe rubs against the ground and the leg is bent. The hands are kept normally (*SUS* 6.79). *SR* : The movement of the feet are as in the *NŚ*. It directs the dancer to place on the chest, the hand that is on the same side as the Kuñcitapāda. This hand should be in Khaṭaka. The other hand should be placed over the head in Alapadma (*SR* 7.698-9).

(146) **Sūcīpāda :** Not explained (*SDām* p. 66).

(147) **Sūcīviddha :** One foot is placed on the heel of the other on the chest (*NŚ* 4.138-9). *VDP* gives two terms : Sūcividdha and Sūcividdhaka (*VDP*

3.20.41.47). *SUS* : The right foot is placed backward and the left foot is put forward. The hands are moved round in Sūcī. (*SUS*. 6.81). *SR* prescribess Pakṣavañcitaka or Ardhacandra for the hand which is placed on the hips. The hand which is placed on the chest should assume Khaṭakāmukha (*SR* 7.700-1).

(148) **Sūcīvṛtta :** Not explained. (*SDām*. p. 66).

(149) **Skhalita :** The dancer performs Dolāpāda and moves her hands round in harmony (*NŚ* 4.146-7; *VDP* 3.20.52; *SDam* p. 66). *SUS* : The dancer moves her feet round and places them on the ground. Her hands are contracted and bent. Her face is brought slightly forward (*SUS* 6.86). *SR* : The hands should be in Haṁsapakṣa. The rest is the same as in the *NŚ* (*SR* 7.716).

(150) **Svastika :** The hands and the feet are in Svastika (*NŚ* 4.75-6; *VDP* 3.20.42; *SDām* p. 67; *SUS* 6.19). *SR* : The hands are placed jin Vyāvartita and moved out in Udveṣṭita. The dancer jumps with her hands and feet in Svastika (*SR* 7.592-3).

(151) **Svastikarecita :** The hands are moved successively in Recita and Āviddha. They are placed in Svastika and then they are separated and placed on the hips (*NŚ* 4.67-8; *VDP*. 3.20.40; *SDām* p. 67). *SUS* : The hands are joined at the wrists and moved in Recita and Svasṭika (*SUS* 6.11). *SR* : The dancer stands in Caturasra, moves her hands quickly in Haṁsapakṣa up and down from the head in Vyāvartita and Parivartita. Then she places them on the chest in Āviddhavakra, crossing each other and then she separates them in Viprakīrṇa. Then she moves her hands in Pakṣapradyotaka and Pakṣavañcitaka successively. Finally, she stands in the Avahittha Sthāna (*SR*. 7.600-2).

(152) **Hariṇapluta :** After doing Atikrānta the dancer jumps up, and on coming down she throws up her shanks which are bent (*NŚ* 4.143-4; *VDP* 3.20.52; *SDām* p. 66). *SUS* : The hands, the feet and the face are bent back and the dancer progresses in jumps (*SUS* 6.85). *SR* : The dancer performs the Hariṇaplutā Cārī with her hands in Dolā and Khaṭaka (*SR* 7.702).

The Utplutikaraṇas

(1) **Añcita :** The dancer stands in Sama and then jumps straight up (*SR* 7.757; *Mānas* 16.4.1384). *SSam* : The description is incomplete as some letters are missing. The first line agrees with *SR* except that it directs the dancer to turn round as well (*ŚSam* 6.187). *SDām* : Describe Añcita as one of the Bhauma-Viṣama-Nṛtyas (*SDām* p. 68).

(2) **Aṅgabhramarī :** The dancer stands and revolves her body with her feet kept one vitasti apart (Vitasti = Twelve aṅgulas or nine inches) (*ADar* 297).

(3) **Aticakrabhramarī :** The dancer moves round placing her right hand on her hips (*SMak* 2.4.26).

(4) **Antarbhramarī :** The Bāhyabhramarī in reverses in Antarbhramarī (*SUS* 6.120; *SSam* 6.190; *SR* 7.776; *NN.* 47b). *SDām* : This again is an Ākāśa-Viṣama-Nṛtya (*SDām* p. 69).

(5) **Antarālaga :** The dancer performs Alaga and comes down to the ground. Then she raises her chest and touches her hips at the back with her head (*SR* 7.762). *SDām* : A form of Ākāśa-Viṣama-Nṛtya (*SDām*. p. 69). *SSam* : Aterālaga : It agrees with the second portion of the action described by *SR*. (*SSam*. 6.183). *Mānas* : Antarālagna : The dancer jumps while arching her back and keeping her head between her shanks (*Mānas* 16.4.1388).

(6) **Alaga :** The dancer jumps with her face lowered and on coming to the front assumes Kukkuṭāsana (*SR* 7.760). *Mānas* : Alagna (*Mānas* 16.4.1387). *ADar* : The dancer jumps with both the sides, placing Śikhara hands on her hips (*ADar* 284). M.M. Ghosh thinks that the dancer jumps with her feet (See his translation of the *NŚ* p. 89). and this seems to be more practical than the description given above. But the actual śloka mentions "pārśva," not the feet.

(7) **Alagabhramarī :** The dancer stands in the Vaiṣṇava Sthāna. Then she stands on the left foot and rotates her body obliquely (*SR* 7.778; *SUS* 6.120).

(8) **Aśvotplavana :** The dancer jumps with both feet and places them together. Her hands are in Tripatākā (*ADar* 286).

(9) **Ākāśabhramarī :** The dancer jumps with her feet stretched and kept wide apart. Then she revolves her body (*ADar* 296).

(10) **Ācchurita :** Not explained. It is a form of Viṣama-Nṛtya (*SDām* p. 69).

(11) **Ucitabhramarī :** To turn round the body obliquely after standing in Sama. It is also described as Añcitabhramarī (*SR* 7.780). *SUS* gives Recitabhramarī which the editor of this text thinks must mean this Bhramarī (*SUS* 6.121, p. 139).

(12) **Uttānalaga :** Described as one of the Ākāśa-Viṣama-Nṛtyas (*SDām* p. 69).

(13) **Utplutabhramarī :** The dancer stands in Sama. Then she jumps and revolves her body (*ADar* 292).

(14) **Ūrdhvālaga :** The dancer comes down after jumping and Praises her feet in Sama (*SR* 7.762). *Mānas* : Ūrdhvālagna (*Mānas* 16.4.1389). *SSam* : The dancer sits down and performs Diṇḍu. Then she

performs Alaga with her face raised (*SSam* 6.182).

(15) **Ekacarnāñcita :** Añcita is done with one foot (*SR* 7.758; *Mānas* 16.4.1386).

(16) **Ekapāda :** Described as Bhauma-Viṣama-Nṛtya (*SDām* 68).

(17) **Ekapādabhramarī :** The dancer revolves alternately on one foot (*ADar* 295).

(18) **Ekapādalohaḍī :** This Lohaḍī done with one foot. It is also described as Ekapādaluṇṭhita (*SR* 7.765). *Mānas* : Ekapādalolita (*Mānas* 16.4.1393).

(19) **Eṇapluta :** The dancer jumps and performs Sūcī in the air. Then she comes down to the ground and performs Utkatāsana above the ground (*SR* 7.771). *Mānas* agrees with *SR* but prescribes stretching the hands and the feet in the air while jumping. (*Mānas* 16.4.1396-7).

(20) **Kapālacūrṇana :** The dancer stands in Sama and touches the ground with her forehead. Then she returns to her original position (*SSam* 6.184; *SR* 7.767).

(21) **Kapālabhramarī :** Not explained (*SSam* 6.191; *SDām*. p. 64).

(22) **Kapālasparśana :** The dancer bends forward and touches the ground with her forehead. This seems to be the same action as Kapālacūrṇana (*Mānas* 16.4.1390).

(23) **Kartarī :** The dancer jumps on her toes with one hand in Kartarī placed the left foot and the other hand in Śikhara is placed on the hips pointing downward (*ADar* 285-6).

(24) **Kartarīlohaḍī :** This is Lohaḍī performed with the feet crossed in Svastika. It is also described as Kartarī-luṇṭhita (*SR*. 7.764). *Mānas* : Kartarīlolita (*Mānas* 16.4.1393).

(25) **Kartaryañcita :** The dancer performs Añcita with her feet crossed in Svastika (*SR* 7.760; *Mānas* 16.4.1385). *ṢDām.* refers to this as a Bhauma-Viṣama-Nṛtya (*SDām* p. 68).

(26) **Karasparśana :** Having performed the Alaga Karaṇa the dancer touches the ground with her hands and revolves in a low position (*SR* 7.770).

(27) **Kuñcitabhramarī :** The dancer bends her knees and revolves (*ADar* 296).

(28) **Kūrmālaga :** The dancer assumes Kūrmāsana while performing Alaga (*SR.* 7.761). *SDām* : A form of *Ākāśa*-Viṣama-Nṛtya (*SDām* p. 69).

(29) **Kurudāyī :** Too obscure to explain (*Smak* 2.4.21).

(30) **Kṛpālaga :** The dancer touches her hips alternately with both heels and between them, places her hands in Ardhacandra (*ADar* 288).

(31) **Garuḍabhramarī :** The dancer stretches one foot obliquely, touches the ground with the other knee and revolves with her hands stretched out (*ADar* 294).

(32) **Ghanarava :** Too obscure to explain (*SMak* 2.4.23).

(33) **Cakrabhramarī :** The dancer spins like a wheel in the middle of Khaṇḍasūcī (*SR* 7.779; *SUS* 6.120; *NN* 47b). *ADar* : The dancer spins round with her feet dragging on the ground and her hands in Tripatākā (*ADar* 293; *SDām* p. 69).

(34) **Citrakulī :** Too obscure to explain (*SMak* 2.4.22).

(35) **Citratara :** Not explained. (*SMak.* 2.4.19).

(36) **Citrabhramarī :** The dancer stands in the pose of Trivikrama and turns to the left (Trivikrama—standing on one leg) (*SUS* 6.121; *SSam* 6.190; *SR* 7.777; *NN* 47b; *SDām* p. 69).

(37) **Jalaśayana** : The Darpāsaraṇa Karaṇa is called Jalaśayana if the dancer after falling to the ground takes the pose of lying in water (*SR* 7.766). *SSam* : Placing the left palm on the ground, resting the head on the left palm and then lying down on the ground on one hip, one thigh and one shank. The other foot should be pointed up (*SSam* 6.180). *Mānas* : Jalaśayī : The dancer jumps as she does in Añcita, comes down obliquely and lies down as if she is lying in the water (Jalaśayī-Viṣṇu). (*Mānas* 16.4.1395).

(38) **Tirayagañcita** : The dancer stands in sama and jumps obliquely (*SR* 7.773).

(39) **Tiryagalagabhramarī** : A form of Ākāśa-Viṣama-Nṛtya (*SDām* p. 69).

(40) **Tiryakkaraṇa** : The dancer jumps obliquely with on foot and upon coming down, stands on the other foot (*Mānas* 16.4.1397; *SR* 7.772).

(41) **Tiryaksvastika** : The dancer crosses her feet in Svastika and jumps obliquely (*SR* 7.774).

(42) **Tiripabhramarī** : The dancer moves round her feet obliquely after crossing the feet in Svastika (*SUS* 6.121: *SR.* 7.773). *NN* : Tirapabhramarī (*NN* 47b). *SMak* : The dancer moves to the left (*SMak* 2.4.25).

(43) **Daṇḍapraṇāmāñcita** : The dancer jumps as she does in Añcita and comes down on the ground straight as a staff (*SR* 7.759). *Mānas* : Daṇḍapraṇataka : Prescribes Alāta for Añcita (*Mānas* 16.4.1394). *SDām* : Daṇḍapraṇāma : A form of Bhauna-Viṣama-Nṛtya (*SDām* p. 68).

(44) **Darpasaraṇa** : The dancer stands in the Vaiṣaṇava Sthāna and falls to the ground sideways (*SR* 7.765; *SSam* 6.179).

(45) **Digbhramarī** : The dancer moves as in Śirobhramarī except that she first revolves on the one side, then

on the other. Then she touches the ground with her hand and revolving on her arm moves successively to four directions (*SR* 7.782).

(46) **Diṇḍu :** The dancer stands in Sama, then she jumps to the front and sits and moves round her body bending to the front. It is also described as Vindu (*SSam* 6.181).

(47) **Natapṛṣṭha :** The dancer performs Kapalacūrṇana and raises her breast doing Calāsana (*ASS* ed. of *SR* omits Calāsana p. 739). It is also described as Baṅkola (*SR* 7.768). *Mānas* : It agrees with *SR* but describes the action in a different way. The dancer is asked to perform Kapālasparśana first and then to repeat Antarālagna in which the dancer raises her breast (*Mānas* 16.4.1391-2).

(48) **Nāgabandha :** Jalaśayana is known as Nāgabandha when the dancer assumes Nāgabandha Āsana (*SR* 7.767). *SMak* : The dancer moves round her head and places her fingers on her shoulders (*SMak* 2.4.24).

(49) **Bāhūbhramarī :** Not explained (*SSam* 6.190).

(50) **Bāhyabhramarī :** The dancer stands on the right leg, bends the left and revolves it on the left (*SR* 7.775; *NN* 47b).

(51) **Bhairavāñcita :** To jump while one foot is placed on the back of the thigh (*SR* 7.758). *SDām* : A form of Bhauma-Viṣama-Nṛtya (*SDām* p. 68). *Mānas* : Suggests jumping with the other foot which rests on the ground (*Mānas* 16.4.1386).

(52) **Bhairavalolita :** Not explained (*Mānas* 16.4.1393).

(53) **Bhrāntapādāñcia :** The dancer turns round her right foot and supports the left shank by the back of the right toe. Then she performs Añcita. She touches the ground with her shoulders and turns round sideways waving her feet (*SR* 7.784-5).

(54) **Matsyakaraṇa :** The dancer jumps and moves round her hips. Then she turns round with her left side like a fish (*SR* 7.769).

(55) **Matsyalolitaka :** The dancer jumps as in Eṅapluta, moves her hips round and comes down to the ground obliquely (*Mānas* 16.4.1398-9).

(56) **Moṭita :** The dancer jumps as in Kartarī on both sides alternately (*ADar* 287-8).

(57) **Laṅkādahana :** The dancer jumps up and comes down as in Añcita with this difference that she comes down obliquely and sits down after moving back (*SSam* 6.188).

(58) **Lohaḍī :** The dancer stands in Sama and turns round her hips. Then she jumps and comes down obliquely. It is also described as Luṇṭhita (*SR* 7.763). *SDām.* : Lohalī : Ākāśa-Viṣama-Nṛtya (*SDām* p. 69). *SSam* : Lohalī and Lohaḍī (*SSam* 6.185). *Mānas* : Loṭita (*Mānas* 16.4.1393).

(59) **Vidhṛtabhramarī :** The dancer moves her whole body and looks down (*SMak* 2.4.27).

(60) **Śirobhramarī :** The dancer stands on her head, raises her feet and turns round thrice (*SR* 7.781).

(61) **Ṣarabhṛta :** The full description of this action can not be found as parts of the text are missing. From what there is left, it appears that the dancer is to jump, and her actions while coming down, should be as in Lohaḍī with the difference that her body should quiver (*SSam* 6.186).

(62) **Samapādāñcita :** The dancer stands in Sama and performs Añcita. Then she touches the ground with one shoulder and turns round sideways waving her feet (*SR* 7.783).

(63) **Sūcyantāni :** If, after the "preceding Karaṇas" the dancer performs "Samasūcī" etc. the conclusion is called Sucyantāni. (The "preceding Karaṇas" are :

1, 4, 5, 11, 13, 15, 16, 17, 21, 22, 23, 25, 31, 32, 34, 35, 37, 38, 41, 42, 45, 48, 52. "Samasūcī etc." denotes all the Sthānas ending with Sūcī (*SR* 7.774).

(64) **Skandhabhrānta** : The dancer assumes Utkaṭāsana and performs Añcita. She touches the ground with her shoulders, lifts her feet in the air and then touching the ground with her hands turns round as in Bhrāntapādāñcita. Finally, she stands facing four directions successively (*SR* 7.786-7).

CHAPTER SIX

Aṅgahāras, or Dance Sequences

Much of the present work is devoted to the movement of parts of the body that are so small that their movement can not be aesthetically pleasing individually. These movements are combined to make up longer movements like the Cārīs, which again are coordinated with others to make the Karaṇas. When the Karaṇas are danced in a series, an Aṅgahāra takes shape. The Aṅgahāras are thus complete dance sequences.

The *NŚ* says that an Aṅgahāra is the combination of the Karaṇas or the Mātṛkās and describes thirty-two varieties of them.[1] Abhg. explains the term in two ways. An Aṅgahāra may either by the proper movements of the limbs or it may be a performance of Hara, characterised by the movements of the limbs.[2]

The *VDP* gives a list of thirty-six Aṅgahāras without discussing them in detail.[3] The names generally agree with those in the *NŚ*. *ND* speaks of thirty-two Aṅgahāras but names only two, Sthirahasta and Paryastaka.[4] *SSam* speaks of thirty-two Aṅgahāras without mentioning details.[5]

SR defines the term Aṅgahāra following Abhg's interpretation of the *NŚ* and says that the proper graceful movements of limbs form an Aṅgahāra and also that it is composed of groups of Mātṛkās. It is further described as movements of Hara. It gives the same list of thirty-two

Aṅgahāras as the *NŚ* does but divides them into two separate clases, each of sixteen, on a basis of the different Tālas employed. One of these classes is performed to a rhythm unit of three beats and the other, to one of four beats. The discussion follows the interpretation of Abhg.[6] *SUS* describes Aṅgahāras as a sequence formed by Karaṇas and gives thirty-two varieties without describing them in detail. In giving some of the names, it does not agree with the *NŚ*.[7]

SDām names the whole section on dancing as Aṅgahāra and describes all the constituents of dancing as parts of the Aṅgahāras. It describes Aṅgahāra as one of the five Nṛtyāṅgas, and enumerates thirty-two varieties following the *NŚ* and *SR*. It gives the same divisions of two classes based on Tālas as *SR* does. Only two of the names given are different from those in the *NŚ*.[8]

The Aṅgahāras are dance sequences and in order to have a full picture of dancing we must look at their detailed descriptions. The *NŚ* and *SR* are the only treatise to discuss them in detail. *SR* follows *Abhg's*.interpretation of the *NŚ* and I have therefore used *Abhg's* interpretation in the account given below.

The account given in the *NŚ*

(1) **Sthirahasta :** The dancer stretches out the hands and lifts them,[9] placing the feet together,[10] and then, after Lifting the hand above the shoulder,[11] changes into the Pratyālīḍha Sthāna. Then the Nikuṭṭaka, Ūrudvṛtta, Ākṣipta, Svastika, Nitamba, Karihasta and Kaṭicchinna Karaṇas are performed successively. This is Sthirahasta, the favourite Aṅgahāra of Hara (*NŚ* 4.175-7).

(2) **Paryastaka :** The dancer performs Talapuṣpapuṭa, Apaviddha, Varitita (Some theorists advise the dancer to change into the Pratyālīḍha Sthāna).[12] The Aṅgahāra is continued by performing the

Nikuṭṭaka, Ūrudvṛtta, Ākṣipta, Uromaṇḍala, Nitamba, Karihasta, and Kaṭicchinna Karaṇas successively. This Aṅgahāra originated from Hara (*NŚ* 4.177-9).

(3) **Sūcīviddha :** The dancer performs Alapallava with the rest of the Ardhasūcī Karaṇas, followed by the Vikṣipta, Āvartita, Nikuṭṭaka, Ūrudvṛtta, Ākṣipta, Uromaṇdala, Karihasta and Kaṭicchinna Karaṇas (*NŚ* 4.179-81).

(4) **Apaviddha :** The dancer performs the Apaviddha and Sūcīviddha Karaṇas. The dancer has to lift the hands in the Udveṣṭita Karaṇa[13] and revolve the back.[14] The hands are to be changed to Uromaṇḍala (which is a part of the Uromaṇḍala Karaṇa). Finally the Kaṭicchinna Karaṇa is performed (*NŚ* 4.181-3).

(5) **Ākṣipta :** Having performed the Nūpura Karaṇa the dancer proceeds to the Vikṣipta, Alātaka and Ākṣiptaka Karaṇas. Ākṣiptaka is again performed.[15] The Aṅgahāra is continued by performing the Uromaṇḍala, Nitamba, Karihasta and Kaṭicchinna Karaṇas. This is known in the profession as the Ākṣiptaka Aṅgahāra (*NŚ* 4.183-5).

(6) **Udghaṭṭita :** In the Udghaṭṭita Nṛtta[16] the hands are moved in Udveṣṭita and Apaviddha[17] and the feet in Nikuṭṭaka. This is to be repeated with the left limbs as well.[18] The hands then change to Uromaṇḍala-hasta[19] and the Aṅgahāra is ended by performing the Nitamba, Karihasta and Kaṭicchinna Karaṇas (*NŚ* 4.185-7).

(7) **Viṣkambha :** The hands are moved alternately in Udveṣṭita and the feet in Nikuṭṭaka.[20] Kuñcitā[21] Añcita and Ūrudvṛtta are performed and the Aṅgahāra is continued by performing the Caturaśra hand and placing the feet in Nikuṭṭaka.[22] The

Bhujaṅgatrāsita Karaṇa follows. The hands are placed in Udveṣṭita. Paricchinna Karaṇa[23] should be performed with the back in Bhramara. At the end the Karihasta and Kaṭicchinna Karaṇas are performed (*NŚ* 3.187-90).

(8) **Aparājita** : This begins with the Daṇḍapāda Karaṇa placing the hand in Vikṣipta and Ākṣipta[24] followed by the Vyaṁsita Karaṇa. The left hand and the left foot are moved at the same time.[25] Two Nikuṭṭakas[26] are performed. The Aparājita Aṅgahāra is finished by performing the Ākṣipta, Uromaṇḍala,[27] Karihasta and Kaṭicchinna Karaṇas (*NŚ* 4.190-2).

(9) **Viṣkambhāpasṛta** : This begins with the Kuṭṭita[28] and Bhujaṅgatrāsita Karaṇas. Patākā hands should be performed with the hands in Recita. The Aṅgahāra is continued by performing the Ākṣiptaka and Uromaṇḍala Karaṇas and finished by performing Latā hands in Kaṭicchinna Karana (*NŚ* 4.192-4).

(10) **Mattākrīḍa** : The dancer revolves the back gracefully[29] and, performs the Nūpura Karaṇa. Bhujaṅgatrāsita should be performed with the left side of the body. The dancer then proceeds to Vaiśākharecita,[30] and ends the Aṅgahāra by performing the Ākṣiptaka, Paricchinna,[31] Bāhyabhramaraka,[32] Uromaṇḍala, Nitamba, Karihasta and Kaṭicchinna Karaṇas successively. This is called the favourite Aṅgahāra of Hara. (*NŚ* 4.194-7).

(11) **Svastikarecita** : In Svastikarecita the hands and the feet are placed in Recita.[33] Vṛścika is also performed. The whole action is repeated, followed again by Vṛścika.[34] The dancer proceeds to Nikuṭṭaka and then performs the Latā hand on the left and on the right sides. The Aṅgahāra is finished with Kaṭicchinna (*NŚ* 4.197-9).

(12) **Pārśvasvastika** : Svastika[35] and then Nikuṭṭaka[36] are performed on one side. The same should be

repeated on the other side. The hand is turned over and placed on the thigh.[37] The Pārśvasvastika Aṅgahāra is finished by performing Ūrudvṛtta, Ākṣipta, Nitamba, Karihasta and Kaṭicchinna successively (*NŚ* 4.199).

(13) **Vṛścikāpasṛta :** The Vṛścika caraṇa[38] accompanies the Latā hand.[39] Bend the hands, in the same position, to touch the tip of the nose.[40] The hands change into the Udveṣṭita Hastakaraṇa. The Aṅgahāra is finished by doing Nitamba, Karihasta and Kaṭicchinna (*NŚ* 4.202-4).

(14) **Bhramara :** Having performed Nūpurapāda[41] the dancer proceeds to the Ākṣipta Karaṇa. Paricchinna,[42] Sūcīviddha,[43] Nitamba, Karihasta, Uromaṇḍala and Kaṭicchina are then performed successively (*NŚ* 4.204-6).

(15) **Mattaskhalitaka :** After the Mattalli Karaṇa the right hand is moved round and bent to touch the cheek.[44] The dancer proceeds to Apaviddha quickly with Talasaṁsphoṭita and finishes the Aṅgahāra by performing Karihasta and Kaṭicchinna. (*NŚ*. 4.206-8).

(16) **Madavilasita :** The hands move in Dolā[45] and the feet in Svastikāpasṛta.[46] Placing the hands in Añcita and Valita,[47] the Talasaṁghaṭṭiata Karaṇa is performed.[48] The Aṅgahāra is finished by performing Nikuṭṭaka, Ūrudvṛtta, Karihasta and Kaṭicchinna[49] (*NŚ* 4.208-10).

(17) **Gatimaṇḍala :** The dancer performs Maṇḍalasthānaka,[50] and then places the hands in Recita,[51] the feet in Udghaṭṭita.[52] The Aṅgahāra is ended by performing Mattalli, Ākṣipta, Uromaṇḍala and Kaṭicchinna (*NŚ* 4.210-2).

(18) **Paricchinna :** The feet are placed together[53] and the dancer performs Paricchinna,[54] followed by

Apaviddha (or, the Sambhrānta Karaṇa).[55] Then the dancer performs Bāhyabhramaraka,[56] proceeding to Vāmasūcī.[57] The Paricchinna Aṅgahāra is finished by performing the Atikrānta, Bhujaṅgatrāsita, Karihasta and Kaṭicchinna Karaṇas (*NŚ* 4.212-4).

(19) **Parivṛttakarecita :** Placing the Svastika and Viprakīrṇa hands over the head[58] the dancer bends the body and moves the left hand in Recita.[59] The body is raised and the Recita hand is repeated. Vṛścika with the Latā hand[60] is performed, followed by Recita.[61] The dancer proceeds to Karihasta, Bhujaṅgatrāsita, Ākṣiptaka and Svastikapāda.[62] He turns round and repeats all the foregoing,[63] finishing the Parivṛttakarecita Aṅgahāra by performing Karihasta and Kaṭicchinna (*NŚ* 4.214-8).

(20) **Vaiśākharecita :** The hands move with the body in Recita. This action is repeated while raising the body.[64] Nūpurapāda,[65] Bhujaṅgatrāsita, Recita and Maṇḍala are performed.[66] The hands are bent to touch the top of the shoulders.[67] The Ūrudvṛtta, Ākṣipta, Uromaṇḍala, Karihasta and Katicchinna Karaṇas are performed (*NŚ* 4.218-21).

(21) **Parāvṛtta :** The dancer performs the Janita Karaṇa first[68] and then stretching out one foot,[69] proceeds to the Alātaka Karaṇa and revolves the back.[70] The left hand is bent and touches the cheek.[71] The Aṅgahāra is finished by performing Kaṭicchinna (*NŚ* 4.221-3).

(22) **Alātaka :** Having performed the Svastika Karaṇa the dancer moves the hands in Vyaṁsita,[72] following this with Alātaka, Ūrdhvajānu, Nikuñcita, Ardhasūcī, Vikṣipta, Udvṛtta, Ākṣipta, Karihasta and Kaṭicchinna successively (*NŚ* 4.223-5).

(23) **Pārśvaccheda** : The dancer moves the hands in Nikuṭṭa[73] on the chest,[74] and performs Ūrdhvajānu. He proceeds to the Ākṣipta and Svastika Karaṇas and after revolving the back, performs the Uromaṇḍala hand.[75] The Aṅgahāra is finished by performing the Nitamba, Karihasta and Kaṭicchinna Karaṇas (*NŚ* 4.225-7).

(24) **Vidyudbhrānta** : The (Ardha) Sūcī Karaṇa is performed with the left side of the body and the Vidyudbhrānta Karaṇa with the right. The same action follows, but in reverse : (Ardha) Sūcī on the right and Vidyudbhrānta on the left. Proceeding to Paricchinna,[76] the dancer performs the Atikrānta Karaṇa on the left and finishes the Aṅgahāra by performing the Latā[77] and Kaṭicchinna Karaṇas (*NŚ* 4.227-9).

(25) **Udvṛttaka** : The dancer performs Nūpurapāda,[78] and stretches the hands downwards on either side[79] and performs with them the Vikṣipta Karaṇa.[80] Sūcī is performed with the hands.[81] The back is revolved.[82] The dancer performs Latā[83] and Kaṭicchinna at the end (*NŚ* 4.229-31).

(26) **Alīḍha** : The dancer performs the Alīḍha Sthāna and moves the hands in Vyaṁsita,[84] touching the top of the shoulders with the hands. Nūpura should be performed with the left foot and Alātaka with the right. Ākṣiptaka is performed with the same side of the body.[85] The hands form Uromaṇḍala.[86] The Aṅgahāra ends upon performing Karihasta and Katicchinna (*NŚ* 4.231-3).

(27) **Recita** : The hands move in Recita, the dancer bends sideways and again moves the hands in Recita. This action is repeated, followed by the Recita Karaṇa.[87] The Aṅgahāra ends with the Uromaṇḍala and Kaṭicchinna Karaṇas (*NŚ* 4.233-5).

(28) **Ācchurita** : The dancer performs Nūpura caraṇa,[88] revolves the back,[89] and moves the hands in Vyaṁsita.[90] The back is revolved again.[91] Alātaka follows on the left side of the body, Sūcī is done at the same place, and Aṅgahāra is concluded by performing the Karihasta and Kaṭicchinna Karaṇas (*NŚ* 4.235-7).

(29) **Ākṣiptarecita** : The dancer performs Svastikapāda in Recita and does the same with the hands. He separates them and lifts them with the same (Recita) movement,[92] and performs Udvṛtta,[93] Ākṣipta and Uromaṇḍala.[94] The Aṅgahāra ends with the Nitamba, Karihasta and Kaṭicchinna Karaṇas (*NŚ* 4.237-40).

(30) **Saṁbhrānta** : The dancer performs the Vikṣipta Karaṇa, moving the hands and the feet in accordance with the expression of the face.[95] Sūcī is performed on the left side of the body and the left hand[96] is thrown outwards while the right hand rests on the chest.[97] The back is revolved.[98] Then Nūpura, Ākṣiptaka, Ardhasvastika, Nitamba, Karihasta, Uromaṇḍala and Kaṭicchinna should be performed successively by the dancer to end the Saṁbhrānta Karaṇa (*NŚ* 4.240-3).

(31) **Apasarpita** : The Apakrānta Karaṇa is first performed, the hands being moved in Vyaṁsita.[99] Udveṣṭita,[100] Ardhasūcī, Vikṣipta, Kaṭicchinna, Udvṛtta,[101] Ākṣipta, Karihasta, and Kaṭicchinna are successively performed (*NŚ* 4.243-5).

(32) **Ardhanikuṭṭaka** : The dancer performs Nūpura-pāda,[102] rapidly moving the hands and the feet in harmony and revolving the back.[103] The hands and the feet are moved in Nikuṭṭa.[104] Finally the Uromaṇḍala, Karihasta and Kaṭicchinna Karaṇas are performed to end the Aṅgahāra (*NŚ* 4.245-7).

The account given in *SR*

(1) **Sthirahasta** : The Līna, Samanakha and Vyaṁsita Karaṇas are performed. The hands are separated. The dancer[105] changes to the Pratyālīdha Sthāna from the Ālīḍha Sthāna, then performs Nikuṭṭaka, ūrudvṛtta, Svastika, Ākṣipta, Nitamba, Karihasta and Kaṭicchinna successively. According to the "devotee of Śiva" (Śārṅgadeva), these ten Karaṇas. constitue the Sthirahasta Aṅgahāra. Some experts on dramaturgy suggest that the portion from beginning up to the Pratyālīdha Sthāna should be performed in all Aṅgahāras (*SR* 7.802-5).

(2) **Paryastaka** : The Talapuṣpapuṭa Karaṇa comes first followed by Apaviddha and Vartita. Then the Nikuṭṭaka, Ūrudvṛtta, Ākṣipta, Uromaṇḍala, Nitamba, Karihasta and Kaṭicchinna Karaṇas are performed (*SR* 7.806-7).

(3) **Sūcīviddha** : Bharata and other scholars explain the Sūcividdha Aṅgahāra as one constituted of the following nine Karaṇas. They are : Ardhasūcī, Vikṣipta, Āvarta, Nikuṭṭaka, Ūrudvṛtta, Ākṣipta, Uromaṇḍala, Karihasta and Kaṭicchinna (*SR* 7.808-9).

(4) **Aparājita** : The nine Karaṇas that are used in the Aparājita Aṅgahāra are Daṇḍapāda, Vyaṁsita, Prasarpita, Nikuṭṭa, Ardhanikuṭṭa, Ākṣipta, Uromaṇḍala, Karihasta and Kaṭicchinna (*SR* 7.810-1).

(5) **Vaiśākharecita** : Vaiśākharecita is performed on either side, followed by the Nūpura, Bhujaṅgatrāsita, Unmatta, Maṇḍalasvastika, Nikuṭṭaka, Ūrudvṛtta, Ākṣipta, Uromaṇḍala, Karihasta and Kaṭicchinna Karaṇas successively. These eleven Karaṇas constitute the Vaiśakharecita Aṅgahāra. (*SR* 7.812-4).

(6) **Pārśvasvastika** : The Diksvastika Karaṇa is first performed, followed by the Ardhanikuṭṭaka Karaṇa on one side. Diksvastika is repeated and Ardhanikuṭtaka performed on the other side. The dancer proceeds to the Apaviddha, Ūrudvṛtta, Ākṣipta, Nitamba, Karihasta and Kaṭicchinna Karaṇas. The Pārśvasvastika Aṅgahāra is said to be made up of these eight Karaṇas, but in actual practice ten are performed, since two are repeated (*SR* 7.814-6).

(7) **Bhramara** : This is constituted of the following eight Karaṇas : Nūpura, Ākṣiptaka, Chinna, Sūcī, Nitamba, Karihasta, Uromaṇḍala and Kaṭicchinna (*SR* 7.817-8).

(8) **Ākṣiptaka** : Nūpura, Vikṣipta, Alāta, Ākṣiptaka, Uromaṇḍala, Nitamba, Karihasta and Kaṭicchinna are performed successively. Normally these eight Karaṇas form the Ākṣiptaka Aṅgahāra, but some experts hold that Vikṣipta, Alāta and Ākṣipta should each be performed twice (*SR* 7.818-20).

(9) **Paricchinna** : Samanakha, Chinna and Saṁbhrānta are performed. Then Bhramara should be done on the left. Finally Atikrānta, Bhujaṅgatrāsita, Karihasta and Katicchinna are performed successively (*SR* 7.820-2).

(10) **Madavilasita** : Madavilasita, Mattalli, Talasaṁsphoṭita are presented in various (pleasing) ways. The Aṅgahāra is concluded by performing Nikuṭṭaka, Ūrudvṛtta, Karihasta and Kaṭicchinna. These are the seven Karaṇas that form the Madavilasita Aṅgahāra though actually thirteen are performed because the first three are done twice. Some theorists suggest repeating these three Karaṇas four or five times (*SR* 7.822-5).

(11) **Ālīḍha :** Beginning with Vyaṁsita and Nikuṭṭa the dancer performs Nūpura with the left foot and with the other (right) foot performs Alātaka and Ākṣipta. The Aṅgahāra is ended by performing Uromaṇḍala, Karihasta and Kaṭicchinna. These eight Karaṇas, done successively, constitute the Ālīḍha Aṅgahāra (*SR* 7.825-7).

(12) **Ācchurita :** The eight Karaṇas in the Ācchurita Aṅgahāra are Nūpura, Bhramara, Vyaṁsita, Alātaka, Nitamba, Sūcī, Karihasta and Kaṭicchinna (*SR* 7.827-8).

(13) **Pārśvaccheda :** The dancer performs Vṛścikakuṭṭita, Ūrdhvajānu, Ākṣipta and Svastika successively, revolving the back. He then proceeds to Uromaṇḍala, Nitamba, Karihasta and Kaṭicchinna (*SR* 7.829-30).

(14) **Apasarpita :** Having performed Apakrānta the dancer moves only the hands in Vyaṁsita, and then proceeds to Karihasta, Ardhasūcī, Vikṣipta, Kaṭicchinna, Ūrudvṛtta, Ākṣipta, Karihasta and Kaṭicchinna. There are seven Karaṇas and a half in this Aṅgahāra, but two more are to be counted as Karihasta and Katicchinna are repeated (*SR* 7.831-3).

(15) **Mattākrīḍa :** The dancer performs Bhramara and Nūpura and then, with the right side of the body, he performs Bhujaṅgatrāsita. He goes on to Vaiśākharecita, Ākṣipta, Chinna, Bhramara, Vyaṁsita, Uromaṇḍala, Nitamba, Karihasta and Kaṭicchinna. These twelve Karaṇas, or eleven if we do not count the repetition of Bhramara, constitute Mattākrīḍa, the favourite Aṅgahāra of Hara (*SR* 7.833-6).

(16) **Vidyudbhrānta :** Ardhasūcī is performed on the left and Vidyudbhrānta on the right. This is repeated

on the other side. The dancer proceeds to Chinna and Atikrānta, then performs Latāvṛścika on the left again. Finally, he performs Katicchinna. These are the six Karaṇas (eight, if we include the repetition of the two) in this Aṅgahāra (*SR* 7.837-9).

The sixteen Aṅgahāras above, have rhythm units of four beats.

(17) **Viṣkambhāpasṛta :** Nikuṭṭaka, Ardhanikuṭṭa, Bhujaṅgatrāsita, Bhujaṅgatrastarecita and Ākṣipta are performed successively. Then the hands are placed in Latā.[105] This is followed by the seventh and the final Karaṇa in this Aṅgahāra, that is, the Kaṭicchinna Karaṇa (*SR* 7.839-41).

(18) **Mattaskhalitaka :** Mattalli, Gaṇḍasūcī, Līna and Apaviddha are performed quickly.[106] Talasaṁsphoṭita, Karihasta and Katicchinna follow. These are the seven Karaṇas in this Aṅgahāra (*SR* 7.841-3).

(19) **Gatimaṇḍala :** In this Aṅgahāra, Maṇḍalasvastika, Niveśa, Unmatta, Udghaṭtia, Mattallī, Ākṣipta, Uromaṇḍala and Katicchinna Karaṇas are used (*SR* 7.843-5).

(20) **Apaviddha :** The dancer performs Apaviddha and Sūcīviddha, and moves the hands in Udveṣṭita.The back is revolved in the Baddhā Cārī. The dancer proceeds to the Ūrudvṛtta and Uromaṇḍala Karaṇas. Kaṭicchina is the fifth and the final Karaṇa in this Aṅgahāra (*SR* 7.845-7).

(21) **Viṣkambha :** The dancer performs Nikuṭṭaka, Nikuñcita, Añcita, Ūrudvṛtta, Ardhanikuṭṭa and Bhujaṅgatrāsita and proceeds to Bhramara with the hands in Udveṣṭita. Karihasta and Kaṭicchinna follow. These are the nine Karaṇas in this Aṅgahāra (*SR* 7.847-9).

(22) **Udghaṭṭita** : Udghaṭṭita, Nikuṭṭa, Uromaṇḍala, Nitamba, Karihasta and Kaṭicchinna are the five Karaṇas in the Udghaṭṭita Aṅgahāra (*SR* 7.849-50).

(23) **Ākṣiptarecita** : In this Aṅgahāra Svastikarecita, Pṛṣthasvastika, Kaṭisama, Ghūrṇita, Bhramara, Vṛścikarecita, Pārśvanikuṭṭaka, Uromaṇḍala, Sannata, Siṁhākarṣita, Nāgāpasarpita, Vakṣasvastika, (this is prescribed by only some of the experts), Daṇḍapakṣa, Lalāṭatilaka, Latāvṛścika, Niśumbhita, Vidyudbhrānta, Ūrudvṛtta, Ākṣipta. Gajavikrīḍita, Nitamba, Viṣṇukrānta, Karihasta and Kaṭicchinna are the twenty-five constituent Karaṇas according to the earlier author. Since Nitamba is repeated after Karihasta and Uromaṇḍala after Ākṣipta, some later authors bring up the number to twenty-seven. But for those who do not accept Vakṣahsvastika and Kaṭicchinna in this Aṅgahāra, there are only twenty-five (*SR* 7.850-5).

(24) **Recita** : This is constituted of Svastikarecita, Ardharecita, Vakṣahsvastika, Unmatta, Ākṣiptarecita, Ardhamattalli, Recakanikuṭṭaka, Bhujaṅgatrastarecita, Nūpura, Vaiśākharecita, Bhujaṅgāñcita, Daṇḍarecita, Cakramaṇḍala, Vṛscikarecita, Vivṛtta, Vinivṛtta, Vivartita, Garuḍapluta, Lalita,[107] Mayūralalita, Sarpita, Skhalita, Prasarpita, Talasaṁghaṭṭita, and Vṛṣabhakrīḍita.These twenty-six Karaṇas are divided into four equal parts the parts being performed in different directions. At the end Uromaṇḍala and Kaṭicchinna are performed (*SR* 7.858-65).

(25) **Ardhanikuṭṭaka** : In the Ardhanikuṭṭaka Aṅgahāra, Nūpura, Vivṛtta, Nikuṭṭa, Ardhanikuṭṭa, Recakanikuṭṭaka, Vaiśākharecita, Catura, Daṇḍarecita, Vṛścikakuṭṭita, Pārśvanikuṭṭaka, Saṁbhrānta, Udghaṭṭita, Uromaṇḍala, Karihasta and Kaṭicchinna are the seventeen constituent Karaṇas (*SR* 7.865-8).

(26) **Vṛścikāpasṛta :** Latāvṛścika is performed first.Then Nikuñcita, Mattallī, Nitamba, Karihasta and Kaṭicchinna should be performed (*SR* 7.869-70).

(27) **Alātaka :** The dancer performs Svastika, Vyaṁsita (twice), Alāta, Ūrdhvajānu, Nikuñcita, Ardhasūcī, Vikṣipta, Udvṛtta, Ākṣipta, Karihasta and Kaṭicchinna succsively. These are the eleven constituent Karaṇas. If we include the repetition of Vyaṁsita, then there are twelve Karaṇas (*SR* 7.871-2).

(28) **Parāvṛtta :** The Janita Karaṇa is performed on the right side of the body. Then after performing the Śakaṭāsya Karaṇa and the Alāta Karaṇa, Bhramara is performed on the left. With hands moving in Nikuṭṭa, the dancer performs Karihasta and finishes the Aṅgahāra by performing the Kaṭicchinna Karaṇa. These are the six Karaṇas in the Parāvṛtta Aṅgahāra given by (Śārṅgadeva), the "son of Soḍhala" (*SR* 7.873-5).

(29) **Parivṛttakarecita :** Having performed Nitamba the dancer goes on to Svastikarecita, Vikṣiptākṣiptaka, Latāvṛścika, Unmatta, Karihasta, Bhujaṅgatrāsita, Ākṣipta and Nitamba. These nine Karaṇas should be performed in all directions with Bhramarī movements. Then these are repeated on another side. Finally, Karihasta and Kaṭicchinna are performed standing in the first position. This procedure of performing the Karaṇas in all directions, except the last two Karaṇas, is common to all the Aṅgahāras according to Śārṅgadeva, who claims to know the views of Bhaṭṭa Abhinavagupta (*SR* 7.875-80).

(30) **Udvṛttaka :** The dancer performs Nūpura, Bhujaṅgāñcita, Gṛdhrāvalīnaka and then performs Vikṣipta twice on either side of the body. Sūcī should be performed between two Udvṛttas. He

proceeds to Nitamba, Latāvṛścika and Kaṭicchinna. These are the nine Karaṇas in the Udvṛttaka Aṅgahāra. The repetition of Vikṣipta and Udvṛtta adds two more to the number (*SR* 7.881-3).

(31) **Saṁbhrānta :** The dancer performs Vikṣipta, Añcita and Gaṇḍasūcī, followed by the last of all Karaṇas, Gangāvataraṇa. The dancer performs Ardhasūcī, and then Daṇḍapāda on the left,[108] and proceeds to Catura, Bhramara, Nūpura, Ākṣipta, Ardhasvastika, Nitamba, Karihasta, Uromaṇḍala and Kaṭicchinna. These are the fifteen Karaṇas in this Aṅgahāra (*SR* 7.883-6).

(32) **Svastikarecita :** The dancer performs Vaiśakharecita and Vṛścika. They are repeated and with the hands in Latā, the dancer performs Nikuṭṭaka. Kaṭicchinna is the fourth and the final Karaṇa in this Aṅgahāra. The repetition of the first two adds two more to the number (*SR* 7.886-8).

These drawings illustrate the Sthirahasta Aṅgahāra, pp. 188, 191. This choreographical sequence is divided into ten Karaṇas, or postures, each having movements of the aṅgas, upāṅgas and pratyangas peculiar to itself. The illustrations show these units of the total sequence. For the process of forming the Karaṇas, and of moving from one into the next, see chapters five and six.

Linaṁ

Samanakhaṁ

Vyamsitaṁ

Nikuṭṭakaṁ

Urūdvṛttam

Akṣpitam

Svastikaṁ

Nitaṁbaṁ

Karihástaṁ

Kaṭicchinnaṁ

CHAPTER SEVEN

A Different Tradition

It will have been noticed that in the tradition of dancing described in the foregoing pages, Bharata's Nāṭyaśāstra occupies an archetypal position. As this happens to be chronologically the earliest text on drama and dance, other works are clearly derived from it. The nature of the relationship is fairly simple. The later treatises accept the framework constructed by the *NŚ* and this acceptance is followed by two things. One is the clarification of Bharata's definitions or descriptions when the later authors feel this to be necessary and the other, an extension of the feeling behind the first is to infer from the original framework a number of details. It is possible that the exhaustiveness achieved in the course of the search for clarity leads actually to a wilderness of details and prevents the reader from seeing the wood for the trees. But in defence of the later authors it may be argued that their aim was to leave nothing unexplored in the vast tradition reported by Bharata.

All this goes indeed to show the vitality of that tradition. This may well be the reason why the attention of the early as well as the present day student has been scarcely drawn to what we may call the missing tradition of Indian dancing. This is the tradition to which Bharata and his followers refer as dancing in the Deśī style. That this form of the art was as powerful socially as the better known form is obvious, for it is defined as the popular—shall we say the lowbrow—form of defined as the popular—shall we say the lowbrow—form of dancing. Surely then, the evolution of Indian dancing has its origin in more sources than Bharata's tradition alone. It is significant that a large number of terms used in modern classical dancing in India are not found in the accounts of Bharata and his followers. From what source are they taken? Common sense points at the unreported tradition, Deśī dancing as that source. Even if it is not the whole source yet it might well have contributed significantly to the shaping of serious dancing in modern India.

What puts the seal on this obvious conjecture is the actual presence in the rare accounts of Deśī dancing, of some technical terms that have descended to our days and do not belong to the tradition represented by the *NŚ*. The importance of this unfamiliar tradition is thus clear, for here we find the missing part of the history of present-day classical dancing in India. This tradition, as we have noted, is not described in the treatises as a rule, though most recognise its existence. Our knowledge of it is derived from two main sources. One is the Nartananirṇaya and the other is the Saṅgīta-Darpaṇa. Some of the dances described in these two texts mentioned are, however, also referred to in a few ślokas of *SSam*[1] while *SR* describes two of these dance sequences, Gauṇḍalī and Peraṇi, in greater detail.[2] *SDām* discusses Peraṇi as a form of Tāṇḍava and mentions Māṇḍālī which may be a corruption for Guṇḍalī.[3] *BhP* discusses Guṇḍalī.[4] All the texts generally agree in describing these dances.

These dances are of the Deśī style and they seem to belong to a tradition that originated and developed in South India.[5] The editor of *Nṛttasaṁgraha* which can be identified with the last part of the *Nartananirṇaya,* an unpublished text has explained some term found in that text, and has shown that they belong to the South Indian tradition of dancing.[6] It should be noted that these dance sequences employ in the main, the same movements of the parts of the body that are used in the classical style though different names are sometimes given.[7] But the combination of movements that they make up, are different and with these, some new positions and gestures are prescribed.

We know that all texts on dancing mention correlated arts such as music, stage-craft and make-up, but the tradition represented by *NN* and *SDar* gives specific instructions as to what songs and instruments should accompany each composition. Since the dancer is asked to use the movements to express her feelings, the compositions involve Abhinaya as well, and this again is an original feature.

NN is more precise than *SDar* in maintaining the order of the descriptions and discuss the tradition under two broad divisions : Bandha and Anibandha Nṛtyas. It should be mentioned that the terms Nṛtta and Nṛtya are used interchangeably to denote dancing.[8] *NN* describes eleven Bandhanṛtyas, some of which have further sub-divisions. Anibandhanṛtyas are twenty-one in number. A Persian dance, Jakkaḍī, and the Rāsa dance are also described at the end.

SDar shows a confusing lack of order. In the course of discussing one subject, the author wanders off to others and often returns after long discussions. But in all essential, there is agrement with *NN*. At the beginning of the chapter on dancing called the Nṛtyādhyāya, the author speaks of Anibaddha and Nibaddha Gītas.[9] He gives a list of twenty dance sequences but in fact discusses more than that number while he passes over some mentioned in the list.[10] Comments on the classification of dance and drama, the difference between Nṛtta and Nṛtya, lists of Aṅgas, Upāṅgas and Pratyaṅgas and other details appear between the descriptions of dance sequences. Gaits and Mukharāgas are also described in detail.[11] The Bandhanṛtya, described in this text has no sub-division as it has in *NN* but some of the forms discussed in *NN* are found here. Most of the dances, discussed in this text are similar to those found in *NN*, only a few being different or new.[12] That the author of this work knew *NN* is obvious, for in describing the dance sequences he frequently borrows words, sometimes even sentences from that text.[13]

Peraṇi and Guṇḍalī seem to be the most important of all the dance sequences described in the two texts, as they are also described in *SR, SSam, SDām* and *BhP. SR* gives the longest descriptions both for Guṇḍalī and Peraṇi, mentioning them as Deśī styles, while *SSaṁ* describes Peraṇi and the instrumental music necessary to Peraṇi and Guṇḍalī.[14] This text mentions a Deśī dance. Pekkhanṇa which is found nowhere else. It also refers to eighteen Deśyaṅgāni[15] and this section has some general components on performance. *SDām* calls Māṇḍalī a Deśī Lāsyāṅga, describing what is known in other texts as Guṇḍalī. Peraṇi is thought by this text to be a form of Deśī Tāṇḍava.[16] *BhP* calls Guṇḍalī a form of Deśī dance.[17] The following is a list of the types of dancing exercises mentioned in these texts:

The account given in NN :

The Bandhanṛtyas

(1) Mukhacāli; (2) Urūpa: (i) Neri, (ii) Karaṇaneri, (iii) Bhitra, (iv) Citra, (v) Natra, (*vi*) Adṛṣtapṛṣṭhatulla, (vii) Tolarūpa (Cakrabandha, Ravicakra, Padmabandha, Nāgabandha, Vṛkṣabandha), (viii) Sīluka, (ix) Turlla, (x) Prasara, (xi) Kartarī, (*xii*) Hollu; (3) Dhuvāḍa : (i) Kalaviṅkavinoda, (ii) Tārkṣyapakṣavilāsita, (iii) Vidyudvilāsita, (iv) Vātyāvartita, (v) Ravisañcara, (vi) Nartanābharaṇa, (vii) Tiryaktāṇḍava, (viii) Raṅgabhūṣaṇa, (ix) Vādiśagajabhairuṇḍa, (x) Rolavāṅgavilāsita, (*xi*) Pakṣiśārdūlaka, (xii) Siṁhaplutaka; (4) Viḍulāgava : (i) Aḍālu, (ii) Rāyaraṅgālu, (iii) Nihśaṅka, (iv) Hormayī, (v) Ḍāṇṭu, (vi) Aṇḍatara, (vii) Diṇḍu, (viii) Rāyādi Pakṣiśāluva, (*ix*) Alaga, (*x*) Ḍheṅkī, (xi) Bīśa, (xii) Alagadiṇḍu; (5.) Bhramarī : (i) Bāhya, (ii) Anta, (iii) Tirapa, (iv) Chatra, (*v*) Cakra; (6) Śabdanṛyta; (7) Svaramaṇṭhanṛtya; (8) Gītanṛtya; (9) Cindunṛtya

(i) Śuddha, (ii) Biṇdu, (iii) Tiruvaṇi, (iv) Mālā, (v) Kolacārī, (vi) Gītamudrā : (10) Dharu: (i) Kaḍḍaḍidharu. (ii) Muktikādharu; (11) Dhruvapada.

The Anibandahanṛtyas

(1) Nāmāvalī; (2) Yati; (3) Neri; (4) Sālaṅganeri; (5) Saṅkīrṇaneri; (6) Bhāvaneri; (7) Naḍaneri; (8) Kaivartana; (9) Muru; (10) Raṭṭamuru; (11) Tālarūpaka; (12) Guṇḍāla; (13) Kamala; (14) Natajānuka; (15) Maṇḍī; (16) Muḍupa; (17) Muraṇḍarī; (18) Kuḍupa; (19) Tiryakaraṇa; (20) Lāvaṇi; (21) Vaṭu.

The two following Nṛtyas are mentioned neither as Anibandhanṛtya nor as Bandhanṛtya:

(1) Jakkaḍi : A Persian dance.

(2) Rāsanṛtya.

The account given in SDar

(1) Mukhacāli; (2) Maṭṭanṛtya; (3) Śabdacāli; (4) Urūpa : (i) Neri, (ii) Karaṇaneri, (iii) Bhitra, (iv) Citra, (v) Natra, (vi) Jāramana, (vii) Ridramuru, (viii) Hulla, (ix) Lāvaṇi, (x) Kartarī, (xi) Tulla, (xii) Prasara; (5) Dhruvāḍa; (6) Lāganṛtya : (i) Rāyarāngala, (ii) Aḍāla, (iii) Niḥśaṅka, (iv) Hurumayī, (v) Aṇḍatara, (vi) Diḍu, (vii) Ḍheṅkī, (viii) Bīśa, (ix) Pakṣiśārdūla; (7) Śabdanṛtya; (8) Vivartananṛtya; (9) Camatkāranṛtya; (10) Gītanṛtya; (11) Svaramaṇthanṛtya; (12) Sūḍanṛtya; (13) Maṇṭha-nṛtya; (14) Rūapakanṛtya; (15) Tṛtīyanṛtya; (16) Adrutālanṛtya; (17) Ekatālanṛtya.

The Deśī Nṛtyavidhi

(1) Cindu; (i) Viḍa, (ii) Kvālacārī; (2) Vaipota; (3) Bandhanṛtya; (4) Kalpanṛtya; (5) Jakkarī, (6) Deśikaṭṭarī; (7) Peraṇi; (8) Gauṇḍalī.

SDar does not discuss Bahurūpa though it is listed at the beginning of the chapter, called the Nṛtyādhyāya.

Mukhacāli

Mukha is the introduction to performance and Cāli is the gait that follows Mukha. This involves Puṣpāñjali. The dancer should perform this in the following manner :

The dancer performs the Samapādā Cārī with Āviddhavakra hands and moves gracefully three steps to the front. She performs Līnaka, Samanakha and moves slowly and obliquely. She moves her sides repeatedly in Sulu simulating the flame of a lamp trembling in the breeze. Or, she presents the Sulu, forming the hood of a snake with her body. She moves her Latā hands simultaneously in Vyāvartita and bends her feet together in Dviśikhara and moves her whole body in harmony with other movements. She moves in Tala, Madhya and Ūrdhvasañcas. Her movements follow Rāgālāpas and Śabdālāpas. Her arms are extended with her hands in Patākā and she performs Savyasūcī with the Sārī Cārī and moves her feet in Agratalasañcara. Her head and feet are simultaneously moved in Recana and then she makes Karihasta and Madhyasañca raising her feet. She moves away her right foot from Karihasta and crosses it with the other to form a Svastika. Then she performs Sulu and Nūpuraviddhikā and makes Caturaśra with Talasañca. Her hands are moved and she performs the Samanakha Sthāna by doing the Svastikā Cārī with Talamukha hands, moving to the third direction and finally by moving to the left in Ūrdhvasañca. She performs the Vaiśakharecita Sthāna with her arms obliquely extended and by doing the Kulīrikā Cārī. She performs the Maṇḍala Sthāṇa and Sulu, one after the other, and she moves to the middle of the stage in the Karihastā Cārī moving her left hand in Udveṣṭita. She folds her hands facing the audience and performs Pārśvarecita, Jānukuñcita, Maṇḍalasthāna and Sulu with the Latā hands. Then she keeps her left hand in a natural way while her right hand in Latā is moved above her body. Then she again performs Svastika with Talamukha hands and moves to the "seventh direction" and moves on her left two or three times.

This series of movements is accompanied by the instrumental music and it is performed seven or eight times. Then she performs the Maralā Cārī with Āviddhavakra hands and moves to the fourth direction and assumes the Maṇḍalasthāna. She performs the Janiṭa Karaṇa and Sulu. She places her right hand near her ear and her left hand at her side in Muṣṭi. The Sthitāvartā and Tiryaṅmukhā Cārīs are performed and moving to the fourth direction, she performs the Pratyālīḍha-Sthāna. Then she performs the Tiryaṅmukhā Cārī with Ardharecita hands and moves to the fifth direction after performing Caturaśra, Viprakīrṇa and Sulu. After doing Sulu once more she assumes the Samanakha Sthāna. Then she performs Śuddhacāli and Kaukkaṭi one after the other and with her hand in Añjali bends her head to bow to the gods, her teacher and the sage. She moves to the centre of the stage doing the Kartarī Cārī and performs the Adhyardhikā Cārī. She takes some flowers in her hands and performing Talapuṣpapuṭa, does Puṣpāñjali on her left, right, at her front and back and throws the flowers into the interior of the stage. Then she acts the Nāndīśloka to a Rāga.

"Bhavatāṁ bhūtaye Bhūyād Bhavānī Bhavaballava,

Aṅgīkṛtasusaṅgītabhṛṅgī muditamānasā."

This śloka is to be acted : *Bhavatāṁ* : one hand in Patākā is placed forward. *Bhūtaye* : "The hands are raised from the front in Alapallava. *Bhūyāt* : One hand in Patākā is moved in Udveṣṭita pointed downwards. *Bhavānī* : One hand in Gomukha is lowered from the left breast to the thigh facing the front. *Bhava* : The Sūcyāsya hand is placed on the forehead. *Ballava* : The Catura hand is palced on the breasts. *Aṅgīkṛta* : The Kapota hand is held near the mouth. *Susaṅgita* : The Haṁsāsya hand is held near the face. *Bhṛṅgī* :[18] The trembling Tripatākā hand is extended. *Mudita* : The left hand in Alapallava is raised from the front. *Mānasā* : The right hand in Sandaṁśa is moved in Vyāvartita and Parivartita near the chest. Then she quickly performs

Kamalavartanikā and Makaravartanikā. She performs Mayūrī, Mainī, Hayalīlā, Mṛgī, Haṁsī, Kukkuṭī, Khaṇjanī and Gajagāminī one after the other, the order varying according to the Sampradāyas or schools of dance. After performing these Gatis she placeds her left hand and left foot forward simultaneously and performs Vaiṣṇava, Hayakrānta and Pratyāliḍha with the left hand placed on the chest in Sikhara while the right is let down by her side in Patākā pointing downwards. Finally, Citrakalāsa is performed (*NN* 40a-43a). *SDar* : Agrees with the descriptions given in the *NN* with the exception that it prescribes Añjali for the hands while acting "Bhavāni." It also directs the dancer to perform Cālakas. The dance is to be performed in the Rāsaka Tāla and three layas : Druta, Madhya and Vilamba. She ends up by doing Haṁsāsya (*SDar* 33-36b).

The Urūpas : The Urūpa is performed with Yati, Tāla, Laya, Sthāna, Cārī and hand gestures. It has twelve varieties :

(1) **Neri** : The dancer stands in the Caturaśra Sthāna and moves her foot in the Rathacakrā Gati and repeats the same with the other. The rhythm is Rāsatala and the tempo is slow. The dancer moves her Patākā hand in all directions simulating the movement of a swinging cord. The dancer moves her limbs harmoniously and Sauṣṭhava is observed. This is known as Śuddhaneri. In all the Urūpas, except Adṛṣtapṛṣṭhaka, Caturaśra is done after Bāhyabhramarī. In the Karaṇaneri, Chatra-bhramarī is performed (*NN* 43b). *SDar* : This agrees with the Anibandhaneri in *NN* (*SDar* 43a-b).

(2) **Karaṇaneri** : The dancer dances in Jhampātāla to the sound of the Gopuccha. Her hands are in Alapallava and she performs the following nine Karaṇas : Pārśvajānu, Ūrdhavajānu, Daṇḍapakṣa, Talavilāsita, Vidyudbhrānta, Candrāvarta, Niśum-bhita, Lalāṭatilaka and Latāvṛścika. She does these facing the left and the right after which she stands

in the Ālīḍha Sthāna. (*NN.* 43b). *SDar* : Does not give the names of the Karaṇas but agrees with the description given in *NN* (*SDar* 43b).

(3) **Bhitra :** The dancer performs various Sthānas and actions with the acompaniment of Gopuccha and other instruments. She performs Cālakas with the Nūpurapādikā Cārī. It is done facing all directions and Trisañca, Rekhā and Sauṣṭhava are its marked features (*NN* 43b-44a). *SDar* : This text mentions Trisañca, Cālaka, Rūpaka tāla and Dhruva and directs the dancer to move in various gaits (*SDar* 43b).

(4) **Citra :** The dancer mostly moves in the Tiryaṅmukhā Gati, though other suitable Gatis are done as well, and moves her Tripatākā hands in Cālaka. She obseves Sauṣṭhava, Trisañca and Pipiṭī to the Mallikāmoda tālas. She stands still after the performance. (*NN.* 44a). *SDar* : It speaks of Cālaka, Sauṣṭhava and Ekatāla done in various beautiful ways (*SDar* 43b-44b).

(5) **Natra :** The dancer moves in the Marālagati, and at intervals some others. Even tālas and proper yatibhedas are followed. She moves in many circles like a boy moving in circles while playing, and she stops when she wants to (*NN* 44a). *SDar* agrees with the portion describing the movement of a boy and says nothing about the rest (*SDar* 45b).

(6) **Adṛṣṭapṛṣṭhatulla :** The dancer performs the Karihastā Gati and others at intervals according to her wish. It is performed to Raccātāla, not too fast nor too slowly and has proper yatis. The hands are moved in various beautiful ways (*NN* 44a).

(7) **Tolarūpa :** The dancer dances quickly in various tālas with various Saṅkīrṇagatis. This is also known as Kuvāda (*NN* 44a).

(a) **Cakrabandha** : The dancer moves her hands, arms and feet. This is done to four to six tālas, one after the other, some fast, some slow, having a regular beat (*NN* 44b).

(b) **Ravicakra** : The dancer dances to six even measured tālas. Each tāla is done twice to form one unit and the units are performed one after another to accompany six Sthānas. Thus altogether twelve tālas are done as in Cakrabandha (*NN* 44b).

(c) **Padmabandha** : Four tālas are followed as in Ravicakra. The hands and the feet meet each other, separately. The left and the right hands and the feet meet each other. It is performed to the Vasutāla. The rest is similar to Ravicakra (*NN* 44b).

(d) **Nāgabandha** : Four tālas, done at the same intervals, are performed separately. Each of them are divided into three and they are done separately. After doing these three, one after the other, the hands and the feet are placed in their normal positions. The rest is similar to Padmabandha (*NN* 44b-45a).

(e) **Vṛkṣabandha** : Four tālas are done as in Padmabandha. The first half of these are done first and the last portions are done together. The hands and the feet are gradually moved forward. The rest is done to a different tāla (*NN* 45a).

(8) **Sīluka** : The dancer moves her Haṁsapakṣa hands and performs Kulīrikā and one other simila to it on all sides and moves forward. She moves th of one foot in Vānarakriḍita. This is also known as Jāramana (*NN* 45a). *SDar* : The dancer performs Sama, Viṣamasūcī and Sulla to Āditāla (*SDar* 45a).

(9) **Turlla :** The dancer performs the Aśliṣṭā Gati and Gajalīlā is quickly done. She moves her hands in the Padmakośa Vartanā and performs Sthānas on all sides (*NN* 45a). *SDar* : Tulla: Gajalīlā, tāla and Sauṣṭhava are followed (*SDar* 45a-b).

(10) **Prasara :** The dancer moves her Āviddhavakra hands and performs the Pārṣṇirecitikā Cārī with other appropriate for the performance. It is done in a slow tempo and to a rhythm of one beat (*NN* 45a). *SDar* : It speaks of the Āviddhavakra hands extended repeatedly and the rhythm is neither too slow nor too fast (*SDar* 45b).

(11) **Kartarī :** The dancer performs the Ūruveṇī Gati and other appropriate Gatis. The hands are moved near the chest and the Laghuśekhara-Sulus are performed. The dancer stands facing different directions each time. This is done with lightning speed (*NN* 45b). *SDar* : The dancer stands in Samapāda and quickly moves to the left and the right with her shanks crossed in Svastika (*SDar* 45a).

(12) **Hollu :** The dancer moves from her breasts her Latā hands to her back. ·She performs the Stambhakriḍanikā Cārī with other appropriate Cārīs. Yatilagna is created by Gatis done on all directions. It is also known as Palāśagṛdhrakrīḍā (*NN* 45b). *SDar* : Hulla : The dancer throws up her leg repeatedly and swings it gracefully in Laghuśekhara tāla (*SDar* 45a).

Dhuvāḍa : The dancer performs Bhramarī at the beginning and at the end of the performance. She does three Sulus near her breasts and performs Bhujaṅgatrāsita. All the Dhuvāḍas have Antarbhramari at the end. Dhuvāḍas can be of the following twelve types : (*NN* 45b):

(1) **Kalaviṅkavinoda** : The dancer performs the Cakrabhramarī, Niḥśaṅka, Ḍāṇṭu, Hormayī successively and finally she ends the performance with a jump (*NN* 45b-46a).

(2) **Tārkṣyapakṣavilāsita** : The dancer performs Cakrabhramarī, Hormayī, Ḍāṇṭu, Niḥśaṅka consecutively (*NN* 46a).

(3) **Vidyudvilāsita** : The dancer performs Cakrabhramarī, Ḍāṇṭu, Niḥśaṅka and Hormayī consecutively (*NN* 46a).

(4) **Vātyāvartitaka** : The dancer performs Cakrabhramarī, Hormayī, Niḥśaṅka and Ḍāṇṭu consecutively (*NN* 46a).

(5) **Ravisañcara** : The dancer performs Bāhyabhramarī, Ḍāṇṭu, Hormayī and Niḥśaṅka consecutively (*NN* 46a).

(6) **Nartanābharaṇa** : Bāhyabhramarī, Niḥśaṅka, Hormayī and Ḍāṇṭu are performed consecutively (*NN* 46a).

(7) **Tiryaktāṇḍava** : Bāhyabhrmaṛi, Aḍālu, Hormayī and Rāyaraṅgālu are performed consecutively (*NN* 46a).

(8) **Raṅgabhūṣaṇa** : Bāhyabhramarī, Rāyaraṅgālu, Hormayī and Aḍālu are done consecutively (*NN* 46a).

(9) **Vādiśagajabhairuṇḍa** : Tirapabhramarī, Ḍāṇṭu, Aṇḍatara and Hormayī are done consecutively (*NN* 46a-b).

(10) **Rolavāṅgavilāsita** : Tirapabhramarī, Hormayī, Ḍāṇṭu and Rāyaraṅgālu are done consecutively (*NN* 46b).

(11) **Pakṣiśārdūlaka** : Tirapabhramarī, Aḍālu, Ḍāṇṭu and Niḥśaṅka are done consecutively (*NN* 46b). *SDar* : It is described as a form of Lāganṛtya. The dancer moves round her hands standing in Maṇḍi[19] (*SDar* 46b).

(12) **Simhapluta** : Tirapabhramarī, Rāyaraṅgālu, Ḍāṇṭu and Hormayī are performed consecutively (*NN* 46b).

ṢDar : Dhruvāḍas consists of jumping steps in Karaṇas done to Tullas. *Or* : Ākāśacarīs are done twice and Tiripa follows. Finally, Muru[20] is performed. *Or* : Two Lāgas and Tiripa are done. Muru and Tiripa are done finally (*SDar* 45b).[21]

Viḍulāgavas : The Lāgas are danced, each accompanied by Sulu, and each being repeated once or twice and sometimes mixed with other Lāgas. At the end the dancer jumps. Viḍulāgava has the following fifteen varieties (*NN* 46b) :

(1) **Aḍālu** : The dancer jumps in Sulu with her feet waving like the wings of a bird and turns round. Then she comes down (*NN* 46b), *SDar* : Aḍāla. (45b-46a).

(2) **Rāyaraṅgālu** : The dancer throws upward one of her feet in Sulu and repeats the same with the other (*NN.* 46b-47a). *SDar* : Rāyaraṅgāla (*SDar* 45b).

(3) **Niḥśaṅka** : The dancer performs Sulu, joins her feet, jumps up and lands at some distance (*NN* 47a; *SDar* 46a).

(4) **Hormayī** : The dancer makes Svastika with her feet and moves one backward. Then she crosses it with the other. *SDar* prescribes Alāta for the feet and agrees with *NN* in describing the rest of the action : Hurumayī (*NN* 47a; *SDar* 46a).

(5) **Ḍāṇṭu** : The dancer performs Sulu, places one foot forward and crosses it with the other (*NN* 47a).

(6) **Aṇḍatara** : The feet are joined at the front. (*NN.* 47a; *SDar.* 46a).

(7) **Diṇḍu** : The dancer jumps with both feet, moves round and jumps again (*NN* 47a). *SDar* (*SDar* 46a).

(8) **Rāyadi Pakṣisālava** : Niḥśaṅka and Diṇḍu are performed in the air (*NN* 47a).

(9) **Alaga** : The dancer jumps up with her face downwards and comes down to the front. Then she stands still performing Kukkuṭāsana (*NN* 47a).

(10) **Ḍheṅkī** : The dancer jumps and moves both feet together from one side to the other (*NN* 47a; *SDar* 46a).

(11) **Bīsa** : The dancer places her feet on the ground and then she jumps (*NN* 47a; *SDar* 46a-b).

(12) **Muṅgaraṇa** : The dancer jumps from the Saṁhata position to the front and sits on the ground in Kukkuṭāsana facing backwards (*NN* 47a).

(13) **Hiṅgaraṇa** : Muṅgaraṇa is reversed (*NN* 47a).

(14) **Kartaridiṇḍu** : The dancer performs Kartarī and Hormayī.

(15) **Lagadiṇḍu** : The dancer jumps in the air (*SDar* 45b).

SDar : Lāga is jumping in Karṇata style (*SDar* 45b).

Śabdanṛtya : This is done in tāla and words beginning with the letter "ta" are sung to such notes as Śaḍga and Ma (*NN* 47b).

The dancer stands in Caturaśra and places her Śikhara hand on her navel and the other hand in Patākā is placed in front of her breasts. Then she performs Subhaga and places one Sūcī foot forward while the other foot is placed backward in Añcita. She moves round her hands keeping them in their own places. She moves the second foot backward and expresses Bhāva with her movements. In this Śabdanṛtya the tāla is indicated by the feet and akṣaras are expressed by the laya (*NN* 47b-48a; *SDar* 46a-47b).

SDar : Says that Karaṇa, Nṛttahastas, Sthānas are applied in the Śabdanṛtya. It has two varieties : Akṣarapradhāna and Svarapradhāṇa. This text describes Śuddhasuḍanṛtya and Sālagasuḍanṛtya as forms of Śabdanṛtyas in the course of which it gives seven kinds of Sālagasuḍas : Dhruva, Maṇṭha,

Rūpaka, Jhampātāla, Tṛtīya, Aṣṭatālī and Ekatālī. It also quotes the view of Ratnākara in describing these Sālagasuḍas. According to this text, Ratnākara gives the following seven kinds of Sālagasuḍas : Dhruva, Maṇṭha, Pratimaṇṭha, Niḥśāruka, Adrutāla, Rāsa and Ekatālī. Śuddhasuḍanṛtya can be of the following eight varities; Elā, Karaṇa, Ḍheṅkī, Vartanā, Jhoṁbāḍa, Lambha, Rāsa and Ekatālī. Some of these Nṛtyas are discussed.

1. **Dhruvanṛtya** : This form of dance begins with Caccatkāra done with Dhruva. The dancer moves her body moving her hands in Āveṣṭita and other Hastakaraṇas. She begins from the right side and gradually moves to the centre of the stage. She performs hand gestures and dances to Dhruva. She begins with Udgrāha and Ābhoga and ends with Udgrāha (*SDar*. 49b).

(2) **Maṇṭhanṛtya** : The dancer dances once in Maṇṭhatāla. Dhruvaka is done two to four times while Ābhoga is done only once. Dhruva is again performed with various hand gestures. Sauṣṭhava must be observed (*SDar* 49b-50a).

(3) **Rūpakanṛtya** : Udgrāha, Ābhoga and Dhruva are sung very quickly and the dance is performed following the tempo (*SDar* 50a).

(4) **Jhampātāla** : The dancer dances in a "middle" tempo following a song sung to the Jhampā tāla. Kalāsa and Lāsyāṅgas are performed with the hand gestures (*SDar* 50a).

(5) **Tritīyanṛtya** : The dancer dances in a fast tempo in the Tṛtīya tāla. Lāsyāṅgas and Kalāsa are performed with appropriate hand gestures (*SDar* 50a).

(6) **Adrutālanṛtya** : The dancer dances in a slow tempo to Adrutāla. Udgrāha and Dhruvaka are sung (*SDar* 50a-b).

(7) **Ekatālīnṛtya :** The dancer dances in a fast tempo to Ekatāla. Bhramarikās are performed in between the Cālakas. Kalāsas and Lāsyāṅgas are performed (*SDar* 50a).

Śabdacāli : Sthānaka, Cārī, Khaṇḍa, Maṇḍala and Karanas are performed with appropriate Hastas. Pramāṇa is observed (*SDar* 43a).

Svarābhinaya : The Rāgas of a particular song is known as Grahasvara. This is one of the six Rāgas and is to be acted with hand gestures (*NN* 48a).

(1) **Ṣaḍga :** The right hand is moved in Alapadma and the left hand in Catura. The dancer moves round in Mayuralalita and Śaḍga is acted (*NN* 48a; *SDar* 48b).

(2) **Ṛṣabha :** The right hand in Haṁsāsya and the left hand in Ardhacandra, are placed on the hips. The head is kept straight and the dancer stands in the Brahmā Sthāna (*NN* 48a). *SDar* : The lines are interchanged by the scribe in the *Bod. ms.* Paris gives the same view (*SDar* 48b; *Paris ms* 107a).

(3) **Gāndhāra :** The dancer looks with Karuṇā Dṛṣṭi, bends her head and moves her Śukatuṇḍa hand. She performs the Aśvakrāntā Cārī (*NN* 48; *SDar* 48b).

(4) **Madhyama :** The dancer crosses her Patākā hands in Svastika and moves her head in Vidhuta. She stands in the Śaiva Sthāna and performs Katicchinna with Hāsyā Dṛṣṭi. The acting should be grave (*NN* 48b; *SDar* 48b).

(5) **Pañcama :** The dancer moves her hand in Alapallava while her head moves in Dhuta. *SDar* prescribes Vaiṣṇava Sthāna and Kāntā Dṛṣti in addition (*NN* 48b; *SDar* 48b-49a).

(6) **Ḍhaivata :** The dancer moves her hands in Kāṅgula, looks with Bībhatsā Dṛṣṭi, moves her head in Parāvṛtta and stands in the Pratyālīḍha Sthāna (*NN* 48b; *SDar* 49a).

(7) **Niṣāda :** The dancer moves her hands in Karihasta and glancing charmingly she moves her head in Vidhuta (*NN* 48b; *SDar* 49a).

Svaramaṇṭhanṛtya : Svarābinaya is performed as a whole or by part to tāla and Yati. Then Śabda, Udgrāha, Śabda, Tena, Śabdakhaṇḍa, Dhruvaka and Sabda are done consecutively. Finally, the dancer in Yatigīta. She dances with the proper Hāva, Bhāva, laya, tāla and Gati (*NN* 48b-49a). *SDar* : A Gīta is set to a Rāga which has three main Svaras. The dancer should follow these Svaras (*SDar* 48a-49b).

Gītanṛtya : The dancer dances with Sauṣṭhava with songs sung to tāla. These Nṛtyas are named after particular songs. The Varṇas are acted with the body. Bhāvas are presented with glances and the meanings are expressed with gestures. Tālas and Grahas are performed by the movements of the feet. Ela, Śuddhasuda, Varṇa, Ālikrama, Śrīraṅga, Viprakirṇa, Sālagasuḍa and other songs are sung and Nṛtya is performed to convey meaning while Nṛtta is done when it does not have any meaning (*NN* 49a). *SDar* : The dancer performs with Sauṣṭhava the following tālas and Varṇas. The words are acted witth the hands and Bhāvas are aroused. The dances are named after the songs (*SDar* 48a).

Cindu : This is a form of Deśī, originating in Drāviḍa. It has six varieties (*NN* 49a). *SDar* gives two varieties (*SDar* 50b).

(1) **Śuddhacindu :** It is done in the Drāviḍa language and consists of Udgrāha and Dhruvapada. Melāpa and Ābhoga do not accompany it (*NN* 49a-b).

(2) **Binducindu :** Udgrāha and Melāpa are sung once and Dhruva follows, done repeatedly with two or three virāmas and it bears the name of the leader of the performance. The performance ends with Dhruva (*NN* 49b).

(3) **Tiruvaṇicindu :** Udgrāha is sung and it bears the name of the leader of the performance. Dhruva

follows, sung to a tempo slower by half to that of the former. The two are repeatedly sung (*NN* 49b).

(4) **Mālācindu :** Cindu is done in an irregular series (*NN* 49b).

(5) **Kolacāricindu :** Ālāpa is done with a series of letters which bring out the meaning and has no tāla. It is done in Paṭarāga. Five or seven Cindus are done at intervals. Pilmirūka and Miruramyakalāsa are done. When this is done with words related to the Śāstras it is known as Kolacāricindu. The same done otherwise is Kaṭṭacindu (*NN* 49b). *SDar* : It varies with different schools (*SDar* 50b) : Kvālacāricindu, Kālacārī.

(6) **Gitamudrācindu :** This is like Gīta and has varieties. Melāpaka, Antarā and Ābhoga sung together or separately, two, three or four times, are known as Cindus. If it begins with Melāpa or Dhruva then it must end in Udgrāha. If it begins with something else then Dhruvaka is sung at the end (*NN* 49b-50a).

(7) **Viḍacindu :** It is done in Pillamuru (*SDar* 50b).

Cindunṛtya : In the Cindunṛtya Syanditā, Apasyanditā, Adhyardhikā and Sthitāvartā Cārīs are performed. Vaiśākha, Āliḍha and Pratyāliḍha Mandalas, Lāsyāṅgas, Recakas of the head, feet and the hands are performed. Rekhā and Sauṣṭhava are observed. It is done with Bhāva and Hāva in Sūlu and Citrakalāsa. It is accompanied by the sound of the Cañcakinkinīs. The dresses and the languages for the presentation are appropriate to the country where it is performed or to the practice of a particular school (*NN* 50b). *SDar* : The dancer moves in various Gatis following tālas, Ghargharas, Tuḍukas and Cindu while the sounds of the Cañcatkinkinīs form an accompaniment. Kalāsas and Lāsyāṅgas are performed. Dhṛtahasta and Triśūla are performed. Udgrāha and Dhruvapadas are sung in the

Drśviḍa language. Ābhoga is never done in Cindunṛtya (*SDar* 50b).

Dharu : Dharu is written in Tailaṅgabhāṣā and is devoid of Udgrāha and Ābhoga. It has two varieties :

(1) **Kaṭṭaḍidharu :** It is a Bandha form of dancing. The dancer enters the stage holding her veil while Ardikā is played. She then dances with Ālāpa. Then she moves with graceful steps taken from Tuṅga, Sulu and Lāsyāṅgas. Pilmurūka is also performed. She dances Lāsyāṅgas with Bhāva and Hāva performing Paṭṭi with Dharu, done two to seven times. After doing Kalāsa and Kaimuraśabda, Citra is performed to a fast tempo. She performs Sulu, Tuṅga, Gharghara in even tālas uttering sounds. Then she dances with Kalāsa Śabda and Padas, done twice, and makes Arddi in the air. This dance, a Deśī form, originated in Telaṅga and is also known as Dharukaṭṭaḍi (*NN* 50b-51a).

***SDar*:** According to this text Tuḍuka is played instead of Arddikā. The dancer acts Nāndī. Sūlupa is also performed. The rest of the action is the same as that described in the *NN*. At the end the text says that Kaṭṭarī emerges out of Niśama, and this is described as Deśī Kaṭṭarividhi. *SDar* states that the description given in it of Kaṭṭarī is only an outline. The movements described are thus the basic features but different schools may add minor details (*SDar* 51a-b).

Ālapa : Ālapa is sung to laya and tāla and the dancer dances with appropriate gestures of the hand done in a series. This gīta is devoid of Dhātu and such other musical elements (*NN* 50b). *SDar* : We find two views: (i) The action is the same as described in the *NN* but the tāla suggested is Ekatāla. (ii) Ālapa should be in the language of Andhra, and Dhruva and Dhātu should be introduced (*SDar* 51b).

Sūlupa : Harmonic combination of stringed instruments and drums like Mṛdaṅgas. This accompanies gay dances

(*NN* 51a). *SDar* : Prescribes Kinnarī tāla and otherwise agrees with the rest. (*SDar*. 52a).

Tuṅga : The dancer jumps up and down with Sauṣṭhava (*NN* 51a).

Pada : This consists of four Virāmpada and may be done to any tāla. It also includes Udgrāha svara (*NN* 51a). *SDar* : The accompanying song is written in the Karṇāṭa language; Virāmas are not mentioned (*SDar* 52a).

(2) **Muktadharu :** The first of Dharu is danced and repeated, followed by the last. The dancer dances several times to a tāla of different layas or she performs a different type of Dharu and does Ḍunnatara. Here the tāla has a fast tempo (*NN* 51a).

Dhruvapada : The accompanying song is written in the languages of the central part of the country and has two to four sentences depicting the ordinary life of people. It has Śṛṅgāra Rasa and is set to Rāgas, tālas and padas. Anuprāsa or Yamaka are used at the end of the lines. Each line is constituted in the above mentioned manner and four such lines with Udgrāha, Dhruvaka and Ābhoga makes a Dhruvapada. This Dhruvapada is sung and the dancer dances Lāsyāṅgas with beautiful Hāvas and Bhāvas in graceful gaits and Kāntā Dṛṣṭi. She moves from one pada to another with a smile and spaces out the performance with occasional shivers. The whole performance is done with Abhinaya in Rekhā and grace. This is Dhruvapada Nṛtya done with different Mukharāgas and movements of the eyes and eyebrows that depict Śṛṅgāra Rasa. The Recaka of Grīvā is also done and Hāvas and Bhāvas are expressed (*NN* 51a-b; *SDar* 53a).

The Anibandhanṛtyas

(1) **Nāmāvalī :** Various graceful gaits characterise this movement. The dance is full of expressive actions.

The rhythm that accompany are named as Tivaṭī and Graha (*NN* 51b-52a).

(2) **Yati :** The dancer dances Lāga with various beautiful rhythmic movements and gaits full of even pauses (*NN* 52a). *SDar* : The dancer dances to the Caccatpuṭa tāla and instruments accompany her (*SDar* 44a).

(3) **Neri :** This is marked by a slow tempo and various gaits that follow Āditāla. (*NN* 52a). *SDar* : Adds Rekhā, Pramāṇa and Mudrā. Although *SDar*. calls Neri an Urūpa, yet its description agrees with that of the Anibandaha Neri described in *NN* and not with the Urūpa-Neri mentioned there (*SDar* 43a-b).

(4) **Sālaṁganeri :** The Neri is performed with single and double-hand gestures. (*NN*. 52a). *SDar* : Speaks of Saṁyuta hands only (*SDar* 43b).

(5) **Saṁkāṇaneri :** The dancer performs the Neri with her hands moved in Nṛttahasta gestures, done with one or both the hands (*NN* 52a; *SDar* 43b).

(6) **Bhāvaneri :** The dancer performs the Neri expressing Rasa and Bhāva (*NN* 52a; *SDar* 43b).

(7) **Naḍaneri :** The same performed quickly (*NN* 52a). *SDar* : Naraneri (*SDar* 43b).

(8) **Kaivartana :** The dancer joins her hands at the wrists and moves them gracefully to her left and right sides (*NN* 52a).

(9) **Muru :** The dancer repeatedly wrings and throws her body in Vikṣipta and Āksipta bringing forward her hands in Tripatāka (*NN* 52a). *SDar* : It says that the dancer does the above mentioned actions in the Utkaṭa Sthāna. The performance can also be done in the Āditāla (*SDar* 45a).

(10) **Raṭṭamuru :** The dancer wrings her body repeatedly and violently (*NN* 52a). *SDar* : Rirdamuru (*SDar* 43a).

(11) **Tālarūpaka :** The dancer dances quickly to a very few tālas. The dance is of various gaits (*NN* 52a).

(12) **Guṇḍāla :** The dancer revolves quickly in time with the beat and moves her shanks in and out (*NN* 52b).

(13) **Kamala :** The dancer moves her arm in various ways such as Alapallavavartanā and keeps her hips, sides and head straight (*NN* 52b).

(14) **Natajānuka :** The dancer moves on her heels (*NN* 52b).

(15) **Maṇḍī :** This seems to mean a dance of which the chief feature is movements in a series (*NN* 52b).

(16) **Muḍupa :** The dancer dance Mudupacārīs following the tāla used in various gaits (*NN* 52b).

(17) **Muraṇḍarī :** The dancer performs Bhramarī in between two Muḍupas (*NN* 52b).

(18) **Kuḍupa :** The dancer trembles and extends her shank quickly with her big toe stretched out while the rest of the toes are curved. Ghargharīs accompany her (*NN* 52b).

(19) **Tiryakaraṇa :** The dancer performs Bhramarī in between some Karaṇas. The whole action is done repeatedly (*NN* 52b).

(20) **Lāvaṇī :** The dancer stands in the Samapāda Sthāna and bends her waist in Ardhacandra. Then she revolves her body, keeping her waist fixed (*NN* 52b-53a; *SDar* 45a).

(21) **Caṭu :** The dancer touches the ground with her knees and describes a circle with her legs. Her hands are in Latā and she revolves (*NN* 53a).

Daṇḍarāsanṛtya : This dance is a part of the Vasantotsava arranged for the pleasure of kings, and is done to the music of such instruments as the Muraja. The dancers holding Daṇḍas in their hands, dance together or separately in a group of four which grows to one of eight, sixteen, thirty-two and sixty-four. The Daṇḍas are sixteen aṅgulas in width and length and made of gold. They are straight, hard and rounded sticks, plain or painted and without joints. The dancers according to their country, hold either Daṇḍacāmara or Daṇḍakṣaumāñcala or Daṇḍakāchurikā. The dancers strike their Daṇḍas four, five or six times at the front, at the back and at the sides to produce sounds. They dance facing the audience on their left and right doing various Cārīs and Bhramarīs and frequently form a circle (*NN* 53a-b.)

Rāsanṛtya : Daṇḍarāsa, performed without the Daṇḍa, is Rāsanṛtya (*NN* 53b).

Jakkaḍī : This form of dance is performed to various rhythms. The accompanying song is in the language of the Yavanas. The dancer holds her veil. The dance is graceful and full of Bhramarīs. Dhruva and Śamya music go with it. There are few movements in this form of dancing. Persian scholars describe it as Jakkaḍī, favourite of the Yavanas (*NN* 53a). *SDar* agrees with the description given in *NN* and prescribes Gajara instruments to accompany the dancer. It has Jakkarī in one place and Jakkaḍī in another (*SDar* 52b-53a).

Maṭṭanṛtya : Mada in the Paris *ms.* (*SDar.* 98a). It is done with Madhyasañca, and Pramāṇa and Rekhā are observed (*SDar* 41b).

Vivartananṛtya : The dancer dances to the Dhruvatāla moving her left or right side of the body. She acts Svaras (*SDar* 47a-b).

Camatkāranṛtya : The hands are joined and the dancer dances to the accompaniment of the Akṣaras. The accompanying tāla is Gārugī (*SDar* 47b).

Vaipota : The dancer moves her head in Vidhuta and Kampita and all the four Recakas. The accompanying song is written in the language of Andhra or Karṇāṭa and sung in

Dhruvadhātu. Kailamuru is performed with Lāsya in between (*SDar* 52a).

Bandhanṛtya : This is done by two dancers moving all the parts of their bodies simultaneously and performing Karaṇas. Three, four or seven dancers may perform it. All must be beautiful girls (*SDar* 52a-b).

Kalpanṛtya : Karaṇas and Sthānakas are performed and their applications depend on the dancer. Usually in this form of Gītanṛtya Kalpatālas accompany (*SDar* 52b). *SDar* discusses Vaipota, Bandhanṛtya, Kalpanṛtya, Jakkarī and Dhruvapadanṛtya as forms of Vaipota (*SDar* 52a-53b).

Peraṇi : The dancer decorates her body with Bhaṣma and dances with Ghargharikā moving rhythmically (*SDar* 53a-b). *SSam* : Nṛtta, Kaivāra, Gharghara, Bāgada and Gīta constitute Peraṇi (*SSam* 6.214). *SR* : Gharghara, Viṣama, Bhāva, Kavicāra and Gīta constitute Peraṇi (*SR* 7.1303-4).

Gauṇḍalī : Complicated instrumental music and Prabandha accompany the performance. Songs, Sālagasuḍas and Dhruvas are performed. Lāsyāṅgas are performed to a fast tempo. She sings and plays the Trivalī. The dancer is known as Guṇdalā and if she does not sing she is called Mūkaguṇḍalī. The dress and make up should be appropriate to the Karṇāṭa country (*SDar* 53b; *SSam* 6.226; *BhP* p. 46). The description of Peraṇi in *SR* agrees with that in *SDar*, but it is discussed in a greater detail. They are translated by K.K. Raja (*Ad Lib Bulletin* pp. 191-8).

Gharghara : A performance done with Kinkinīs is called Gharghara : which can be of these six types (*NN* 50a) :

(1) **Piḍibāṭa :** The dancer stamps the ground alternately with the sole of one or both feet (*NN* 50a). *SR* : Paḍibāṭa (*SR* 7.1306-7).

(2) **Śiripiḍī :** The dancer repeatedly moves forward and backward touching the ground with her soles (*NN* 50a). *SR* : Śiripaṭa (*SR* 7.1308).

(3) **Paṭava :** The dancer stamps on the ground with one foot (*NN* 50a). *SR* : Apaḍapa (*SR* 7.1307).

(4) **Lagapāṭa :** Both the feet are shaken delicately in the air (*NN* 50a-b). *SR* : Alagapāṭa (*SR* 7.1309).

(5) **Śirihira** : The dancer places one foot in Sama, puts the other forward and shakes her shank. *Or* : The dancer shakes her shanks standing on the ground in a natural position (*NN* 50b; *SR* 7.1310-1).

(6) **Khalu-hula :** The dancer stamps the ground with the heel of her left foot touching the ground with the forepart of the sole and moves round to the left and the right with the other touching the ground with the forepart of the sole (*NN* 50b; *SR* 7.1312).

Epilogue

The great number of early treatses in Sanskrit devoted to the analysis and exposition of dance techniques indicates the self-conscious artistry that attended upon the development of the dance. The many accounts of the origin of the dance in India show that this art had its roots in folk-culture and was not entirely an artifical product of court-life or academic research. But there would seem to have been a constant endeavour to mould the art into a vehicle of a highly sophisticated aesthetics. There is no doubt that in the absence of a controlling principle of beauty mere movements become meaningless gymnastics. Also, in concentrating upon the individual movements one may wholly lose the rhythm of the sequence. It is perhaps with these contingencies in mind that the Sanskrit theoreticians of the dance have repeatedly sought to impress upon the dancer the importance of artistic unity. The intense effort required for mastering individual movements may very well blind one to the total effect. That is why the Sanskrit treatises reiterate, while imposing upon the dancer the rigour of difficult gestures or stances, the need for gearing those movements to Sauṣṭhava and Pramāna,[1] that is, grace and harmony. Even more significant is their insistence upon the necessity of the movements of the dancer conforming to the Rekhā.[2] This may be defined as the composite image of the lines along which the movements flow at any given moment. Their concern for this alone shows that the lovers of the dance were not obsessed, as it may appear, with only gymnastic skill. It is therefore only fair that the treatises should be considered in a background of the dance of reality.

It is difficult to understand the exact relationship of the "classical" dances of modern India to the ancient tradition in view of the conflicting claims of authenticity made by the present-day artistes. That the technique followed by modern artistes is based on some tradition is beyond doubt. Many changes are apparent, yet we may find exciting traces of an older art. The term Sabdaṁ that is so well-known to Bharatanāṭyaṁ dancers, connects this dance to the Śabdanṛtya of *NN* and *SDar*. The Śakatāsya Karaṇa can be found in the Odiṣī dance. Similarly, the Cāli of Manipurī, a preliminary dance sequence, is very possible derived from Cāli, the Deśi Lāsyāṅga which is described in *SR*.

However, since in most cases the descent of the tradition has been oral, the possibility of corruption and radical change must not be overlooked. It is in this context then that an account of the details of the original techniques of classical dancing in India can be the most useful. The present work has been prepared in the hope that it may be of some help in formulating a creative examination of this ancient art.

Appendix

Two more texts on dancing have been edited and published since the previous chapters were sent to the press. One is *Nṛtyādhyāya* of Aśokamalla, edited by Dr. Priyabala Shah and the other is *Nṛtyaratnāvalī* of Jāyasenapati, edited by Dr. V. Raghavan. This latter text has not been available to me. Another text, *Nṛtyaratnakośa,* edited by R.C. Parikh and Dr. Priyabala Shah, is a part of *Saṅgītarāja* of Mahārāṇā Kumbha. I have mentioned it previously (Chapter 1, p. 6) but since it was not available to me then, I take the opportunity of setting down my notes on it here.

Nṛtyādhyāya, a 14th/15th century text, mainly follows *SR.* It is an incomplete text in which Aṅga, Upāṅga, Pratyaṅga, Cārī, Māṇḍala, Sthāna, Karaṇa, Aṅgahāra and Kalāsa are discussed. It begins with the description of hand gestures and ends with Kalāsa. It is this description of Kalāsa that lends to this text a special importance, for it seems to be here that this class of movements is described for the first time. This text also describes Muḍupacārī, which is, as noted by the editor, P. Shah, obviously another name for Madhupacārī, an ākāśacārī mentioned by Kohala according to Kallinātha's commentary on *SR. Nṛdh,* is the only extant text that I have come across which describes Vartanās and Cālakas fully. These movements are described by Kohala, as quoted by Kallinātha in his commentary on *SR* and those descriptions are the same as those found in *Nṛdh*. Since they do not appear in the actual text of *SR*. I have given their descriptions in the context of *Nṛdh*. Incidentally, it describes several Vartanās and Cālakas that are not mentioned by Kohala. Besides Kalāsas, Muḍupacārīs, Vartanās and Cālakas, *Nṛdh* also describes some new forms of Deśī Lāsyāṅgas, Sthānas and Utplutikaraṇas.

Saṅgitarāja by Mahāranā Kumbhakarṇadeva is a work on music, dance and instrumental music. *Nṛtyaratnakośa* is the section that deals with dancing. The first part of *NRK*, the only part available to me, is divided into four ullāsas. The first ullāsa deals with the stage, pūrvaṁga, four different abhinayas (āṅgika, vācika, sāttvika and āhārya). Āṅgika describes movements of different aṅgas. Here *NRK* follows the *NŚ* and *SR*. Cālakas and Vartanās are described after Kallinātha. The second ullāsa describes Cārī, Sthānaka and Recaka.

The few variations are recorded later in this chapter.

Kālāsa : This is a special type of sequence. There is no textual definition although its various forms are described. Kay Ambrose states that the word is derived from the Arabic word Xalāsa which means 'conclusion.' Ambrose also reports that Kalāsa occurs in Kathakali and that it has the vigorous movements typical of pure Tāṇḍava.[1] Kalāsas are six in number : Vidyutkalāsa, Khaḍgakalāsa, Mṛgakālasa, Bakakalāsa, Plavakalāsa and Haṁsakalāsa. The first two are done in plutamāna, the next two are done in gurumāna, the fifth is done in laghumāna while the sixth is done in drutamāna.[2] Vidyutkalāsa can be of six kinds, Khadgakalāsa can be of four kinds, Mṛgakalāsa has only one variety Plava and Baka can be of four kinds while Haṁsa can be of three kinds.

Vidyutkalāsa : Movements of this class are characterised by their great speed which is likened to that of lightening. The body is placed obliquely and moves up and down. Some hand-gestures are also prescribed, but only Patākā is specifically named (*Nṛdh* 1570-71).

(1) The left hand in Patākā is placed on the right ear. The other hand is placed on the left hip and on the left shank. Then this is done in reverse with the hands moving quickly (*Nṛdh* 1572-3).

(2) The right hand moves in Ardhacandra. The dancer looks to the front and bends her knee in the form of a bow (*Nṛdh* 1574).

(3) The dancer performs Añjali with her hands and her glance is in sama. Then she stretches her fingers and changes her hands into Śikhara in front of her (*Nṛdh* 1575).

(4) The Keśabandha hands are moved alternately on the forehead. Then they are placed on right and left sides in Patākā (*Nṛdh* 1576).

(5) One hand in Puṣpapuṭa is placed above the head. The dancer puts her hands together and glances at her sides. Then she quickly touches her right foot with the right hand and the left foot with left hand (*Nṛdh* 1577-8).

(6) The dancer dances in plutamāṇa with her hands in Makara (*Nṛdh* 1579).

Khaḍgakalāsa

(1) The dancer looks quickly to her front and behind her with her head (or possibly the whole body) turned left and right. Her hands are moved in various ways such as Ardhacandra and she dances in plutamāna (*Nṛdh* 1580-1).

(2) The left hand is placed on the hips, presumably the left. The other hand assumes Khaḍga and is shaken. It is then changed to Ardhacandra. This is followed by Kapota with the hands raised. Finally, one hand is placed below in Muṣṭi while the other hand is placed obliquely in Patāka (*Nṛdh* 1582-3).

(3) The feet are placed forward and the hands perform Tripatākā (*Nṛdh* 1584).

(4) The hands assume Svastika, Karkaṭa, Muṣti, Patākā and Catura. They express firmness, delusion, the action of killing and the action of falling (*Nṛdh* 1585).

Mṛgakalāsa

The dancer dances on her toes, raises her knees and strikes the ground repeatedly with her hands in Mṛgaśīrṣa. She jumps like a deer in gurumāna (*Nṛdh* 1587-8).

Bakakalāsa

The dancer's hands which are in Sandaṁśa and Mukula are moved at the same level from the left and right like the wings of a stork. The dancer gets up from a sitting position in laghumāna and dances with Sauṣṭhava (*Nṛdh* 1589-90).

(1) The dancer stands in Saṁhata after doing Bhrahmarī. The hands are in Alapadma and Arāla. The feet are brought in alternately or shaken one at a time. One hand is in Mukula. The dancer moves like a stork looking for a fish. She moves slowly on her toes to the front and at the back (*Nṛdh* 1591-3).

(2) The dancer stands in Viṣamāsana with her hands in Tripatākā. She proceeds step by step with her feet in Maṇḍikā and changes her hands to Sandaṁśa. She looks quickly at her front and at both sides (*Nṛdh* 1594-5).

(3) The right knee is quickly brought from the left and placed on the ground and the left knee is also quickly brought from the right and placed on the ground. This is described as Maṇḍikā by Aśokamalla. Then one hand assumes Mukula. The dancer at first moves quickly and then slowly. She stumbles and strikes the ground like a fish freed from the clutch of a stork. The

hands are changed to Alapadma, Arāla and Mukula (*Nṛdh* 1596-7).

(4) The hands assume Uttānavañcita first and then changed to Ardhacandra. Then they are placed on the hips. The dancer moves to the front and to the back (of the stage) in different gaits. The hands touch the big toes and thus the dancer assumes the figure of a stork (*Nṛdh* 1600-1).

Plavakalāsa

The dancer stands in Viṣamasthāna and jumps up in Sama feet. She wanders around with her hands in Tripatākā (*Nṛdh* 1602-3).

(1) The hands rest on the navel in Tripatākā or Patākā (*Nṛdh* 1603-4).

(2) The dancer stretches her left knee and the left hand with the hands in Tripatākā. She moves to the left in laghumāna and assumes either Sama or Visaṁasthāna. Then she jumps up with her feet in Sama (*Nṛdh* 1605-6).

(3) The hands are placed on the hips and the dancer assumes Sama or Viṣamāsana. Then she jumps up and comes down to the ground. She moves in laghumāna to the front or to the back with down cast eyes (*Nṛdh* 1607-8).

(4) The dancer moves to the front, to the back, to the right and to the left. These four movements may be done one after the other (*Nṛdh* 1609).

Haṁsakalāsa : The dancer moves in different gaits like a swan with her hands in Haṁsāsya (*Nṛdh* 1610).

(1) One hand in Makara is placed at the right side. The other hand is probably in Patākā[3] (*Nṛdh* 1611).

(2) The Mukula hand is moved from the feet to the back. The dancer moves in Lāsya (*Nṛdh* 1612).

(3) The Haṁsāsya hands are placed at the sides. The dancer dances to Ālāpa, Varṇa and rhythm (*Nṛdh* 1613).

Muḍupacārī

'Muḍûpa is the upper side of a toe and the cārī done with the Muḍupa is called Muḍupacārī. It involves Nikuṭṭana.[4] Kohala mentions Nikuṭṭana only but say nothing about toes. *NRK* describes them as Deśīcārīs.

1. **Puraḥ Paścātsarā :** Nikuṭṭana is done in front of the body and at the back. Then with the back of the toes Nikuṭṭana is done at the same positions (*Nṛdh* 1089; *NRK* 2, 3, 11-2).
2. **Paścāt Puraḥsarā :** The same is done first at the back then in front (i.e. in reverse). (*Nṛdh* 1090; *NRK* 23.13).
3. **Madhyacakrā :** The dancer stands after doing Nikuṭṭana. Then she again performs Nikuṭṭana after turning round (*Nṛdh* 1091; *NRK* 2.3.36).
4. **Ekapadakuṭṭitā :** One foot performs Nikuṭṭana at its own side with the toes followed by similar movements of the other foot (*Nṛdh* 1092; *NRK* 2.3. 16).
5. **Padadvayanikuṭṭā :** Nikuṭṭana is done with both feet (*Nṛdh* 1093).
6. **Pādasthitinikuṭṭitā :** The dancer stands on the toes with one foot in Nikuṭṭana. This is repeated several times (*Nṛdh* 1094; *NRK* 2.3.17).
7. **Kramapādanikuṭṭikā :** The same as above is done with both feet (*Nṛdh* 1095; *NRK* 2.3.18).
8. **Samapādanikuṭṭitā :** Nikuṭṭana is done with same feet on the toes (*Nṛdh* 1096; *NRK* 2.3.32).
9. **Ḍamarukuṭṭitā :** One foot is placed in Nikuṭṭana after which the toes are dragged, Nikuṭṭana is resumed (*Nṛdh* 1097; *NRK* 2.3.20).

10. **Ḍamarudvayakuṭṭitā :** The same is done with both feet (*Nṛdh* 1098; *NRK* 2.3.21).

11. **Puraḥkeṣepanikuṭṭitā :** Nikuṭṭana is done in front on the back of the toes. After resting the feet for a while Nikuṭṭana is done again (*Nṛdh* 2.3.22).

12. **Paścātkṣepanikuṭṭitā :** The same is done at the back. (*Nṛdh* 1100; *NRK* 2.3.23).

13. **Pārśvakṣepanikuṭṭitā :** The same is done at the side (*Nṛdh* 1101; *NRK.* 2.3.24).

14. **Cakrakuṭṭanikā :** One foot in Nikuṭṭana is turned round from the side followed by a normal Nikuṭṭana (*Nṛdh* 1102; *NRK.* 2.3.33).

15. **Madhyasthāpanakuṭṭā :** Nikuṭṭana is done in front and at the back. Then after placing them in the middle Nikuṭṭana is again performed (*Nṛdh* 1103; *NRK* 2.3.26).

16. **Catuṣkoṇanikuṭṭitā :** Nikuṭṭana is done in front and at the back. This is repeated thrice. (*Nṛdh* 1104; *NRK* 2.3.25).

17. **Trikoṇacārī :** One foot rests on the toes. Then Nikuṭṭa is done in front, at the side and at the back. Finally Nikuṭṭana is done on the toes with the foot back in its original position (*Nṛdh* 1105-6; *NRK* 2.3.14-5).

18. **Tiraścinakuṭṭitā :** Nikuṭṭa is done by the foot first at its own side and then at the other side. Then it is placed in the middle and finally Nikuṭṭa is done obliquely (*Nṛdh* 1107-8; *NRK* 2.3.16).

19. **Anulomavilomā :** Trikoṇacārī is done in the regular way and then in reverse. Then the feet are placed in the original position and Nikuṭṭana is done (*Nṛdh* 1108; *NRK* 2.3.30).

20. **Pratilomānulomakā :** The order of Anulomavilomā is exactly reversed (*Nṛdh* 1109; *NRK* 2.3.31).

21. **Purastātluṭhitā** : The feet are dragged to the front (*Nṛdh* 1110; *NRK* 2.3.29).

22. **Pṛṣṭhaluṭhitā** : The feet are in Kuñcita while the toes are moved to the back. Then they are moved to the original position in front (*Nṛdh* 1111; *NRK* 2.3.28).

23. **Cakrakuṭṭitā** : After doing Nikuṭṭana the feet are turned round followed by Nikuṭṭana again in the original position (*Nṛdh* 1112). *NRK* : Vaktrakuṭṭanikā (*NRK* 2.3.35).

24. **Pārśvadvayacarī** : The dancer stands on the toes and performs Nikuṭṭana followed by Svastika from which she moves her feet to Nikuṭṭana first at one side and then at the other (*Nṛdh* 1113; *NRK* 2.3.19).

25. **Madhyaluṭhitā** : The dancer performs Nikuṭṭa and after a rest drags her feet and performs Nikuṭṭa (*Nṛdh* 1114; *NRK* 2.3.34).

Deśī Lāsyāṅga : Nṛtyādhyāya describes thirty-seven Deśī Lāsyaṅgas of which ten are taken from *SR*. The discrepances between the two texts are minor. *Nṛdh*, has Trikaṁ for Sūkaṁ, Leḍhi for Laḍhi, Thasaka for Dhasaka and Uyāraṁ for Oyārakaṁ.

1. **Cāli** : Same as in *SR* (*Nṛdh* 1519).
2. **Cālibaḍa** : Same as in *SR* (*Nṛdh* 1520).
3. **Tūkaṁ** : Same as in *SR* (*Nṛdh* 1521).
4. **Mana** : Same as in *SR* (*Nṛdh* 1522-3).
5. **Ledhi** : Same as in *SR* (*Nṛdh* 1524-5).
6. **Uroṅgaṇa** : Same as in *SR* (*Nṛdh* 1526-9).
7. **Ḍhillāi** : A dance of soft movements performed with Sauṣṭhava and full of Bhāva and Helā (*Nṛdh* 1530).
8. **Trikali** : The distinctive characteristics of this dance are Gati and Cārī. The head is moved in the following five way—Vidhuta, Ākampita, Dhuta, Parivāhita and Kampita (*Nṛdh* 1531-2).

9. **Kiṇṭu :** A dance in which movements of the eyebrows, breasts and hips follow the accompanying song and the rhythm (*Nṛdh* 1533).
10. **Deśīkāra :** A sequence of refined movements which avoid anything coarse or vulgar. Its exact naturre varies from one region to another and it may be presented in various modes (*Nṛdh* 1534).
11. **Nijāpana :** This is distinguished by Sauṣṭhava and Rekhā and Gati and is full of beautiful Bhāvas. The dancer looks at her hands (*Nṛdh* 1535).
12. **Ullāsa :** A rhythmic dance expressing Bhāvas. The movements are repeated, first at double the speed then at three times the speed of the first sequence (*Nṛdh* 1536-37).
13. **Thasaka :** Same as in *SR* (*Nṛdh* 1538).
14. **Bhāva :** This is a dance of the Nṛtya type in which great attention is paid to the tempo and songs (*Nṛdh* 1539).
15. **Sukalāsa :** This is also known as Meni. Cārīs are used in this dance involving considerable movements of the feet while songs are sung and instruments played. *Or,* Shānas and Cārīs are performed and the hands are moved in harmony with songs and music (*Nṛdh* 1540-1).
16. **Laya :** A dance of fast tempo expressing astonishment (*Nṛdh* 1542).
17. **Ḍhāla :** The dancer moves her body like the movement of a drop of water on a lotus. This is also known a Tāna (*Nṛdh* 1543).
18. **Cheva :** The dancer expresses emotions with the corners of her eyes and the eyebrows. (*Nṛdh.* 1544).
19. **Aṅgahāra :** Same as in *SR* (*Nṛdh* 1545).
20. **Laṅghita :** This is danced to the music of instruments. The dancer stops at intervals (*Nṛdh* 1546).

21. **Vihāsī :** Same as in *SR* (*Nṛdh* 1547).

22. **Nīki :** A dance in which the dancer takes stumbling steps rhythmically and a uniform tempo (*Nṛdh* 1545).

23. **Namanikā :** The dancer bends her body easily and slowly adopting difficult postures (*Nṛdh* 1549).

24. **Śaṅkā :** The dancer quickly whirls round and moves her body towards the front and the sides (*Nṛdh* 1550).

25. **Vitaḍa :** A graceful dance using Cārī and Karaṇa (*Nṛdh* 1551).

26. **Gītavādyatā :** The dancer dances in harmony with Gīta, Vādya, Akṣara[5] and Laya (*Nṛdh* 1552).

27. **Vivartana :** Cārīs, Karaṇas and Bhramarīs are performed with appropriate hand gestures while Vādya, Prabandha[6] and Varṇas[7] are arranged in harmony with the dance (*Nṛdh* 1553).

28. **Tharahara :** The dancer shakes her body quckly and the arm are moved gracefully (*Nṛdh* 1554).

29. **Sthāpanā :** The dancer stands gracefully with an expressive face. The whole action is aimed at achieving Rekhā (*Nṛdh* 1555).

30. **Sauṣṭhava :** Too obscure to explain (*Nṛdh* 1556-7).

31. **Sruvā :** The dancer moves her body like a flame in a breeze. (*Nṛdh.* 1558).

32. **Masṛṇatā :** The dancer gestures with her hands and her eyes express Rasa through Snigdhā Dṛṣṭi (*Nṛdh* 1559).

33. **Upāra :** The different parts of the body are moved one after the other and the whole body is moved round in rhythm (*Nṛdh* 1560).

34. **Aṅgānaṅga :** A mixture of Lāsyāṅga and Tāṇḍava (*Nṛdh* 1561).

35. **Abhinaya :** The use of a Karaṇa to express emotions (*Nṛdh* 1562).
36. **Komalikā :** The dancer moves round and performs Aṅgānaṅga thus indicating a soft heart (*Nṛdh* 1563).
37. **Mukharasa :** While dancing the dancer utters words in order to express emotions (*Nṛdh* 1564).

Strīsthāna : Pronnata is a new name of Strīsthāna that occurs in this text. The other seven are the same as in other texts.

Pronnata : The toes are kept at the same level with the instep. The body is in Āyata (*Nṛdh* 920).

Nṛdh has thirty-eight Utplutikaraṇas of which twenty-seven are the same as in *SR*. It does not include Bhramarīs in Utplutikaraṇas but gives eleven new varieties (*Nṛdh* 1306-1382).

1. **Laṅkādāhāñcita :** The dancer moves round in Añcita and sits down in Utkaṭāsana, with her face towards the back of the stage (*Nṛdh* 1324).
2. **Samakartaryañcita :** The dancer stands in Sama and then crosses her Añcita feet in Svastika (*Nṛdh* 1325).
3. **Balibandhāñcita :** The dancer performs Añcita after moving her hands in Gajadanta (*Nṛdh* 1326).
4. **Kṣetrāñcita :** With her feet in Añcita, the dancer sits in Utkaṭāsana at the beginning and at the end of the movement (*Nṛdh* 1327).
5. **Skandhāñcita :** The dancer performs Añcita and touches the ground with her shoulders. Then she jumps obliquely and quickly comes down (*Nṛdh* 1328).
6. **Vicitralohadī :** The dancer stands sidewise to the audience and moves her body obliquely like a wheel (*Nṛdh* 1335).

7. **Bāhubandhalohaḍī :** The same is done with Gajadanta hands. (*Nṛdh*. 1336).
8. **Samakartarīlohādi :** The same feet are crossed in Svastika at the beginning and at the end of the performance (*Nṛdh* 1338).
9. **Caturmukhalohaḍī :** Lohaḍī is done turning to all four sides (*Nṛdh* 1339).
10. **Alagāñcita :** The dancer performs Alaga first and quickly moves doing Añcita (*Nṛdh* 1340).

The descriptions of Nāgabandha, Matsyakaraṇa, Triryakkaraṇa, Tiryaksvastika, Kapālacūrṇana, Nataprṣṭhaka, Karasparśa, Skandhabhrānta, Eṇapluta, Lohaḍī and Sūcyantāni are missing. The editor has quoted *Bharatakośa* (pp. 138-9) which agrees with *SR*.

11. **Lohaḍyañcita :** The dancer performs Añcita after Lohaḍī (*Nṛdh* 1341).

Cālaka

1. **Viśliṣṭavartita :** The hands are crossed in Svastika and one hand is obliquely lowered. Then they are moved up and down at the sides (*SR* p. 113; *Nṛdh* 767).
2. **Vepathuvyañjaka :** The hands are moved alternately near the navel (*SR* p. 113; *Nṛdh* 768).
3. **Apaviddha :** The hands are rotated near the throat and the navel at the left and right sides of the dancer (*SR* p. 113; *Nṛdh* 769).
4. **Laharīcakrasundara :** One hand is moved obliquely near the navel. The other hand is upturned and moved up to the left shoulder and stretched out. Then they are moved to the left and right side of the head and then gently brought down (*SR* p. 113; *Nṛdh* 770-2).

5. **Vartanāsvastika** : One hand having been separated from the other, is moved sideways with lightening speed and joined with the other. This is done repeatedly (*SR* p. 113; *Nṛdh* 773).

6. **Sanmukhīnarathāṅga** : The Recita hands are obliquely moved facing each other. They are moved inwards at the sides with their elbows pointing. Then they are again moved in Recita (*SR* p. 114; *Nṛdh* 775-6).

7. **Purodaṇḍabhrāmya** : One hand in Musṭi is obliquely moved in and out while the other hand is moved gracefully. The hands are alternately stretched forward. (*Nṛdh.* 777-8). *SR* : Purodaṇḍabhrama (*SR* p. 114).

8. **Tribhaṅgīvarṇasāraka** : The hands are rotated obliquely forward and at the sides. This may be done with both hands at the same time or alternately (*Nṛdh* 779). *SR :* Tribhaṅgīvarṇasaraka (*SR* p. 114).

9. **Dola :** Each hand is moved up and down obliquely in a graceful way. This is done alternately (*Nṛdh* 780). *SR* : Ḍola (*SR* p. 114).

10. **Nīrājita :** The hands are crossed in Svastika and then separated by moving them outwards. They are obliquely moved round together near the head at the right and the left sides (*SR* p. 114; *Nṛdh* 781).

11. **Svastikāśleṣa** : The Svastika hands are moved away from the shoulders (*Nṛdh* 782). *SR* Svastikā-śleṣacālana (*SR* p. 114).

12. **Mithaḥsaṁvikṣyabāhya :** One hand is moved straight up and placed on the shoulder on the other side.Then it is brought back to its own side and rotated (*SR* p. 115; *Nṛdh* 785).

13. **Vāmadakṣatiraścīna** : The hands in Svastika are obliquely moved at the right and the left sides. (*Nṛdh* 783), *SR* : Vāmadakṣavilāsita (*SR* p. 115).

14. **Maulirecitaka** : One hand rests on the hip and the other is stretched forward. Then they are moved upwards gracefully and brought to the ears (*SR* p. 115; *Nṛdh* 786).

15. **Vartanābharaṇa** : One hand is taken near the ear while the other is rotated. Then they are moved in Udveṣṭita (*SR*. p. 115; *Nṛdh* 784).

16. **Kūrmāvatāra** : The hands are placed together or one after the other on the right and the left near the head. They are rotated and crossed in Svastika. The hands form Svastikavartanā and are rotated at the sides. They describe a large circle (*SR* p. 115; *Nṛdh* 773-4).

17. **Aṁsavartanaka** : The arms are raised and moved in Vartanā near the wrists, shoulders, elbows and the fore-arms. The head is a little bent and the hands, with the palms turned down are moved on the ground in front. They are moved simultaneously or one after the other at the sides, to the left and the right (*SR* p. 116; *Nṛdh* 790-1).

18. **Manibandhāsikarṣa** : The hands are raised to the shoulders and moved together or one after the other. The elbows are again moved outwards and inwards in Muṣṭi. Then they quickly describe a circle. They are rotated at the sides and then they are thrown outwards gracefully (*SR* p. 116; *Nṛdh* 787-9).

19. **Kalviṅkavinoda** : The hands are rotated one after the other over the head and the sides. They are moved quickly and beautifully up and down (*SR* p. 116; *Nṛdh* 795-6).

20. **Catuṣpatrābja** : One hand is raised at first and it describes a circle. Then it is stretched to all the four sides while the other hand rests on the navel (*SR* p. 116; *Nṛdh* 799-800).

21. **Maṇḍalāgra** : One hand is Muṣti while the other hand is raised. They are moved at the sides, to the front and at the back. Then the whole action is repeated with the order reversed (*SR* p. 117; *Nṛdh* 797-8).

22. **Vālavyajanacālana** : The fore-arms are raised to the shoulders alternately. Then they describe a circle near the ground (*SR* p. 117; *Nṛdh* 801).

23. **Viruḍibandhana** : One hand forms a triangle and describes circles in front and at the sides. (*Nṛdh* 802) : *SR*. Vīrudhabandhana (*SR* p. 117).

24. **Viśṛṅgāṭakabandhana** : The same is done first in reverse and then in regular order (*SR* p. 117; *Nṛdh* 803).

25. **Kuṇḍalicāra** : The hands are moved to the left, right and to all sides. Then they are obliquely moved (*SR* p. 117; *Nṛdh* 804).

26. **Murujāḍambara** : The hands are moved round at the middle of the body, at the right and the left and at the sides. The right hand is raised to the left shoulder and quickly brought to the middle and then to the left while the other hand touches the navel (*SR* p. 118; *Nṛdh* 808-10).

27. **Hāradāmavilāsaka** : The hands touch the opposite shoudlers and then they are lowered together at the sides (*SR* p. 118; *Nṛdh* 806).

28. **Dhanurākarṣaṇa** : The Svastika hands are quickly and obliquely brought to the sides. Then with a sudden movement one hand touches the ear (*SR* p. 118; *Nṛdh* 805).

29. **Sādhāraṇa :** The hands rest on the hips and then they are obliquely moved. They describe a circle together moving inward and outward (*SR* p. 118; *Nṛdh* 816).

30. **Samaprakoṣṭhavalana :** The fore-arms are rotated. *SR* adds that the hands should be in Āviddha or Apaviddha (*SR* p. 118; *Nṛdh* 807).

31. **Devopahāraka :** The Arāla hands are moved at both sides. One hand is stretched out while the other points at the elbow (*SR* p. 118-9; *Nṛdh* 813-4).

32. **Tiryakjātasvastikāgra :** The hands are stretched at the sides and then they form a Svastika facing each other. Finally they are moved gracefully in front. *SR* : Tiryggatasvastikāgra (*SR* p. 119; *Nṛdh* 811-2).

33. **Maṇibandhagatāgata :** One wrist rests on the other and they move in and out forming circles (*SR* p. 119; *Nṛdh* 818).

34. **Alātacakra :** One hand moves towards the body and away (*SR* p. 119; *Nṛdh* 815).

35. **Vyastotplutanivartaka :** The hands are quickly moved out to the sides and the elbows point at each other. Then they are joined while being turned to the ground (*SR* p. 119; *Nṛdh* 823).

36. **Urabhrasaṁbādha :** The Svastika hands are quickly separated, moved out and away and then turned towards each other (*SR* p. 120; *Nṛdh* 817).

37. **Tiryaktāṇḍava :** One hand is raised first and then obliquely placed on the navel while the other hand is moved obliquely to the side (*Nṛdh* 822); *SR* : Tiryaktāndavacālana (*SR* p. 120).

38. **Dhanurvallīvināmaka :** The hands are raised with palms turned down and rotated alternately. Then they are again moved near the head, the hips and at the sides with palms turned downwards (*SR* p. 120; *Nṛdh* 820-1).

39. **Tārkṣyapakṣavinodaka** : The hands are moved together in Vartanāsvastika at the sides. *SD* : Tārkṣyapakṣavirasāka *(SR* p. 120; *Nṛdh* 819).

40. **Kararekaratna** : The hands move to the sides and then brought to the middle of the body. Then they are placed on the hips in Svastika and moved in Vālavyajanacālana. They form Vartanāsvastika with the palms turned down. They are raised describing circles and brought down in Svastika. One hand touches the shoulder while the other is swung in Rathacakra. Then they are stretched straight, raised and bent. Then they are again brought to the shoulders with a circular motion and then moved out to the front. After doing this they are moved up and down alternately from the head to the hips. Then they are moved round to the right and the left in Svastika and with the elbows crossed in Svastika rotated inward and outward. Or, the hands are moved sraight in a quick tempo to the right, the left and at the back. Then they are raised obliquely with palms turned down in Svastika simultaneously or one after the other (*SR* p. 120-1; *Nṛdh* 824-33).

41. **Śarasandhāna :** One hand is moved to the back while the other hand is repeatedly raised to the head (*SR* p. 121; *Nṛdh* 839-40).

42. **Maṇḍalabharaṇa** : The hands describe a circle moving inward and then they are moved downard in Dolā. This can also be done with the order reversed (*SR* p. 121; *Nṛdh* 836).

43. **Aṁsaparyāyanirgata :** The hands form a Svastika while doing Kalāsa and then they are stretched out alternatiely from the shoulders to the hips (*SR* p. 122; *Nṛdh* 842).

44. **Aṣṭabandhavihāra :** The hands are moved round first to the left and the right, then to the front and

towards the back and then to the "eight quarters," that is, on all sides of the body (*SR* p. 122; *Nṛdh* 837-8).

45. **Karṇayugmaprakīrṇaka** : The hands are moved obliquely and alternately upto the ears and then are brought to the sides and to the front. *SR* says of this movement that the hands are moved near the chest (*SR* p. 122; *Nṛdh* 846).

46. **Paryāyagajadanta** : One hand is moved obliquely while the other hand is stretched alternately (*SR* pp 122-3; *Nṛdh* 841).

47. **Rathanemi** : The hands in Rathacakra are crossed in Svāstika and held obliquely (*SR* p. 123; *Nṛdh* 844).

48. **Trikoṇasvstika** : The hands are crossed in Svastika and then raised upto the left shoulder in Kuñcita. *SR*: Svastikatrikona (*SR* p. 123; *Nṛdh* 843).

49. **Latāveṣṭitaka** : The hands are raised and moved in Udveṣṭita towards the body and out to the sides. This is done obliquely and alternately (*SR* p. 123; *Nṛdh* 845).

50. **Navaratnamukha** : The hands are moved in Cālakas such as Viśliṣṭavartita and then while doing a Vartanā raised up to the hair, forming a Svastika. The palms are turned down. The hands are then rotated in Āviddha and Apaviddha together or alternately with a swinging movement (*SR* p. 123; *Nṛdh* 847-9).

The following five Cālakas are mentioned in *Nṛdh* as entirely new ones :

1. **Digvarṣābhidhacālana** : The hands are moved to the front, at the sides and at the back. They are also raised and moved obliquely. (*Nṛdh.* 851-2).

2. **Anaṅgāṅgamoṭana** : The hands are moved round near the shoulders. Then they are moved in the same way near the head (*Nṛdh* 852-3).

3. **Toraṇacālaka :** The hands are crossed in Svastika and then they are separated. They are kept at the sides and again crossed in Svastika. They are placed on the head and separated (*Nṛdh* 845-6).

4. **Anaṅgoddīpana :** The hands are kept on the chest. Then they are moved round one by one and brought near the shoulders. Finally, they are moved in Udveṣṭita with palms downwards (*Nṛdh* 856-7).

5. **Murajakartarīcālaka :** The hands are moved round from the chest to the shoulders. Then they are quickly brought from the chest to the sides. One hand is moved downwards while the other is moved round. Then they are placed on the hips facing each other and moved (*Nṛdh* 858-9).

Vartanā

1. **Patākāvartanā :** The wrists are moved to the right and left in Patākā (*Nṛdh* 715; *SR* p. 106; *NRK* 12.32).

2. **Alapadmavartanā :** The Alapadma hands are moved in Vyāvṛtta (*Nṛdh* 716; *SR* p. 106; *NRK* 1.2.35).

3. **Arālavartanā :** The hands are moved in Āveṣṭita and then they are moved in Udveṣṭita forming Arāla (*Nṛdh* 717; *SR* p. 106; *NRK* 1.2.33).

4. **Śukatuṇḍavartanā :** One hand in Āviddha is moved near the chest with the palm turned down while the other hand forms Śukatuṇḍa and is placed near the knee (*SR*. p. 106; *Nṛdh* 718; *NRK* 1.2.34).

5. **Avahithavartanā :** The hands move in Avahittha (*Nṛdh* 719).

6. **Makaravartanā :** One hand in Makara is moved in Āvartita to the front and at the sides (*SR* p. 106; *Nṛdh* 720; *NRK* 1.2.37).

7. **Khaṭakāmukhavartanā :** The wrists are moved to the left and the right of the body and near the navel in

Khaṭakāmukha (*S.R* p. 106; *Nṛdh.* 721; *NRK* 1.2.36).

8. **Ūrdhvavartanā** : The Udvṛtta hands are moved upward (*SR* p. 106; *Nṛdh* 722; *NRK* 1.2.38).
9. **Recitavartanā** : The Haṁsapakṣa hands are separated from Svastika and quickly moved round forming Recita (*SR* p. 106; *Nṛdh* 723; *NRK* 1.2.40).
10. **Āviddhavartanā** : The Āviddhavakra hands are moved in Vyāvartita alternately and then they form Āviddha (*SR* p. 107; *Nṛdh* 724; *NRK* 1.2.39).
11. **Keśabandhavartana** : The Keśabandha hands are brought away from the hair alternately (*SR* p. 107; *Nṛdh* 725; *NRK.* 1.2.43).
12. **Bhālavartanā** : Phāla in *SR.* The Ūrdhvamaṇḍalahastas are rotated. This is also known as Cakravartanā (*SR* p. 107; *Nṛdh* 726); *NRK* : Phalgu (? Phāla) (*NRK* 1.2.44-45).
13. **ūrusthavartanā** : The Uromaṇḍala hands are moved. *SR* : *NRK* : Urovartanikā (*SR* p. 1087; *Nṛdh* 727; *NRK* 1.2.47).
14. **Kakṣavartanā** : The Pārśvamaṇḍala hands are moved together or alternately at their own sides (*SR* p. 108; *Nṛdh* 728; *NRK* 1.2.46).
15. **Khaḍgavartanā** : One hand in Muṣṭi moves in Kuñcita while the other hand in Khatakāmukha moves in Añcita. Kohala himself suggests Muṣṭikasvastika for the hands while the above-mentioned action is suggested by Kīrtidhara, quoted by both the authors (*SR* p. 108; *Nṛdh* 729; *NRK* 1.2.48).
16. **Daṇḍavartanā** : The Daṇḍapakṣa hands are rotated round. Kohala suggests that one hand in Haṁsapakṣa is moved from one side in Vyāvṛtta and brought near the chest in Parivartita. The other hand is stretched out obliquely. This is also

done with Daṇḍapakṣa hands (*SR* p. 108; *Nṛdh* 730; *NRK* 1.2.49-53).

17. **Padmavartanā** : The Nalinīpadmakośa hands are moved gracefully. Kohala suggests Padmakośa for the hands which are first moved in Vyāvṛtta and Parivartita and then crossed in Svastika. Finally, they assume Nalinīpadmakośa facing opposite sides (*SR* p. 108, *Nṛdh* 731).

18. **Nitambavartanā** : The hands assume Nitamba from Alapallava and move down from the shoulders and brought near the hips (*SR* p. 107; *Nṛdh* 733; *NRK* 4. 1.2.41-2).

19. **Pallavavartanā** : The Pallava hands are gracefully moved round. Kohala says that the Patākā hands are separated at the wrists and then crossed in Svastika (*SR* p. 109; *Nṛdh* 734; *NRK* 1.2.54).

20. **Lalitavartanā** : The hands are moved in Lalita. Kohala says that the hands in Lalita are moved to the head and then each touches the tip of the other's fingers and move near the head in Khaṭakāmukha (*SR* p. 109; *Nṛdh* 735; *NRK* 1.2.60).

21. **Ardhamaṇḍalavartanā** : Uraḥpārśārdhamaṇḍala hands are rotated. Kohala says that the Alapallava hands are stretched and moved round, each from its own side of the chest and after moving in Āveṣṭanā assume Arāla. The other hand moves to its own side in the same way. Then both hands move in Uraḥpārśvārdhamaṇḍala (*SR* p. 109; *Nṛdh* 736; 1.2.55-7).

22. **Valitavartanā** : Valita hands are rotated. Kohala suggests that the elbows are crossed in Svastika. Or, the Khatakāmukha hands are joined at their tips with their elbows bent and raised (*SR* p. 109; *Nṛdh* 737; *NRK* 1.2.61.)

23. **Ghātavartanā :** The Ulvaṇa hands are moved round. Kohala suggests that the Alapallava hands are moved in Udveṣṭita.Then they are raised together from the chest and the shoulders and finally they are moved near the shoulders (*SR* p. 109; *Nṛdh* 738; *NRK* 1.2.58-9).

24. **Gātravartanā :** The hands in Alapallava are moved inwards in Vyāvṛtta and then, placed back to back, they assume Alapallava. (*SR.* p. 110; *Nṛdh.* 739; *NRK.* 1.2.62).

25. **Prativartanā :** The Alapallava hands are thrown backward and rotated (*SR* p. 110; *Nṛdh* 740; *NRK* 1.2.63).

The following eleven Vartanās are mentioned in *Nṛdh* as entirely new ones :

1. **Caturasrākhyavartanā :** The Caturasra hands are moved along with the shoulders and elbows. The arms first assume Udveṣṭita and then placed on the chest (*Nṛdh* 744).
2. **Talamukhavartanā :** The Talamukha hands are moved with Sauṣṭhava (*Nṛdh* 745).
3. **Svastikavartanā :** The hands are moved in Vyāvartanā and crossed in Svastika (*Nṛdh* 746).
4. **Viprakīrṇavartanā :** The hands are moved in Udveṣṭita and separated. The left is then placed on the left side, the right on the right (*Nṛdh* 747).
5. **Puṣpapuṭavartanā :** One hand in Puṣpapuṭa is moved in Parivartanā and then placed on the chest after moving it in Vyāvartanā (*Nṛdh* 748).
6. **Tripatākāvartanā :** The Tripatākā hands are moved to the right and to the left. The wrists are also moved (*Nṛdh* 749).
7. **Kartarīmukhavartanā :** The same action is done with the hands in Kartarīmukha (*Nṛdh* 750).

8. **Muṣṭivartanā :** The Muṣṭi hands are moved to the right and to the left in Vyāvartanā (*Nṛdh* 751).
9. **Śikharavartanā** 10, **Kapitthavartanā,** 11, **Sūcimukhavartanā :**

   These are done like Muṣṭivartanā with appropriate hands such as Śikhara in Śikharavartanā (*Nṛdh* 752).

NRK. also mentions seven new forms of Vartanās. They are as follows : Śikhara, Tilaka, Nāgabandha, Siṁhamukha, Vaiṣṇava and Talamukha (*NRK* 1.2.64-5).

Nṛtyaratnakośa names different types of Venīdhammilla without discussing them in detail. They are : Veṇīkṛtā, Muktā, Baddhā, Stabdhakacā, Moṭaka, Jutaka, Vīragranthi, Dviphalaka, Nāriṅgi, Saṁnivṛntaka, Yāvagranthi, Kuśagranthi, Brahmagranthi, Gumphita, Mūlagranthi and Madhyapranatagranthi. It also describes a few new hand gestures. They are as follows :

1. **Upadhāna :** An Asaṁyutahasta. The fingers of the Patākā hand are separated (*NRK* 1.1.635).
2. **Kadamba :** Asaṁyutahasta. The fingers are joined to form a circle (*NRK* 1.1.637).
3. **Prayogaprada :** Saṁyutahasta. The Patākā hands are joined at their tips (*NRK* 1.1.674).
4. **Āliṅgana :** Saṁyutahasta. The Patākā hands are crossed (*NRK* 1.1.675).
5. **Kalāpa :** Saṁyutahasta. The hands are interlocked with the fingers separated and raised. The thumbs are kept out (*NRK* 1.1.678).
6. **Kirīṭa :** Saṁyutahasta. Kalāpa is done above the head (*NRK* 1.1.679).
7. **Caṣaka :** Saṁyutahasta. Puṣpapuṭa hands are joined at the elbows (*NRK* 1.1.680).
8. **Lekhana :** Saṁyuta-hasta. The left hand in Patākā is raised while the right is placed on it in Sañdaṁśa (*NRK* 1.1.681).

9. **Añjana :** Nṛtta-hasta. The Lalita hands are placed on the chest. Then they assume Kapota near the ear. Finally, Saṅdaṁśa is done (*NRK* 1.1.775).

10. **Candrakānta :** One hand assumes Makara after performing Ardhacandra while the other hand assumes Śukatuṇḍa. Then both the hands touch the knee and move up to touch the head (*NRK* 1.1.776).

11. **Jayanta :** The left hand assumes Makara while the right assumes Ardhacandra. Then the left hand is moved and placed at the right in Patāka. The other hand in Tripatāka is placed on the shoulder (*NRK* 1.1.777).

References

CHAPTER ONE

1. *History of Sanskrit Poetics,* P.V. Kane. 1961. p. 47.
2. *VDP,* G.O.S. ed., vol. I, p. xxvi.
3. *ADar.* M.M. Ghosh, ed., p. 38.
4. Winterniz. *A History of Indian Literature,* vol. I. p. 566.
5. *NŚ,* M.M. Ghosh, ed., p. lxvii.
6. S.N. Dasgupta and S.K. Dey *A History of Sanskrit Literature.* vol. I, p. 550.
7. *NŚ,* M.M. Ghosh, ed., p. lxviii.
8. *ND,* G.O.S. ed., Preface, p. 3.
9. *Mānas,* G.O.S. ed., vol. I, p. vi.
10. *BhP,* G.O.S. ed., Introduction, p. 76.
11. *SMak,* G.O.S. ed., Introduction, p. iv.
12. S.N. Dasgupta and S.K. Dey. op. cit., p. 564.
13. *SUS,* G.O.S. ed., p.x.
14. *SUS,* G.O.S. ed., pp. v-vi.
15. *SUS,* 6. 129-32.
16. *SUS,* G.O.S. ed., p. xxix.
17. *SDām,* Preface, p. 15.
18. *NN,* 53b.
19. *NN,* 26b-27a, 32b; *NŚ,* 10. 3-6. 49.
20. *SDar,* 113a. (*Paris ms*).
21. *SDar.* 41b, 40b, *SR,* 7.27. *ADar,* 36-7. *SSam,* 6.234, 236-7.
22. *NN,* 54a.
23. *SDar,* 51a, 52a.
24. *NŚSam,* vol. I, Introduction, p. ii.

25. *NŚSam,* vol. II, Introduction, p. 15.
26. *NŚSam,* vol. I. Introduction, p. iii.
27. *HR,* Ia.

CHAPTER TWO

1. *NŚ,* 4.264.
2. *DR,* 1.9;1 *SR,* 7.26.8; *SDām,* p. 69; *SSam,* 6.1; 6.167.
3. *NŚ,* 4.13, 4.30.
4. *NŚ,* 9.163-4.
5. K.M. Varma. *Nāṭya, Nṛtta änd Nṛtya,* p. 21.
6. *Cosha,* Amar Sinha. H.T., Colebrooke, ed., 1808, p. 42.
7. *BhP,* p. 297.
8. *ND,* p. 214.
9. *Mālavikāgnimitraṁ,* R.D. Karmakar, ed., Act, I, pp. 3, 6.
10. *Cosha,* op. cit., p. 42.
11. *Mānas,* 16.4.959-60.
12. *SR,* 7.31.
13. *SR,* 7.18.
14. *BhP,* p. 46.
15. *NN,* Ia.
16. *SDar,* 36b.
17. *DR,* 1.7.9; *SR,* 7.17.26, 27.
18. *BhP,* p. 296.
19. *BhP,* p. 296.
20. *BhP,* p. 181.
21. K.M. Varma, op. cit., p. 9.
22. *SSam,* 6.167; *SDām.* p. 69.
23. *DR,* 1.9.
24. *SR,* 7.27; *SDar,* 41b.
25. *NŚ,* 4.261.
26. *NŚ,* 4.250; 269.
27. *NŚ,* 4.13.
28. *NŚ,* 19.120.
29. *NŚ,* 5.27.
30. *VDP,* 3.20.2-3.
31. *ADar,* 3.4.

32. *DR,* 1.10.
33. *Mānas,* 16.4.959-60.
34. *BhP,* p. 301.
35. *SR,* 7.28, 1.206.
36. *SUS,* 5.8.
37. *SDām,* p. 69.
38. *NN,* 1a.
39. *SDar,* 43b.
40. *NŚ,* 4.269; 13.
41. *Mānas,* 16.4.962-3.
42. *SR,* 7.29-30.
43. *VDP,* 3.20.2, 4.
44. *ADar,* 4.
45. *DR,* 1.10.
46. *Mānas,* 16.4.961-2.
47. *BhP,* p. 46.
48. *BhP,* p. 246.
49. *NŚ,* 4.287-90; 253-8.
50. *VDP,* 3.20.55.
51. *ND,* p. 214.
52. *SR,* 7.30.
53. *NŚ,* 19.118.
54. *DR,* 3.47-8.
55. *ND,* p. 127.
56. *SDām,* p. 73.
57. Guṇḍalī seems to be likelier, as this name can be found in *SR. BhP. SSam. NN,* and *SDar.* The descriptions agree. There can be found another reading of the term "Maṇḍalī" which can be interpreted as being a confused form of "Gu" if the scribe has dropped "u."
58. *SDām,* p. 74.
59. *SR,* 7.1216.
60. *SDām,* p. 75; *SR.* 7.1213.
61. *SDām,* p. 75; *SR.* 7.1214-5.
62. *SDām,* p. 75.
63. *NŚ,* 13.59.
64. *VDP,* 320.54.

65. *Mānas,* 16.4.963-6.
66. *SR,* 7.31.2.
67. *SDām,* p. 68.
68. *BhP,* p. 296.
69. *NN,* 1a.
70. *SDar,* 36b.
71. *AP,* 338.
72. *DR,* p.4.
73. *NLR,* pp. 131-4.
74. *ND,* pp. 213-5.
75. *BhP,* p. 256.
76. *SD,* 6.4-6.
77. *SDām,* pp. 79-80.

CHAPTER THREE

1. *NŚ,* 8.14; *VDP,* 3.24; *ADar,* 42; *AP,* 341; *ND,* p. 189; *Mānas,* 16.4.974; *SR,* 7.38; *SSam,* 6.6.; *SUS,* 5.18; *SDām,* p. 69.
2. *NŚ,* 8.14; 40; 105; 97; 110.
3. *VDP,* 3.25.
4. *ADar,* 45-7.
5. *AP,* 341. 9-12.
6. *ND,* p. 189.
7. *Mānas,* 16.4.975-6.
8. *SR,* 7.40-2.
9. *SSam,* 6.9.
10. *SUS,* 5.18-9.
11. *SDām.* p. 63.
12. *NN,* 15a-17b.
13. *SDar,* 40b.
14. *NŚSam,* 41-2.
15. *NŚ,* 8.13.
16. *ADar.* 43-5.
17. *AP,* 341.12-20.
18. *Mānas,* 16.4.76-7.
19. *SR,* 7.39-40.
20. *SSam,* 6.12.

21. *SUS,* 5.19-20.
22. *SDām,* p. 64.
23. *NŚSam,* p. 64.
24. *NN,* 18a-b; 17b.
25. *SDar,* 40b.

CHAPTER FOUR

1. *NŚ,* 10.1-5; 5.15; 10.8-10; 11-13.
2. *VDP,* 3.20.22.
3. *ADar,* 298-300.
4. *SMak,* 2.4.42.
5. *Mānas,* 16.4.1331-5.
6. *SR,* 7.898; 902-16.
7. *SUS,* 6.123-7.
8. *SDām,* p. 65.
9. *NŚSam,* 2.86-234.
10. *NN,* 27a-28a.
11. *NŚ,* 10.6; *NN.* 27a.
12. *NŚ,* 5.15.
13. *SDām.* p. 64.
14. *NŚ,* 10.51; 12.160-1; 12.228.
15. *VDP,* 3.21; 22; 23.
16. *ADar,* 274.
17. *Mānas,* 16.4.
18. *SR,* 7.1019-30.
19. *SSam,* 6.128-30.
20. *SUS,* 5.135; 137.
21. *SDām,* p. 64.
22. *NN,* 25a-26b.
23. *NŚSam,* 2.11-64.
24. *NŚ,* 11.2-5.
25. *VDP,* 3.20-23-7.
26. *ADar,* 261.
27. *SR,* 7.1143-5.
28. *SDām,* pp. 67-8.
29. *NŚ,* 12; *VDP,* 3.39.

30. *ADar*, 309-10.
31. *NŚ*, 4,248-9.
32. The śloka is not very clear. The ASS. ed. of the *SR* gives "Udhṛta" for "Udvṛtta" foot which seems to be likelier.
33. All but three Bhūmīcārīs in *SDām* (Kubīrā, Cārurecikā and Samanakhā) agree with those in *SR* (*SDām*, p. 65.).
34. All but four Ākāsacārīs in *SDām* (Bhramarī, Bhramarikā, Uru-āndolitā and Jaṅghā-āndolitā) agree with those in *SR* (*SDām*, p. 65).
35. Bracketted portions occur only in the G.O.S. ed. of the *NŚ*..
    Paricchinna denotes the Chinna Karaṇa.
    Bāhyabhramaraka means Bhramara done by the left foot.
    Bhramarī Gārī is denoted by the turning round of the hips.
    Udvṛtta denotes the Urudvṛttā Cārī.
    Āspanditā denotes the Spanditā Cārī.
    Nikuṭṭa denotes the Talasañcarapāda.
    Pṛṣṭhāpasarpī and Apasarpī seem to mean the Adhyardhikā Cārī.
    Apaviddha means the Āviddhā Cārī (*NŚ*, vol. II. pp. 119-22).

CHAPTER FIVE

1. *NŚ*, 4.30.
2. *NŚ*, vol. I. pp. 90-1.
3. *NŚ*, 10.45.
4. *VDP*, 3.20.40-54.
5. *ND*, pp. 189-90.
6. *Mānas*, 16.4.1384-98.
7. *SR*, 7.468-748; *SR*, 7.750-88.
8. *SSam*, 6.170-91.
9. *SUS*, 6.110; 6.120-2.
10. *SDām*, pp. 66-7.
11. *SDām*, pp. 68-9.
12. *ADar*, 283-97.
13. *NN*, 32b, 47b.

CHAPTER SIX

1. *NŚ*, 4.19-27; 31; 33.
2. *NŚ G.O.S.* ed., vol. I, p. 89.
3. *VDP*, 3.20; 28-34.
4. *ND*, p. 189.
5. *SSam*, 6.15.
6. *SR*, 7.790-1; 794-800.
7. *SUS*, 6.114-119.
8. *SDām*, p. 61, 64, 68.
9. The result is the Līna Karaṇa (*NŚ*, 4.66).
10. This implies placing the feet in the Samanakha Karṇa, (*NŚ*, 4.65).
11. The Viprakīrṇa hands are performed in the Vyaṁsita Karaṇa (*NS*, 4.108).
12. Some commentators, according to Abhg, think that, the portion in the text from the mention of the hands stretched out to the change to the Pratyālīḍha Sthāna applies to all the Aṅgahāra indicating their appropriateness, while others think that each Aṅgahāra should be confined to the definition under its name (*NŚ*, *GOS*, ed., vol. I, p. 140.).
13. This is the Karaṇa of the hand. (*NŚ* 9.216).
14. Abhg tells the dancer to revolve the back doing the Cārī, including in it, the Udveṣṭita Karaṇa of the hand (*NŚ* GOS ed., vol. I, p. 142).
15. According to Abhg, some commentators interpret again as twice (*NŚ*, vol. I, p. 143).
16. Nṛtta is equated with Aṅgahāra.
17. Udveṣṭita is a Hasta-Karraṇa, Apaviddha is not mentioned in any list of hand-gestures. According to Abhg, the Nikuṭṭaka Karaṇa is implied by the first śloka. In the commentary on the Nikuṭṭaka Karaṇa, moving one hand in Udveṣṭita and the other in Āviddhavakravartanā is mentioned (*NŚ*, vol. I, pp. 143, 101).
18. The result is the Nikuṭṭaka Karaṇa (*NŚ*, 4.69).
19. The Uromaṇḍala Karaṇa is to be performed, (*NŚ* 4.115).
20. The result is the Nikuṭṭaka Karaṇa (*NŚ*, 4.69).
21. The same as Nikuñcita.

22. The result is the Ardhanikuṭṭaka Karaṇa (*NŚ*, 4.70).
23. Paricchinna implies Chinna which is followed by the Bhramara Karaṇa.
24. The result is the Daṇḍapāda Karaṇa (*NŚ*, 4.143).
25. The result is the Prasarpita Karaṇa (*NŚ*, 14.149).
26. Nikuṭṭaka and Ardhanikuṭṭakas are the two Karaṇas.
27. The next gives "Maṇḍalorasī" which means "in Uromaṇḍala" (*NŚ*, 4, Vol. I, p. 145).
28. Kuṭṭita implies the Nikuṭṭaka and Ardhanikuṭṭaka Karaṇas.
29. The result is the Bhramara Karaṇa (*NŚ*, 4.99).
30. This should be performed with the right side of the body, (*NŚ*, vol. I, p. 146).
31. The same as the Chinna Karaṇa (*NŚ*, 4.106).
32. Bāhyabhramaraka is explained as Vāmabhramaraka by Abhg, which means that the Brahmara should be done on the left (*NŚ*, vol. I, p. 146).
33. The result is the Vaiśākharecita Karaṇa (*NŚ*, 4.98).
34. Both Karaṇas are repeated, followed by Vṛścika again.
35. This implies the Diksvastika Karaṇa (*NŚ*, Vol. I, p. 147).
36. Abhg. says that Ardhanikuṭṭaka should be performed on one side and repeated on the other (*NŚ*, Vol. I, p. 147).
37. The result is the Apaviddha Karaṇa (*NŚ*, 4.64).
38. There is another reading: "Karaṇa" The G.O.S. ed. of the *NŚ* has accepted the reading "Karaṇa," but "caraṇa" is likelier as Abhg accepts that term (*NŚ*, Vol. I, p. 147).
39. The result is the Latāvṛścika Karaṇa (*NŚ*, 4.105).
40. The result is Nikuñcita (*NŚ*, 4.87).
41. The result is the Nūpura Karaṇa (*NŚ*, 4.97).
42. Paricchinna seems to be the same as the Chinna Karaṇa. The author has used this term for the Chinna Karaṇa in the seventh and the tenth Aṅgāhāra also.
43. Sūcīviddha Karaṇa is implied by Sūcipāda (*NŚ*, 4.139).
44. According to Abhg, this implies performing the Gaṇḍasūcī and Līna Karaṇas (*NŚ*, vol. I, p. 148).
45. This implies the Madakshalitaka Karaṇa (*NŚ*, 4.159).
46. The result is the Mattalli Karaṇa (*NŚ*, 4.88).

47. The word "Valita" implies that the three Karaṇas, Madaskhalitaka, Mattalli, and Talasaṁsphoṭita, should be performed in various ways (*NŚ*, vol. I, p. 149).
48. AbhG thinks that the Talasaṁsphoṭita Karaṇa is also suggested here (*NŚ*, vol. I, p. 149).
49. According to Abhg, some commentators suggest repeating the first three Karaṇas thrice. This would give thirteen Karaṇas to the Aṅgahāra. Others are said to suggest that all the seven Karaṇas should be repeated thrice bringing the number upto twenty-one Karaṇas, of which the Aṅgahāra consists (*NŚ*, vol. I, p. 149.
50. The Maṇḍalasvastika and Niveśa Karaṇas are suggested here (NŚ, vol. I, p. 149).
51. The result is the Unmatta Karaṇa (*NŚ*, 4.74).
52. The result is the Udghaṭṭita Karaṇa (*NŚ*, 4.163).
53. The result is the Samanakha Karaṇa (*NŚ*, 4.65).
54. The same as Chinna.
55. Apaviddha implies the Aviddhapādā Cārī which is a part of the Sambhrānta Karaṇa (*NŚ*, vol. I, p. 149).
56. Bhramaraka is to be performed on the left side.
57. Ardhasūcī is to be performed with the left foot (*NŚ*, vol. I, p. 150).
58. The text is very complicated. According to Abhg, Nitamba and Svastikarecita Karaṇas are suggested here. Actually, in the Nitamba Karaṇa, the hands are lifted over the head and in Svastikarecita, Svastika and Viprakīrṇa hands are place on the waist (*NŚ*, vol. I, p. 150; 4.67; 148).
59. Bending the body implies the Vikṣiptākṣitaka Karaṇa (*NŚ*, vol. I, p. 150).
60. The result is the Unmatta Karaṇa (*NŚ*, vol. I, p. 150, 4.74).
61. The result is the Unmatta Karaṇa (*NŚ*, vol. I, p. 150, 4.74).
62. Svastikapāda implies the Baddhā Cārī in the Nitamba Karaṇa (*NŚ*, vol. I, p. 151).
63. Abhg says that according to (Bharata) Muni, in all the Aṅgahāras, leaving the last two Karaṇas, all Karaṇas should be performed on all sides. At the end, the last two should be performed facing the audience only (*NŚ*, vol. I, p. 151).

64. The result is the Vaiśākharecita Karaṇa in which this is performed on both the sides. The meaning of "Apavidha" is not very clear (*NŚ*, vol. I, p. 151, 4.98).
65. This refers to the Nūpurapādikā Cārī in the Nūpura Karaṇa.
66. Recita refers to the Unmatta Karaṇa and Maṇḍala refers to the Maṇḍalasvastika Karaṇa (*NŚ*, vol. I, p. 151, 4.74; 68).
67. This refers to the Nikuṭṭaka Karaṇa (*NŚ*, vol. I, p. 152).
68. "First" indicates the right side of the body (*NŚ*, vol. I, p. 152).
69. The result is the Sakaṭāsya Karaṇa (*NŚ*, vol. I, p. 152; 4.168).
70. The result is the Bhramara Karaṇa (*NŚ*, vol. I, p. 152; 4.99).
71. This is Karihasta in which the left hand is placed on the chest. This is a variation (*NŚ*, vol. I, p. 152).
72. The Vyaṁsita Karaṇa is to be performed twice (*NŚ*, vol. I, p. 153).
73. While explaining the Nikuṭṭaka Karaṇa, Abhg quotes Kohala in order to explain the term Nikuṭṭa that denotes moving the body up and down (*NŚ*, vol. I, p. 101).
74. The result is the Vṛścikakuṭṭita Karaṇa (*NŚ*, vol. I, p. 153).
75. The result in the Uromaṇḍala Karaṇa (*NŚ*, vol. I, p. 153).
76. The same as the Chinna Karaṇa.
77. Latā implies the Latāvṛścika Karaṇa (*NŚ*, vol. I, p. 155).
78. The result is the Nūpura Karaṇa (*NŚ*, vol. I, p. 155; 4.97).
79. According to Abhg, this refers to the Bhujaṅgāñcita and Gṛdhrāvalīnaka Karaṇas (*NŚ*, vol. I, p. 155).
80. Vikṣipta should be performed twice on either side (*NŚ*, vol. I, p. 155).
81. This refers to the Udvṛtta Karaṇa, (*NŚ*, vol. I, p. 156; 4.146).
82. The result is the Nitamba Karaṇa (*NŚ*, vol. I, p. 156; 4.146).
83. This implies the Latāvśṛcika Karaṇa (*NŚ*, vol. I, p. 156; 4.105).
84. The result is the Vyaṁsita Karaṇa (*NŚ*, vol. I, p. 156; 4.109).
85. That is, the right side of the body.
86. The result is the Uromaṇḍala Karaṇa (*NŚ*, vol. I, p. 156; 4.115).

87. This Aṅgahāra has a long commentary to it. Recita here means all the Karaṇas in which the hands are moved in Recita. They are Svastikarecita, Ardharecita, Vakṣasvastika, Unmatta, Ākṣiptarecita, Ardhamattalli, Recakanikuṭṭaka, Bhujaṅgatrastarecita, Nūpura, Vaiśakharecita, Bhujaṅgāñcita, Daṇḍārecita, Vṛścikarecita, Vyaṁsita, Vivṛtta, Vinivṛtta, Vivartita, Garuḍapluta, Mayūralita, Sarpita, Skhalita, Prasarpita, Talasaṁghaṭṭita, Vṛṣabhakrīḍita and Lolita. These twenty-five should be performed gracefully. These should be divided into four sections, the sections being performed in four different directions (*NŚ*, vol. I, pp. 156-8). The result of bending the body is the Cakra-maṇḍala Karaṇa (*NŚ*, vol. I, p. 158; 4.114).
88. This implies the Nūpura Karaṇa (*NŚ*, vol. I, p. 158; 4.97).
89. The result is the Bhramara Karaṇa (*NŚ*, vol. I, p. 158; 4.99).
90. The result is the Vyaṁsita Karaṇa (*NŚ*, vol. I, p. 158; 4.109).
91. The result is the Nitamba Karaṇa. Abhg suggests that the Nitamba Karaṇa should be performed after the Alātaka Karaṇa (*NŚ*, vol. I, p. 158).
92. All the Karaṇas that require simultaneous performance of Svastika and Recita, should be performed in this Aṅgahāra. They are : Svastikarecita, Pṛṣṭhasvastika, Diksvastika, Kaṭisama, Ghūrṇita, Bhramara, Vṛścikarecita, Pṛsthanikuṭṭaka, Uromaṇḍala, Sannata, Simhākarṣitaka, Nāgāpasarpitaka, Vakṣasvastika (to be applied only if Recana is suggested). The following Karaṇas are also to be performed wherever raising or lifting the hands and the feet is required. They are Daṇḍapakṣa, Lalāṭatilaka, Talavilāsita, Niśumbhita, Vidyudbhrānta, Gajakrīḍita, Nitamba and Viṣnukrānta (*NŚ*, vol. I, pp. 158-60).
93. Urudvṛtta is the Karaṇa suggested here. Abhg thinks that since it is to be performed with the Ākṣiptaka Karaṇa, covering is necessary (*NŚ*, vol. I, p. 160).
94. Abhg says that "ca" after Uromaṇḍala, according to some, denotes Kaṭicchinna after Uromaṇḍala (*NŚ*, vol. I, p. 160).
95. Abhg thinks that this indicates three Karaṇas; Añcita, Gaṇḍasūcī and Gaṅgāvataraṇa, which are to be performed (*NŚ*, vo. I, p. 160).

96. The Ardhasūcī and Daṇḍapāda Karaṇas are to be performed with the left side of the body (*NŚ*, vol. I, p. 160).
97. The result is the Caturaśra Karaṇa (*NŚ*, vol. I, p. 161).
98. The result is the Bhramara Karaṇa (*NŚ*, vol. I, p. 161).
99. Movements of the hands are emphasised to imply that the hands should be moved as they are moved in the Vyaṁsita Karaṇa.
100. Udveṣṭita implies sthe Karihasta Karaṇa (*NŚ*, vol. I, p. 161).
101. Udvṛtta implies the Urdudvṛtta Karaṇa (*NŚ*, vol. I, p. 161) as it does in the Ākṣiptarecita Aṅgahāra.
102. The result is the Nūpura Karaṇa (*NŚ*, vol. I, p. 162; 4.97).
103. The result is the Vivṛtta Karaṇa (*NŚ*, vol. I, p. 162; 4.122).
104. The word Nikuṭṭa means moving the body up and down. Whenever Nikuṭṭa of the hands and the feet mentioned, Nikuṭṭaka and Ardhanikuṭṭaka Karaṇas are implied (*NŚ*, vol. I, p. 162).
105. This seems to be the same as the Viprakīrṇa hand.
106. This implies the Latāvṛścika Karaṇa (*SR*, p. 266).
107. Sudhākara says that these three Karaṇas should be performed quickly. Apparently, this excludes the Mattallī Karaṇa. The translation of this Aṅgahāra in the Ad. Lib. Bulletin shows that the Talasaṁsphoṭita Karaṇa is to be performed at the same speed as Apaviddha. This agrees with Abhg's interpretation of this Aṅgahāra in the *NŚ*, but not with the view of Sudhākara (*SR*, p. 266; *SR*, Ad. Lib. Bulletin, p. 133; *NŚ*, vol. I, p. 149).
108. Only Mayuralalita, and not Lalita, is mentioned in the text, but as this does not make up twenty-six Karaṇas, the Commentator adds Lalita.
109. Between Daṇḍapāda and Catura, it is not clear which should be done on the left. According to Abhg, it is Daṇḍapāda. But Ad. Lib. Bulletin says that it is Catura which should be done on the left (*SR*, p. 2.73; *SR*, Ad. Lib. Bulletin, p. 137; *NŚ*, vol. I, p. 160).

* The sixteen Aṅgahāras mentioned above, rhythm-units of three beats.

CHAPTER SEVEN

1. *SSAm,* 6, 128.
2. *SR,* 7, 1273-1302; 1303-25.
3. *SDām,* p. 69; see p.
4. *Bhp,* p. 297.
5. *NN,* 49a, 50b; *SDar,* 51a, 52a.
6. *Nṛttasaṁgraha,* p. 38.
7. See *Mukhacāli,* p.
8. *NN,* 49a.
9. *SDar,* 33b.
10. *SDar,* 33.
11. Gati : *SDar,* 41b-42a. Mukharāga : *SDar,* p. 42b.
12. *SDar,* 33a.
13. Mukhacāli : *SDar,* 4-a-43a.
14. *SSam,* 6. 214-26.
15. *SSam,* 6, 191.
16. *SDām,* p. 69.
17. *Bhp,* p. 297.
18. Bhṛṅgī in *Nṛttasaṁgraha.*
19. Manrī for Maṇḍī in Bod ms 46b.
20. Bod. ms speaks of Guru (45b).
21. Three lines are missing in Paris Ms.

EPILOGUE

1. *NŚ,* 10.94; *NN,* 36a.
2. *SR,* 7.1216.

APPENDIX

1. Ambrose, Kay, *Classical Dances and Costumes of India,* p. 68.

   In describing Gaundalī, a Lāsyānga, *SR* mentions Kalāsa as a part of the concluding movements (*SR,* 7.1291-1292).
2. These terms refer to tempo and measure.

3. The description is incomplete in this text but has been conjecturally completed by the editor with the help of *NRK.*
4. Nikuttana means pounding by the feet.
5. Akṣara, p. 173; the better (of the alphabet) to which the music is set.
6. Prabandha, p. 173; a musical composition.
7. Varṇa, p. 173; a steady note sung or played as accompaniment.

Bibliography

MANUSCRIPTS

Dāmodara, *Sangīttadarpaṇa,* Bodleian Library, Oxford, MS. No. Mill, 47d.

Dāmodara, *Sangītadarpaṇa,* Bibliotheque Nationale, Paris, MS. No. 771.

Puṇḍarika Viṭṭhala, *Nartananirṇaya,* India Office Library, London, Ms. No. 5197.***

Puṇḍarīka Viṭṭhala, *Nartananirṇaya,* Asiatic Society Library, Calcutta, MS. No. III, D. 5.

TEXTS

Agnipurāṇa, ed. Hari Narayan Apte, Anandashrama Sanskrit Series, No. 41 (Poona, 1900).

Ajñātakartṛka, *Nṛttasaṁgraha,* ed. Priyabala Shah, Rajasthan Oriental Research Institute, No. 17 (Jaipur, 1956).

Amarsiṁha, *Cosha, or, Dictionary of the Sanskrit Language,* with an interpretation and annotations, ed. H.T. Colebrooke, 2nd ed. (1825).

Aśokamalla, *Nṛtyādhyāya, A Work on Indian Dancing by Aśokamalla,* ed. Priyabala Shah, Gaekwad Oriental Series, 141 (Baroda, 1963).

Bharatamuni, *Nāṭyaśastra of Bharatamuni with the Commentary Abhinavabhāratī by Abhinavaguptācārya,* ed. Manavalli Ramakrishna Kavi, Gaekwad Oriental Series, I-IV, (Baroda, 1934-1964).*

Bharatamuni, *Nāṭyaśāstra,* ed. Batuk Nath Sharma and Baldev Upadhyaya, Kashi Sanskrit Series, 60 (Varanasi, 1929).

Bharatamuni, *The Nāṭyaśāstra of Bhratamuni,* ed. Pandit Shivdatta and Kashinath Pandurang Parab, Kavyamala, 42 (Bombay, 1894).

Bharatamuni, *The Nāṭyaśāstra of Bharatamuni,* with an introduction and various readings with translations, ed. Manomohan Ghosh, Vols. I-II (Calcutta, 1950).

Bhāmaha, *Kāvyālankāra,* ed. Batuk Nath Sharma and Baldev Upadhyaya, Kashi Sanskrit Series, No. 61 (Benaras, 1928).

Catura Dāmodara, *Sangīta Darpaṇam,* ed. K. Vasudeva Sastri, Saraswathi Mahal Series, No. 34 (Tanjore, 1952).

Caturbhāṇi, ed. Moticandra and Vasudevasaran Agarwal, Hindi Grantha Ratnakar (Bombay, 1959).

Daṇḍin, *The Kāvyādarśa of Daṇḍin,* with the commentary of Taruṇavācaspati and also with an anonymous commentary known as Hṛdayaṁgamā, ed. Rangācārya (Madras, 1910).

Dattila, *Dattilam, Dattilamuni Praṇītam,* ed. K. Sambashiva Shastri, Trivandrum Sanskrit Series, No. 102 (Trivandrum, 1930).

Dhanañjaya, *Daśarupaka,* ed. G.C.O. Haas (New York, 1912).

Govindacarya, Utke, *Nāṭyaśāstra Śastra Saṁgraha,* ed. A.K.M. Row Sahib, K.B. Shastri and G. Nagaraja, Vols. I-III, (Bombay, 1953-1961).

Hemacandra, *Kāvyānuśasana* with Alaṁkāracuḍāmaṇi and Viveka by Ācārya Hemacandra, ed. R.C. Parikh, Shri Mahavir Jaina Vidyalaya, I-II (Bombay, 1938).

Hemacandra, *The Kāvyānuśāsana of Hemacandra,* ed. Pandit Shivadatta and Kashinath Pandurang Parab, Kavyamala, 71 (Bombay, 1901).

Kālidāsa, *Abhijñānaśakuntalā of Kālidāsa,* with a commentary styled Arthadyotanikā of Rāghavabhaṭṭa, ed. M.R. Kale (Bombay, 1902).

Kālidāsa, *Mālavikāgnimitram* with commentary of Kāṭayavema, ed. Kashinath Pandurang Parab (Bombay, 1912).

Kālidāsa, *Mālavikāgnimitra of Kālidāsa,* ed. R.D. Karmakar, Bhandarkar Oriental Research Institute (Poona, 1950).

Kālidāsa. *Vikramorvaśīyam,* ed. H.D. Velankar (New Delhi, 1961).

Kauṭilya, *Arthaśāstra,* ed. R. Sharma Shatri. Government Oriental Library Series, No. 37 (Mysore, 1909).

Matanga, *Bṛhaddeśī,* ed. K.S. Shastri, Trivandrum Sanskrit Series (Trivandrum, 1928).

Mahārāṇā Kumbhā, *Nṛtyaratnakośa,* ed. R.C. Parikh, Vol. I, No. 24, Rajasthan Oriental Research Institute (Jaipur, 1957).

Mahārāṇā Kumbhā, *Nṛtyaratnakośa,* ed. R.C. Parikh, Vol. II. No. 25, Rajasthan Oriental Research Institute (Jodhpur, 1968).

Nandīkeśvara, *Abhinayadarpaṇa,* ed. and tr. by M.M. Ghosh, 2nd ed. (Calcutta, 1957).

Nārada, *Sangītamakaranda of Nārada,* ed. M.R. Telang, Gaekwad Oriental Series, No. 16 (Baroda, 1920).

Pāṇini, *Aṣṭādhyāyīsutrapāṭha,* ed. Narayan Ram Acharya, Nirnaya Sagar Press, 1954.

Pārśvadeva, *Sangītasamayasāra,* ed. T.G. Ganapati Shastri, Trivandrum Sanskrit Series (Trivandrum, 1925).

Rājaśekhara, *Karpuramāñjarī,* ed. M.M. Ghosh (Calcutta, 1939).

Rājaśekhara, *Karpuramāñjarī*, ed. Sten Konow, Harvard Oriental Series (Boston, 1901).

Rājaśekhara, *Kāvyamīmāṁsā*, ed. C.D. Dalal and R.A. Shastri, Gaekwad Oriental Series, No.1, 3rd ed. (Baroda, 1934).

Rāmacandra and Guṇacandra. *Nāṭyadarpaṇa of Rāmacandra and Guṇacandra* with their own commentary, ed. G.K. Shrigodekar and L.B. Gandhi, Gaekwad Oriental Series, No. 48 (Baroda, 1929).

Śārngadeva, *Sāngitaratnākara*, . ed. S.S. Shastri, Adyar Library, Vols. I-IV (Madras, 1943-1953).**

Śubhankara. *Sangītadāmodara, ed.* G. Shastri and G. G. Mukhopadhyaya, Sanskrit College Series, No. 11 (Calcutta, 1960).

Śubhankara, *The Hastamuktāvalī*, ed. Mahesvar Neog, Journal of the Music Academy (Madras, 1952-59), pp. 23-30.

Śudraka, *The Mṛcchakaṭika of Śudraka*, ed. Hiranand Mularaj Sharma Shastri and Kashinath Pandurang Parab (Bombay, 1910).

Śrīharṣadeva, *The Ratnāvalī of Srīharśadeva*, ed. N.B. Godbole and Kashinath Pandurang Parab (Bombay, 1890).

Sāgaranandin, *The Nāṭakalakṣaṇaratnokośa*, ed. Myles Dillon, Vol. I (1937).

Sāgaranandin, *Nāṭakalakṣaṇaratnakośa*, tr. Myles Dillon, Murray Fowler and V. Raghavan (*Philadelphia, 1960).

Śāradātanaya, *Bhāvaprakāśanam of Śāradātanaya*, ed. Y.Y. Svami of Melkote and K.S. Ramasvami Shastri Shiromani, Gaekwad Oriental Series, No. 45 (Baroda, 1930).

Sudhākalaśa, *Sangītopaniṣatsāroddhāra*, a work on music and dancing by Vācanācārya Sudhākalaśa, ed. U.P. Shah, Gaekwad Oriental Series, No. 133 (Baroda, 1961).

Suttāgame, ed. Pupphabhikkhu, Part II (Gurgaon, 1954), pp. 55-56.

Somadeva, *Kathāsaritsāgara,* ed. Pandit Durgaprasad and Kashinath Pandurang Parab (Bombay, 1930).

Someśvara. *Mānasollāsa,* ed. G.K. Shrigondekar, Gaekwad Oriental Series, No. 138 (Baroda, 1961).

Skanda Purāṇa, ed. K.R. Shrikrisnadasa (Bombay, 1908).

Vāgbhaṭa, *The Kāvyānuśāsana,* ed. Pandit Shivadatta and Kashināth Pandurang Parab, Kavyamala, 43 (Bombay, 1894).

Vātsyāyana, *Kāmasutra,* ed. Mahesh Pal, Tridivnath Roy (Calcutta, 1911).

Viśvanātha, *Sāhityadarpaṇa,* ed. P.V. Kane (Bombay, 1923).

Viṣṇudharmottarapurāṇa, ed. Dr. Priyabala Shah, Gaekwad Oriental Series, Vols. I and III (Baroda, 1958, 1961).

* All references to the *Nāṭyaśāstra* are to the G.O.S. edition of the *Nāṭyaśāstra* unless otherwise stated.

** All references to the *Sangītaratnākara* are to the Adyar Library edition of the *Sangītaratnākara* unless otherwise stated.

*** All references to the *Nartananirṇaya* are to the India Office Library Ms. unless otherwise stated. References corresponding to the published edition of *Nartananirṇaya* appear in the Additional Notes.

GENERAL WORKS

Ambrose, Kay, *Classical Dances and Costumes of India* (London, 1950).

Aufrecht, Theodore, *Catalogi Codicum Manuscriptorum Bibliothecae Bodleianae pars octava, Codices Sanscriticoes Complectens* (Oxford, 1864).

Bachhofer, L., Early Indian Sculpture, Vols. I-II (1929).

Bose, Mandakranta, *A Critical and Comparative Study of Sanskrit Texts Dealing with Dancing,* Ms. B. Litt. Thesis, D1008, Oxford University, 1964.

Bowers, Faubion, *The Dance in India* (New York, 1953).

Burrow, Thomas and M.B. Emeneau, *A Dravidian Etymological Dictionary* (Oxford, 1961).

Classical and Folk Dances of India (Bombay, 1953).

Coomaraswamy, Ananda, *The Dance of Śiva,* Essays on Indian Art and Culture (New York, 1917).

Coomaraswamy, Ananda and Gopala K. Duggirila. *The Mirror of Gesture,* Being the Abhinaya Darpaṇa of Nandikeśvara (Cambridge, Mass., 1917).

Dasgupta, S.N. and S.K. De, A History of Sanskrit Literature, Vols. I-II (Calcutta, 1961).

De Zoete, Beryl, *The Other Mind* (London, 1953).

Ghosh, M.M., *Contributions to the History of Hindu Drama* (Calcutta, 1958).

Iyer, K. Bharata, *Kathakali : The Sacred Dance-drama of Malabar* (London, 1955).

Jacob, Colonel G.A. *Laukikanyāñjali, A Handful of Popular Maxims in Sanskrit Literature* (Bombay, 1900).

Kavi, Ramakrishna, *Bharatakośa* (Tirupati, 1951).

Kane, P.V., *History of Sanskrit Poetics* (Delhi, 1961).

Keith, A.B., *The Sanskrit Drama* (Oxford, 1924).

Krishnamachariar, M., *History of Classical Sanskrit Literature* (Madras, 1937).

Levi, Sylvain, *Le Theatre Indien* (Paris, 1890).

Mankad, D.R., *The Types of Sanskrit Drama* (Karachi, 1936).

Monier-Williams, Monier, *A Sanskrit English Dictionary* (Oxford, 1899, repr. 1960).

Naidu, V. Narayanasvami, Naidu, P. Srinivasulu and Pantulu, V. Rangayya, *Tāṇḍava Lakṣaṇam* (Madras, 1936).

Prajñanānanda, Swamī, *Sangīt Saṁskṛti,* Bhāratīya, Sangīter Itihās, Vol. I, (Calcutta, 1953).

Prajñānānanda, Swami; *Historical Development of Indian Music : A Critical Study* (Calcutta, 1960).

Raghavan, V., *Bhoja's Śṛngāra Prakāśa* (Madras, 1963).

Shastri, Surendranath, *The Laws and Practice of Sanskrit Drama,* Chowkhamba Sanskrit Series, No. 14 (Varanasi, 1961).

Varma, K.M., Nātya, *Nṛtta and Nṛtya: Their Meaning and Relation* (Calcutta, 1957).

Winternitz., M.A., *A History of Indian Literature,* Vol. I (1927).

ARTICLES

Agarwala, V.S., "The Śiva Tāṇḍava Stotra of Rāvaṇa," *Journal of the Oriental Institute,* M.S. University of Baroda, No. X (Barodā 1960), pp. 18-21.

Gode, P.K., ""Notes on Indian Chronology, *The Poona Orientalist* (Poona, 1936-37), pp. 26-29, 33-42, 47-49, 55-64.

Iyer, E.K. "Bhagavata Mela Dance Drama of Bharatanatya," *Sangeet Natak,* No. 13 (New Delhi, 1964), pp. 46-56.

Kalyanpurkar, M.S., "The Technique of Kathak: Nrtta", in *Classical and Folk Dances of India,* Part III (Bombay, 1963).

Khokar, Mohan, "Technique and Repertory," *in Classical and Folk Dances of India,* Part III (Bombay, 1963), pp. 28-31.

—"Natya : Bhagavata Mela and Kuchipudi," *in Classical and Folk Dances of India,* Part I (Bombay, 1963), pp. 27-36.

—The Tradition : Brief Historical Survey," in *Classical and Folk Dances of India,* Part II (Bombay, 1963).

Menon, Devaki, "The 'Kuttu' of the Kerala Theatre, *Journal of the Music Academy,* No. XXV (Madras, 1954), pp. 122-129.

Raghavan, V., "Writers Quoted in the Abhinavabhāratī," *Journal of Oriental Research* (Madras, 1932).

Raghavan, V., "Nāṭyadharmī and Lokadharmī," *Journal of Oriental Research,* No. XXV (Madras, 1933), pp. 359-375.

—, "A Note on the Name Daśarūpaka," *Journal of Oriental Research* (Madras, 1933).

—, "The Hastamuktāvalī of Śubhankara : A Brief Note," *Journal of the Music Academy,* No. IV (Madras, 1933), pp. 16-24, 50-84.

—, "Bhagavata Mela Nāṭaka," *Journal of the Indian Society of Oriental Art* (Calcutta, 1937), pp. 167-70.

—, "Śabdas," *Journal of the Music Academy,* No. XX (Madras, 1949), pp. 160-62.

—, "Uparūpakas and Nṛtyaprabandhas," *The Samskrita Ranga Annual,* No. XXI (Madras, 1950), p. 37.

—, "Some Corrections and Emendations to the Text of the Abhinavabhāratī, *Adyar Library Bulletin* No. 18 (Madras, 1984), pp. 196-209.

—, "Some Names in Early Saṅgīta Literature," *Bulletin of the Sangit Natak Academy,* No. 5 (New Delhi, 1956), pp. 19-28; No. 6 (New Delhi, 1957), pp. 23-30.

—, "Later Saṅgīta Literature," *Bulletin of the Sangit Natak Academy,* No. 17 (New Delhi, 1960), pp. 1-24; No. 18 (New Delhi, 1961), pp. 1-18.

Ragini Devi, "Indian Dance," *Journal of the Music Academy,* No. IV (Madras, 1933), pp. 153-154.

Raja, Kunjunni, "Kṛṣṇaāṭṭam," *Journal of the Music Academy,* No. XXIX (Madras, 1958), pp. 121-29.

Ramachandran, K.V., "The Grace Notes of Dance," *Journal* of The Music Academy, No. XXV (Madras, 1933), pp. 93-100.

—, "Music and Dance in Kālidāsa," *Journal of Oriental Research,* No. XVIII (Madras, 1948), pp. 116-35.

Rao, Maya, "The Hastas in Kathak," in *Classical and Folk Dances of India,* Part III (Bombay, 1963), pp. 44-47.

Sandesara, B.J. "Cultural Data of Vasudeva Hindi," *Journal of the Oriental Institute,* M.S. University of Baroda No. X (Baroda, 1960), pp. 7.17.

Sharma, V. Venkatarama, "Bharata Nāṭya," *Journal of the Music Academy* (Madras, 1930), pp. 32-37.

Shastri, K.V. "Literature and Other Sources in Indian Classical Dances," *Journal of the Tanjore Saraswathi Mahal Library,* No. XII (Tanjore, 1958), pp. 1-12.

Vatsyayan, Kapila, "Kathak," *Journal of the Music Academy,* No. XXVII (Madras, 1956), pp. 74-88.

—, "Classical Indian Sculpture and Dancing", *Journal of the Oriental Institute,* No. XI (Baroda, 1962), pp. 247-59.

Index

A

Ā

I

Ī

U

Gha

Ca

Cha

Ja

Jha

Ḍa

Ḍha

Tā

Tha

Da

Dha

Na

Pa

Ma

Ya

Ra

Ha